Sacred Drums of Liberation

Sacred Drums of
LIBERATION

Religions and Music of Resistance in Africa and the Diaspora

by
Don C. Ohadike

Africa World Press, Inc.

P.O. Box 1892
Trenton, NJ 08607

P.O. Box 48
Asmara, ERITREA

Africa World Press, Inc.

P.O. Box 1892　　P.O. Box 48
Trenton, NJ 08607　　Asmara, ERITREA

Book and Cover design: Saverance Publishing Services

Library of Congress Cataloging-in-Publication Data

Ohadike, Don C.
　Sacred drums of liberation : religions and music of resistance in Africa and the Diaspora / by Don C. Ohadike.
　　p. cm.
　Includes bibliographical references and index.
　ISBN 1-59221-516-5 (hardcover) -- ISBN 1-59221-517-3 (pbk.)
　1. Africa--Religion. 2. Africans--Music. 3. Africans--Civil rights. 4. Politics and culture--Africa. 5. African diaspora. I. Title.

BL2400.O33 2007
299.6--dc22
　　　　　　　　2006035247

To my grandkids

Obina Jason Ohadike
Nneka Casandra Ohadike-Sidle
Olisemeka Emmanuel
Oluchukwu Emmanuella Ohadike

Table of Contents

Preface
by Toyin Falola

Professor Don Ohadike was working on this manuscript at the time of his untimely death on Sunday, August 28, 2005. His children recovered the manuscript and sent it to me to bring the project to completion. As to be expected, many questions have to remain unanswered. Hopefully, another generation of scholars will elevate his scholarship to a new level. We appreciate the great legacy that he has left behind.

That he left behind a manuscript is a testimony to an active life. Born in 1941, he lived in different African countries before relocating to Cornell University in 1989 where he distinguished himself as an historian and administrator. He served as the Director of the Africana Studies and Research Center from 2001 to 2005.

Trained in Nigeria and England, he held academic appointments and prestigious fellowships at several institutions, including Stanford University in 1988 and Northwestern University in 1988-1989; as a lecturer at the School of Humanities, University of Port Harcourt in Nigeria from 1977 to 1979; and the University of Jos in Nigeria as Chair of History Department from 1984 to 1988.

His career saw the publication of a number of successful books, most notably *The Ekumeku Movement: Western Igbo Resistance to the British Conquest of Nigeria, 1883-1914* (Athens: Ohio University Press, 1991), *Anioma: A Social History of the Western Igbo People* (Athens: Ohio University Press, 1994), and *Pan-African Culture of Resistance: A History of Liberation Move-*

ments in Africa and the Diaspora, (Binghamton: Institute of Global Cultural Studies, Binghamton University, 2002).

I am grateful to Don's children for their cooperation to see this book in print, to Dr. Salah Hasan the Director of Cornell's Africana Studies and Research Center for his encouragement, to Adam Paddock who assisted with proof-reading, to those who agreed to write the commentaries, and to Sam Saverance and the publishers.

Toyin Falola
Fellow of the Nigerian Academy of Letters
The University of Texas at Austin

INVINCIBLE VOICES
Connections Between African Retentions and Black Freedom Struggle

Toyin Falola and Kwame Essien

Don Ohadike's insightful book examines how African religious practices and retention aided Blacks in Africa and those in the diaspora in their struggles against white oppression and domination. The work is divided into eight chapters, with overlapping and related themes. The chapters do not necessarily follow a specific thematic pattern or transition, thus allowing each to be read on its own terms. Dr. Ohadike is specifically interested in the ways in which the descendants of African slaves depended on magic, music, dance, prayers, charms and other forms of cultural practices as vehicles for liberation in their pursuit for freedom. Almost half of the book demonstrates how African cultural practices remained intact and traveled with slaves across the Atlantic. Ohadike's strongest argument is that although slaves might have left Africa, symbols of African cultures did not leave them, especially in the New World. Not only did the dependence on cultural elements pave the way for their autonomy, Ohadike posits that African deities, priests and priestesses also served as a binding agent for mobilizing various Black communities both in Africa and the diasporas. He shows how the people of African descent engaged with spiritual forces and negotiated with community leaders who acted as intermediaries between the gods and the community.

In chapter one, "Traditional African Religious Beliefs and Anti-colonial Protests in Africa," Ohadike delves into the heart of African religions to demonstrate how Africans armed themselves with traditional practices such as magic, charms, prayers and amulets as a shield to combat European weaponry. Here, Ohadike mentions diversity within various ethnic groups in Africa and how these communities embraced various spiritual oracles and divine powers. He argues that most Africans held on to traditional practices as a guide and as an outlet for obtaining divine powers prior to Islamization and Christianization religious projects in Africa. Ohadike notes that although premodern Africans did not have written documents and historical stations for recording religious beliefs and practices, Africans "sacred manuscripts were embodied in their music, oral history, religions, rituals, and ceremonies, as well as in the hearts of the people, their priests, their elders, and their chiefs."[1] He relates that New World African slaves did not only carry their skills through the Middle Passage, but they carried their religious beliefs and practices as well.

To show how Africans responded to European colonization in the continent, Ohadike outlines numerous deities and oracles located in different geographical regions of Africa. For example, he makes reference to Ogun, the god of war among the Yoruba, and Amadioha, the god of Igbo people of eastern Nigeria. In East Africa, Ohadike mentions Kinjikitile Ngwale of Tanzania as the leading deity in the struggle against white hegemonic powers. Ohadike includes Nanny, a deity in Jamaica who fought alongside Kinjikitili, the charismatic diviner who effectively mobilized Africans against the European invaders and slave owners. We need to see the links between these deities and why they merged across continents to oppose Europeans.

Ohadike does not underestimate the role of female priestesses in his analysis, explaining why he pays homage to them. The author talks about two female priestesses, Siofume and Maria, who organized their communities in Kenya and Congo to repel European weapons through charms. According to Ohadike, although the deities could not stop the European penetration into African communities, their mobilization efforts and spiritual powers left an indelible mark in the history of religious mobilizations in many African locales, especially within peasant communities where farmers were vulnerable to forced plantation slavery. Divine powers, as Ohadike stresses, created a broad-based spiritual cesspool that provided other forms of protection against European weaponry. For example, "holy water," as Ohadike describes it, became a protective mechanism and an integral element of resistance. Citizens who made pledges to the gods were also assured of life after death. The "holy water" is described as the reservoir for empowering traders and guiding them against exploitation by European traders. In fact, Kinjikitile's role as protector and a guide went beyond physical needs—the people of the community placed their destiny in the hands of their gods and made lifetime commitments to the laws that were established by the deities.[2] Others went through initiations and pledged their allegiance to the gods, Ohadike says.

Despite the commitments by the local people, Ohadike points out that the relations between the gods and their followers were not always peaceful. Whenever the gods failed to provide timely divine instructions and directions, their followers placed their destiny in their own hands. Such disobedience to their gods led to spontaneous attacks on Europeans. The common attacks against slave owners occurred in plantations where peasants destroyed cotton fields. Rebellions, according to Ohadike, created ripple effects in other communities controlled by slave owners and planters. As Ohadike shows, the untimely and pre-mature attacks on Germans in Tanzania created a double jeopardy: one between the gods and their disobedient followers, and the other between Europeans and peasants. In addition to the tensions between the gods and the community, Ohadike argues that the failures by the gods to predict the future accurately led to a mass desertion of their followers. He cites the case of Gussi, a prophetess in Kenya whose spiritual powers failed to withstand the powerful arms of the British in 1908. The community mocked their spiritual leader as a form of protest.[3]

Ohadike creates a complication from page twelve because he introduces terms like maroon in the body of his argument without fully locating the significance to the chapter. Thereafter, he compares the guerilla style attacks that were employed by the Maji Maji and Ekumeku freedom fighters as templates that could have been copied by the followers of Kinjikitile. In other words, he notes that the Maji Maji, Ekumeku and maroons thrived because of their effective warfare tactics. By creating a dichotomy between powerful European weaponry and unreliable divine interventions, Ohadike is suggesting that the gods of the land were powerless. What would have happened if the peasants who rebelled against their gods were successful in their mobilization and attacks on Europeans? Is African *juju* powerful? Could it be that the people did not respect their gods which was why they were defeated? Is obedience tied to victory? Can we theorize that the powers of African gods and Maji Maji medicine were restricted or were designed to destroy non-European weapons? Why did the gods of Tanzania allow Europeans to conquer Africans if they knew the long-lasting effects of colonization? If the conditions that Ohadike describes in Tanzania and Kenya are the same as the context of divine powers in Yorubaland, where the incantations of gods were specific to a specific location and defined to destroy a specific group of people, then we need to know a wide range of other issues.

Ohadike vindicates the gods and divine powers in Tanzania by showing how the Nyabingi cult emerged in East Africa to unify a divided people and to provide a hopeful site for resisting European powers at the same time. Among the priestesses who surfaced around a crucial moment is Muhamusa who "declared herself the liberator of the Africans and instigated many uprisings." Other successful rebellions led by new priests and priestesses against heavy taxes and levies imposed on Africans occurred around this period. Religion, as Ohadike contends, became an important impetus for rallying support for uprisings and rebellions from 1918 through 1928. Ohadike narrates how Christianity was introduced into Africa during this era and how foreign religion overshadowed traditional religions, especially those led by priests and priestesses. Ohadike takes side in his conclusion, and credits Europeans for imposing Christianity on Africans.

In the following pages, Ohadike provides similar synopses, and he analyzes the influence of religion in the decolonization process, especially the Mau Mau movement in Kenya and how they fought violently against British domination. Ohadike is particularly concerned about the fate of the Kikuyu. He shifts his analysis from one region to the other by comparing the Mau Mau movement and the Ekumeku movement in Southern Nigeria. To end chapter one, he provides a long narrative of the Mau Mau movement and explores ceremonial religious practices as well as the political rhetoric of the movement. Such practices appropriated Christian songs and Bible references to empower their followers. Ohadike has to explain why the Mau Mau movement embraced Christianity—a western imposed religion which was resisted in the initial phase of the armed struggle. Like the priest and priestesses earlier described, disloyal followers were punished by the gods in Kenya.

Ohadike's conclusion does not follow the theme of chapter one. In this chapter, he sets out to show how traditional practices aided decolonization and became a shield for resisting European deadly weapons. Paradoxically, Ohadike contends that "religion did not cause resistance, it was European violence and economic exploitation that did. All that religion did was to unify the oppressed and instill in them a sense of purpose."[4] His conclusion is bold. In the first place, he wants us to believe that charms, prayers, amulets and other spiritual powers were elements of resistance against European weaponry. Yet, he later states that religion did not aid in resisting oppression. If this argument holds true, then the entire discussion and long narratives about the role of priests, priestesses, deities and other divine interventions will need a rethinking. Also, Ohadike has to explain why the communities he describes resisted Christianity in the beginning of their crusade, why they embraced them at a point in time and resisted them once again when the resistance movements became more successful. In other words, why is the element of Christianity important to this chapter?

Chapter two seeks to show how Africans in the diasporas relied on similar religious forms of resistance by Africans. Ohadike debunks the notion that Africans in the New World had no traces or retentions of African cultures, and he shows how slaves were guided and motivated by the marks of their African past and common sufferings in captivity. He provides streams of religious practices such as *candomblé* in Brazil, *voodoo* in Haiti, and *sango* in Cuba. Ohadike asserts that the descendants of slaves were tied spiritually to their gods, goddesses and ancestors. He also looks at the ways in which both men and women depended on spiritual powers to aid them in rituals, politics and medical practices. For maroon and other slave communities, spirituality was a vital ingredient and a source of strength for their rebellions and escape. Ohadike points out that spiritual protection was also necessary for slaves who were subjected to whipping and other forms of physical attacks.

Contemporary religious practices in the New World can be traced to Africa. To strengthen his arguments about African retentions and religious practices in the slave plantations and beyond, Ohadike explores the use of poison as a form of resistance and traditional African rituals that are performed during burial services in the New World. Also, he traces the various regions where slaves were captured in Africa and how the geographical differences infused diverse religious practices in the plantations.

The beginning of chapter two is very complicated because Ohadike tries to tackle multiple themes which he fragments into many ideas. He makes an interesting link between African and European languages as a basis for explaining how this process made it easy for slaves from one region (Anglophone) to communicate with others (Francophone), but some readers may ask for more historical evidence. He provides a richer analysis when he talks about specific African religions such as Yoruba practices. He asserts that many slaves embraced Yoruba religion because of the strong Yoruba presence and due to the fact that Yoruba religion was "tied less to object and place than were the beliefs of other African groups."[5] In his effort to explain why some African cultures were easily sustained and why others slowly faded, he claims that population size was crucial to this process. For example, he argues that the African presence in Brazil was stronger because of the high density of African slaves in the region. In the case of North America, Ohadike suggests that due to the limited number of slaves in the area Black American Churches appropriated African cultural practices such as songs and dances into their activities and became the new spiritual voice for slaves as African retentions faded out slowly between generations.

Ohadike had no time to prop up his claims. How did the Black American Church emerge and what is the transition between the periods when African cultural practices were at their zenith? What other historical circumstances explains this phenomenon? A timeline is needed in this chapter to explain the occurrence of events that he relates. Historian Michael Gomez's book, *Exchanging Our Country Marks*, discusses the religious retentions of African slaves and how slavery evolved both culturally and racially. This book would be a great reference point for this chapter.

Ohadike associates *Santeria*, a Cuban cultural practice, with Yoruba practices. He focuses on Oba Oduduwa and other supreme beings and deities. Ohadike explores spiritual intermediaries such as Obatala, Esu, Orunmila, Esu, Sango, Osun and Yemonja who are stationed in heavenly realms. He provides a long narrative about the role of "lesser gods" who acted as agents for connecting the community to their gods. Furthermore, Ohadike underscores religious rituals and ceremonies that occurred during this time. As we have stated earlier, Ohadike does justice to his analysis and provides his readers with ample evidence and details whenever he talks about religious practices or references to Nigerian religious history. So far, this is the best part of his book. He should also be credited for his treatment of *candomblé* and the multiple role it plays in Catholicism and as a form of resistance. The discussion on voodoo deserves a similar praise because of the way the arguments are organized and supported by historical evidence.

Chapter three is the continuation of the previous chapter because it addresses themes of retention and resistance. Ohadike's greatest task here is to show why the *Rumba* dance could be traced to Yorubaland rather than to other geographical regions on the African continent.[6] According to him, in Cuba, African slaves used *Rumba* dance and singing as a therapy against white racism and oppression, as avenues for maintaining self-control and self-pride, as well as a symbol of cultural resistance. He talks about how the *Rumba* dance is organized and the public places where they were commonly held in Cuba. However, Ohadike fails to talk about how the *Rumba* got to Cuba. His strongest point is that while slavery stripped Afro-Cubans of their humanity and pride, the *Rumba* became a vehicle for restoring them. He contends that through singing and dancing, the *Rumba* provided a platform for women to attract men sexually.[7]

He also introduces the *Samba* dance in Brazil, and shows how *Samba* was appropriated by Brazilian white elites to mask racial discrimination. In other words, he claims that *Samba* provided a false image of Brazil as a country with racial harmony. He provides the historical background of *Samba* and how it is demonstrated through body movements. Ohadike believes that *Samba* has religious significance in Brazil and plays a role in politics.

Although his thrust about *Samba* is warranted, we can complicate his thematic and methodological approach by raising a number of points: 1) how did *Samba* become a major source of revenue for Brazil? 2) how did the *Samba* evolve from Afro-Brazilian history and how did the dance gradually become part of white capitalist culture? 3) the preparations towards yearly carnival celebrations which the *Samba* dance forms a key part. 4) an examination of how the Brazilian government has invested in the *Samba* schools as part of white elite's long-term plan to take total control over carnival festivities. In fact, one could write a chapter on this subject by showing the differences between the *Samba* dance and carnival celebrations in Bahia and Rio de Janeiro. There is an avalanche of historical sources for such a project.

Despite Ohadike's limitation to delve deeper into the *Samba* in Brazil, he does a great job in investigating the role of *capoeira* in Brazilian socio-political cultures. He corrects most of the earlier criticisms that we raised regarding chapters one and two. The subject is well treated and organized with cohesive arguments and evidence. His discussion on the steel band music of Trinidad, although short, follows a similar thread as his take on the capoeria in terms of its organization and as space of resistance.

In chapter four, Ohadike's interest is the progress of traditional African religions in Jamaica, and how this progress changed steadily to Christianity, then to Rastafarianism, and finally to *Reggae*. Similar to his examination of deities, priests, priestesses and other divine powers in Tanzania and other African countries, he attempts to show how *Obeah* and *Myal*, the two powerful spiritual agents in Jamaica, influenced Jamaicans. He explains that Nanny was a powerful religious figure in Jamaica during the struggle for independence. He shows how Nanny situates herself in different circumstances to exercise her authority over her followers and colonial powers alike. Ohadike references the strategies employed by the Mau Mau leaders to show how spiritual leaders also appropriated Christian practices to challenge the Anglican Church and other religious institutions in Jamaica.[8]

The fusion of African traditional religious practices and Christian doctrines is emphasized in this chapter. He notes that baptism by immersion and the gift of the Holy Spirit were twin experiences that Jamaicans embraced in the religious ceremonies because of the common roots they shared. For example, Jamaicans saw the anointing of the Holy Spirit and baptism by immersion as two parallel elements that connected them to the sea and their ancestral home.[9] Once again, Ohadike goes back and forth spreading his ideas but asking us to supply the historical backing on our own terms. He attributes the gradual demise of Myaism and other religious engines in Jamaica to the period of intense persecution by the Europeans. The abolition of slavery in 1834, as he describes it, did not guarantee freedom for Jamaicans; rather, it diffused mobilization efforts and forced traditional religions underground. The strategy of a random narrative creates a problem in the attempt to formulate ideas around the genesis of Rastafarianism and *Reggae*.

Rastafarianism, as Ohadike defines it, "is a movement that seeks to establish its own identity."[10] He searches for ways to tie Rastafarianism to African cultural practices, especially to Myalism. Ohadike does a better job when he interrogates Rastafarianism and how it offers sanctuary to poor people and other subaltern groups. He grapples with this subject as he tries to use African cultures, religions, music and dance as a lens for gauging the popularity of Rastafarianism. Finally, he finds an outlet for his argument and explores it to its fullest. Ohadike reaches the zenith of his analysis when he unearths the historical resemblance or the connections between Rastafarians and Ethiopianism. He claims forcefully that Rastafarians trace their roots to Ethiopia, the cradle of civilization and Christianity in Africa,[11] but it is still not clear how the movement connects to other African religious practices. If Ohadike admits from the outset of the chapters that Christianity was denounced by many African cultures, and that Rastafarianism is a movement but not a religion then he has to explain the ties between Ethiopia, the cradle of Christianity, and a non-religious movement like Rastafarianism.

Like other scholars who pursue similar projects, Ohadike also falls into the same trap of trying to force undistinguishable historical ties or events between the two geographical regions: Africa and the New World. For example, he uses Marcus Garvey's prophecy that a "Black King would be crowned in Ethiopia" as a justification for showing the validating linkages between Rastafarians and Ethiopia. He provides extremely long narratives about Ethiopian history and the nation's glorious defeat of Italians in 1896. The additional four pages talk about Marcus Garvey's ideological and spiritual relationship with Ethiopia. Subsequent discussions look at how Rasta and *Reggae* serve as the bedrock for Rastafarianism and how the movement attracts both the working class and middle class population. Dreadlocks and *Reggae*, as he describes them, have become the symbol of resistance and Black pride internationally because of the influence of Rastafarianism. He treats *Reggae* better in his analysis and explains how its lyrics remain the leading voice in resisting all forms of white power.[12]

In chapter five, Ohadike shifts to another contentious terrain: Islamic resistance to European domination. This chapter, without doubt, is the most organized, coherent and well argued in the entire book. The methodology and the thematic approach leave no doubt that it could have been added to the manuscript after the rest of the chapters were developed. It treats the subject of African retentions in the New World differently and covers a more detailed scope. He successfully constructs historical accounts that outline the contentions between Islam and Christianity in their quest to convert and control Africans and their resources. Students interested in the relation between Muslims and Christians in Africa will find it very useful.

According to Ohadike, Islamic resistance to European intrusion is very complex because of the long-standing historical conflicts between the two groups for religious space, conversions and recognition. Muslims did not only see the penetration of Europeans into Africa and other regions as a threat, but foremost the religion perceived Europeans as unbelievers or *Kafiri*.[13] He links Islamic rebellions to Islamic liberation theology and uses a chunk of the narrative explaining why, when and how Islamic jihad emerged in Africa. The teachings of the Prophet Mohammad, the role of the caliphs, emirs, mallams and other significant actors in Islamic rebellions against Europeans around the globe is also underscored. European plans to end Muslim monopoly over trading routes in East Africa and their attempts to convert Muslims into Christianity are also included. Ohadike contends that for many Muslims, European penetration into Islamic realms was perceived as an extension of the crusade. We would like to see a comparative analysis with European response to Islamic enslavement of Africans in this chapter. If Ohadike's project aspires to show how Africans and people of African descent resisted European domination of Africans why did he leave out the response of Africans to Islamic enslavement? If they did, did they consult the same divine interventions African gods, priests, priestesses and deities leaned upon?

Ohadike continues by examining subsequent or earlier Muslim rebellions in the Sokoto Caliphate in Nigeria, Brazil, Haiti, North America and other regions. This chapter consists of a wide range of data, mostly secondary sources. In fact, he leans heavily on Joao Reis' thought-provoking book, *Slave Rebellion In Brazil*, to show how African slaves from Nigeria capitalized on their large population size and their retentions of Africa as a tool for liberation.[14]

Beside spontaneous resistance in Portuguese colonies, Ohadike explores other uprisings in Francophone and Anglophone colonies where Muslims used similar tactics to end white oppression. He extends his detailed analysis to the rise of the Mahdi movement, an Islamic radical group in the Sudan. In North America he examines the role of the Nation of Islam in combating economic and racial inequalities. Ohadike does an excellent work here when he shows that the Nation of Islam, as an ideological group, was not as radical as other resistance movements that depended heavily on arms and guerilla style approaches. Also, the Nation of Islam, as he describes it, did not advocate for the integration of Blacks in America but for separation from the oppressive racist system.

Chapter six delves deeply into how Europeans and people of African descent appropriated Christianity as a vehicle for oppression or as a tool for freedom. While Europeans leaned on Christian doctrines to infuse notions of racial inequality and white hegemony, Africans on the other hand, as Ohadike posits, did not only embrace Christianity as an outlet for liberation but they sustained their traditional beliefs alongside Christianity during the process.[15] His investigation of Christianity dates back to the Byzantine era, where he makes the argument that European missionaries became agents of Christian enterprise in Africa. According to Ohadike, Europeans' emphasis on obedience permitted them to coax their subjects into enslavement. He notes that the history of European enslavements in Africa helps to explain why most Africans in the New World were pessimistic about, or despised some aspects of, Christianity.

Ohadike describes African theology as a tool that was devised by Africans for liberation. Liberation theology, as he shows, aims at reclaiming Christianity and appropriating Christian doctrine to suit African ideological schemes. Racially, liberation theology endeavors to "relate God and Christ once more to the black man and his daily problems."[16] Ohadike's approach is praise worthy. European ethnocentrism is visible in the process of commodifying Christian symbols such as water baptism to guarantee salvation. Although Europeans did not see Africans as a people with souls, they manipulated those they enslaved in order to force them to submit to their selfish and racist desires. In addition, he shows how Africans incorporated Christian doctrines and teachings in their worship and how others volunteered to be members of Christian churches. The list includes Denmark Vessel, Nat Turner and others who participated in Christian religions but used their experience as a platform for liberation.

In his analysis of liberation theology in Africa, Ohadike follows a similar approach to show how Ethiopia became the center of Black liberation theology because of its historical past. As Ohadike shows, tensions between African Christians over liberation theology created divisions that eventually influenced many Africans to apply African interpretations to Christian issues.[17] For many new African Christians, liberation theology allows them to emphasize self-empowerment, self-rule and political rights. Like Africans in the New World who used their retention and cultural practices such as voodoo, *candomblé, Samba* and others as a form of resistance, the new African liberation theology that mushroomed across the continent empowered Africans to adopt warfare tactics to end white control. He provides a long list of names and narratives to show how liberation theology spread in Africa and the African diaspora. Ohadike uses eight pages to chronicle the life of Dona Beatriz, a famous Congolese woman who opposed Catholicism and Portuguese imperialists. The rest of the chapter cites comparable crusades to prop up liberation theology and to repel white oppression.

For chapter seven, "Black Popular Music of Resistance in the USA: From Blues to Rap," Ohadike brings back some of the themes that he explores in the earlier chapters. He begins with Blues and argues that in order to differentiate one form of performance from the other, it is imperative that one evaluates the cultural context, the historical underpinnings and the socio-political messages they convey.[18] Thereafter, Ohadike traces the origins of Blues to Africa. Similarly to his assertion about the significance of music in chapter three, he repeats the notion that music was a source of comfort and remedy for combating loneliness and distress in many plantations. According to Ohadike, scholars grapple with the exact historical moment that Blues evolved but the consensus is that the era of emancipation of slaves best describes how Blues surfaced and how it was sustained by slaves. Despite the freedom that slaves lost after emancipation, he notes that Blues became synonymous with freedom. New Orleans, as Ohadike describes it, became the center for developing and for nursing Blues in the United States, a practice which persists till today.

Language and communication are two vital elements in the expansion of Blues in the United States. According to Ohadike, Blues musicians who were mostly lowly educated Blacks who joined the mass exodus to Northern cities in the early 1900s were compelled by their circumstances to move away from what was perceived as "primitive" Blues to a "more refined" Blues in order to reach their diverse audience. It was through this transformation that Classical Blues emerged. According to Ohadike, in spite of major national socio-economic tragedies such as the Great Depression in 1929, the crusade to sustain and expand Rhythm and Blues flourished in many cities. In fact, Ohadike continues that contemporary Blues was born after World War II and gained more momentum during the civil rights era.[19]

Also, he analyzes the roots of Rap music in the United States in the 1970s and shows how the ghettos became the core musical station for spreading the message they communicate.

Thereafter, he looks at the ways in which Rap music contributes to socio-political ideas in the United States and abroad. He then credits major Rap musicians such as Tupac Shakur, Talib Kweli, Lauryn Hill and other musicians in the entertainment business. He claims that many poor people have been attracted by Rap musicians because the messages they convey echo poverty, crime, poor health and other issues that affect the daily lives of the working class communities. In fact, he contends that while Rap music gravitates towards social issues it also serves similar projects pursued by major media outlets such as the CNN: Rap music also broadcast and disseminate news about crisis in Black America, Ohadike asserts.[20]

He notes that a large percentage of working class and "liberal" Americans embrace Rap music. Despite the criticism that Rap music corrupts the morals of the youth, promotes violence, perpetuates pre-marital sex and devalues women, many conservatives have joined the musical bandwagon in recent times. According to Ohadike, while critics of Rap music continue to launch campaigns to taint the image of Rap musicians, many young and poor people see Rap music as an outlet for instilling self-pride, self-identity and self-respect among the youth.

In the last chapter, "Black Music of Resistance in South Africa, 1818-1994," Ohadike sets out to complete a daunting task. His objective is to chronicle the history of Black music in South Africa during the last one hundred and fifty years. He races through the chapter to articulate his argument. The thrust of chapter eight is visible in the first three pages as he devotes the introduction to talk about colonial experiences in various parts of Africa, wage labor in Nigeria and anti-colonial crusade by the Mau Mau movement. Instead of interrogating the core of his topic, Ohadike deals with the crust area. To make this chapter more complex, he provides Nigerian songs as evidence to support his claims. After all, there is nothing wrong academically to insert other ideas that support an argument, but a Zulu song or a song from South Africa could prop up his arguments better. Ohadike probes the central theme and shows how European discovery of

Gold in South Africa simultaneously led to enslavement, genocide and the systematic placement of the local people on the
peripheral of her national treasure.

He believes that *capoeira* and voodoo in the New World,
and dance and music in South Africa were the most common
weapons of resistance, for mobilization, for creating Black consciousness, and for injecting racial pride. Ohadike describes the
functions of various musical instruments and argues that many
African nationalist leaders including Nnamdi Azikiwe, Jomo
Kenyatta and Kwame Nkrumah were influenced by *Ngoma*, a
form of musical performance.[21] Regarding how and when these
leaders were influenced by *Ngoma*, Ohadike does not tell us.
Did they travel to South Africa? Did they hear or participate in
Ngoma music and dance because the performance spread across
other countries across the continent? He provides a long narrative about Miriam Makeba, a music legend in South Africa. He
describes her as the vital link between the struggle against apartheid and Jim Crow laws in the United States.[22]

As if Ohadike is undertaking a biographical project of Makeba,
he places his earlier objective on the back burner and talks extensively about her. He documents the family tree of Makeba, and
how she became interested in music, the various jobs she secured
as a musician, her activism and her contacts with various foreign
artists and nationalist leaders in the United States. Ohadike
should be praised for including some of the revolutionary songs
of Makeba that speaks to the struggle of South Africans and for
demonstrating how Makeba rallied support internationally.

CONCLUSION

This is a splendid synthesis that leans heavily on secondary
sources. Ohadike's book performs several tasks, especially the
analysis of African retentions in the New World. In most of the
chapters, he makes a salient and a compelling case that although
slaves were forcefully removed from their ancestral homelands,

the Middle Passage experience could not strip them of their memories of Africa. He challenges us to take African retentions in the New World seriously. The book is part of a body of emerging diasporic literature that seeks to interrogate how some historical narratives are configured, the production of knowledge, its methodological underpinnings, and, most significantly, how some authentic historical voices are either silenced or systematically erased to favor other paradigms. Ohadike's journey to participate in this important project is laudable. He is remarkably successful when he interrogates issues relating to Nigerian history and when he provides broad overviews about his themes.

In chapter one, Ohadike generates a religious debate. Is it safe to say that the European conquerors depended on the "god of the white man" during the enslavement and colonization of the African? If so, can we suggest that African gods were more effective when they had to operate within their socio-cultural and political boundaries rather than contesting with European gods? To put it in another way, is the ammunition of Europeans powerful than the spiritual oracles of African gods? What does oral tradition offer us as we deal with this stimulating religious issue? One problem still remains—can scholars reconstruct academic framework to address these questions? Now that Ohadike lives in the unseen world, perhaps, he could find an answer to this epistemological problem.

Notes
1. Chapter 1.
2. Ibid.
3. Ibid.
4. Ibid.
5. Chapter 2.
6. Chapter 2.
7. Ibid.

8. Chapter 3.
9. Ibid.
10. Ibid.
11. Ibid.
12. Ibid.
13. Chapter 6.
14. We recommend other books to expand the argument: Mieko Nishida, "Slavery and Identity: Ethnicity, Gender and Race in Salvador,Brazil, 1808-1888" (Bloomington: Indiana University Press, 2003); and James Sweet, "Recreating Africa: Culture,Kinship and Religion in the African Portuguese World, 1441-1770"(Chapel Hill: University of North Carolina Press, 2003).
15. Chapter 6, 3.
16. Ibid.
17. Ibid.
18. Chapter 7.
19. Ibid.
20. Ibid.
21. Chapter 8.
22. Ibid.

CHALLENGING OPPRESSION WITH SACRED DRUMS AND DANCE

Raphael Chijioke Njoku[1]

Sacred Drums of Liberation is a moving account of Black people's quest for freedom from the various forms of European plunders and domination. Here is a multidisciplinary study focusing on religion, music and dance as some of the dominant and successful strategies through which enslaved and colonized Africans survived several centuries of alien acts of brutality and perfidy. The miseries experienced by the Africans started early in the fifteenth century with the rise of trans-Atlantic slavery and the making of the African diaspora. This would later expand and deepen with the dawn of colonialism and racialist ideologies against people of African descent. In a way, this book offers the reader with the reasons for the survival of Africans from the inhuman conditions of plantation labor, the brutal wars of European conquest and colonization, the depressing civil rights struggle in the United States, the bloody anti-Apartheid movements in South Africa, and the humiliations of outright racism. In their spirited fights with each of these forms of alien threats, the Africans held strongly to the trilogy of religion, music and dance as a mode of dialogue with their ancestors, a symbol of strength, a means of cultural expression, and an idiom of identity. From an African epistemological viewpoint, religion and music, which are always accompanied by dance, tied up together instrumental sounds, body movements, and soul rejuvenating spirituals as a distinctive form of self-narrative.

While several studies have analyzed different dimensions of the African encounters with Europe and the historical outcomes of that contact, this book is unique because it is the first to bind the idioms of religion, music and dance in a Pan African context of resistance, while highlighting the dynamics of culture, adaptations and continuities. This history started early on the Portuguese slave ships leaving the continent in the 1440s. As the victims of the trans-Atlantic slave trade were hauled across the ocean, they quickly began to construct a new sense of common identity irrespective of the obvious problem of language barriers. Where some scholars like P. O. Esedebe have claimed that Pan-Africanism, as an ideological movement, "originally began in the so-called New World, becoming articulate during the century starting from the declaration of American independence,"[2] Ohadike looks beyond this projection. In this book, and also in his *Pan African Culture of Resistance: A History of Resistance Movements and the Diaspora*, our able historian pins down the birth of the Pan African idea on the European-owned slave ships. Confronted with the language barrier, Ohadike reasons that music and dance provided the Africans with a viable mode of communication.

In the African indigenous society, religion, music and dance are part of everyday life. No festival (both religious and secular) was complete without music and dance and certain genres of African music are communal properties whose spiritual qualities are shared by all. Consecrated drums and other instruments provided the music and dance that often accompany religious worship. For the oppressed Africans, consecrated drums interspersed with sacred powers provided them with hope, energy, and boldness to stand up against oppression. Music created the emotive spirit for political awakening and war against the white culture of domination. In other words, it was religion and music that first defined the African exiles in the Americas and helped rediscover their broken manhood. From the sacred drums oozed the secrecy, and coded messages that summoned Black freedom fighters to action. Thus, through instrumentation, singing and dancing, African traditional religion communicated a defining message—namely, that religion is not about going to heaven or hell as Christianity claims, but about healing bruised souls and mending tortured bodies; about making peace between individuals and the supernatural forces; and about finding solace in communion with the ancestors.

Carefully divided into eight chapters which drew from a variety of sources, *Sacred Drums of Liberation* immerses the reader into a nuanced accounts of the survival, adaptations and continuities of African cultural elements in the face of the white man's acts of intimidations, hostility and botched legislations aimed at expurgating them. Chapter one lays the foundation for subsequent chapters with a lively discussion on the role of African traditional religious belief system as an instrument of colonial resistance. It narrates how the Africans deployed charms, prayers, amulets, and curses to counter European maxim guns and other instruments of terror including evangelical subterfuge. In the absence of sacred documents, the indigenous charms and amulet, oral history, rituals, and poetry served as sacred documents. In East Africa, more than any other area on the continent, diviners, and charismatic leaders led revolts against the European presence. Chapter two explains how religion served diaspora Africans as a binding force of identity and mobilization in the face of language barrier. Within the Black churches in the United States, *Santerias* and voodoo worshippers in Cuba, religion served as an instrumental force of political awakening.

Chapter three focuses on the use of rumba, samba, *capoeira* and steelband as instruments of resistance in Cuba, Brazil and Trinidad. Particularly, rumba served as a form of therapy loaded with defiant displays of sexuality. It permitted Black men to recommence their protective role on women. Samba in Brazil combined secular and spiritual practices and oral literature to communicate what the mouth could not. In Brazil also, *capoeira* (a blend of martial art and a dance of dialogue) strived towards liberty under the cover of secrecy. Similarly, steelband music, invented by the Trinidadian poor and oppressed (or panmen), served as a mode of resistance against the dominating upper class.

Chapter four examines Jamaica's social history in the context of change. This chapter educates the reader on the dynamics of syncretism involving elements of traditional African religion, Christianity Rastafarianism, and *Reggae*. Each of these genres of spiritual movements produced a unique form of opposition against white domination. Along with them came the practice of *Pukumina* or *Pokomanie*, an amalgam of elements of African traditional religious practices and Christian values. Religious syncretism in Jamaica brought about the emergence of over two hundred Afro Christian cults in the 1860s.

While chapter five analyzes the contributions of Black jihadists in the struggle against European stranglehold in Africa, Brazil and the United States, chapter six focuses on African theology and Black liberation theology as resistance movements in Africa and the United States respectively. The latter, which drew its form from elements of continental African indigenous religious practices, expanded dramatically from being a religion of succor for the oppressed, to a theology of confrontation and liberation. Chapter seven dealt with Black popular music of resistance in the United States, including Blues and Rap. Blues, in particular, symbolizes the Black person's expression of loneliness and isolation and his new challenges in a post-abolition American society. Chapter eight, revisits the role of religion, music and dance as idioms of African resistance against the evils of Apartheid policies in South Africa.

Overall, this educative book reflects the snowballing experience of a multi-talented African historian, teacher and distinguished scholar. It will appeal to a wide variety of interests, including students of African colonial and nationalist history, diaspora studies, comparative religion, and African-American history. Those in music, theater arts, and the general readers will find this book a useful companion.

Notes

1. Raphael Chijioke Njoku, PhD., is a first class history graduate of the University of Nigeria, Nsukka (UNN). He holds two PhDs in African-history from Dalhousie University, Canada and in African Politics from

Vrije (Free) University, Brussels, Belgium. He is a recipient of numerous academic awards and holds a joint position as Assistant Professor of African History in the Departments of History and Pan African Studies, University of Louisville, Kentucky, USA. He has previously taught at the Department of History, Alvan Ikoku College of Education, Owerri, Nigeria. Njoku is the author of *Culture and Customs of Morocco* (Greenwood, 2005), and *African Cultural Values: Igbo Political Leadership in Colonial Nigeria, 1900-1966* (Routledge, 2006). He has also been published in several international journals and edited.

2. P. Olisawuchukwu Esedebe, *Pan-Africanism: The Idea and the Movement, 1776-1991* second ed. (Washington D.C.: Howard University Press, 1994), 8.

"DON WAS 'DONATUS' AND HE WAS 'OHADIKE'"[1]

Apollos O. Nwauwa[2]

Of all the tactics that the Europeans use to subvert African cultures, especially African religions and music, none is more ingenious than the principle of assimilation. Outwardly, assimilation is harmless yet its consequences could be devastating. One of the aims of assimilation is to achieve political and cultural control by mounting a vicious attack on the victim's consciousness and self-esteem. When put in motion, the victim begins to hate the customs of his people, their language, music and religion. Now, he listens to Mozart and Beethoven, rather than Fela Kuti and Sunny Ade. And rather than visit his relatives and ancestral shrines in the countryside, he spends his vacations in Paris, London and Rome (p. 14)

For those in search of the best way to understand or characterize Don Ohadike's intellectual disposition, the above citation culled from *Sacred Drums of Liberation* is unmistakably instructive. It is the best way to grasp his philosophy on the destructive effects of psychological alienation on black cultures, personality and identity. His analysis of the policy of divide-and-conquer, which Europeans effectively used against Africans of the continent during colonial rule, and which European slave owners used against Africans in the diaspora during slavery through the process of assimilation is very compelling. Colonial and slave mentalities are two deadly combination. Their impact on the progress of Africans and the diaspora cannot be underestimated. *Sacred Drums of Liberation* exposes the extent of the ongoing black struggle to overcome. Don Ohadike must be placed in the center of this struggle and scholarship for that is where he belonged.

Although my acquaintance with Don Ohadike was more on a scholarly than personal level, it may well not be a coincidence to be invited to comment on his last but very compelling book, *Sacred Drums of Liberation.* Yet, it was not because Ohadike and I are both Igbo for there are, perhaps, other scholars better qualified for this role. But there is, probably, more to it. We are both historians of modern African history with intersecting research fields of interest and focus on Igbo resistance to British colonial incursion. While I focused on the Aro-Igbo, Ohadike concentrated on Anioma-Igbo; and as Ohadike later broadened his scope to include the African diaspora in his study of resistance movements, my effort equally shifted to include continental African resistance to colonial education and the consequent agitation for indigenous higher educational institutions. Coincidentally, also, and without any premeditation, we both shifted our research attention to the role of Igbo intellectuals in the making of African intellectual tradition, with Ohadike working on Maazi Mbonu Ojike and I focusing on Professor Kenneth Onwuka Dike. Our papers on these two remarkable individuals were concurrently presented at the African Studies Association conference in Nashville, Tennessee, in 2001 on a panel chaired by Ohadike himself. In a sense, I have always threaded in the shadows of Don Ohadike until his dignified passing in 2005. As a scholar, it was an honor to be associated with him, and, for me, making this commentary on his works is inestimable.

I knew Don before I met him. For more than twenty years before I actually met him for the first time, Don Ohadike's name had lingered on my mind. It was in 1985 that Ohadike's name was first introduced to me during my third year as an undergraduate history student at the Bendel State (now Ambrose Alli) University, Ekpoma, Nigeria, by the Professor A. C. Unomah (now late), then professor of history and deputy vice chancellor at the university. Unomah informed my class that he had finalized plans to bring to the university a well-respected historian. But who was this scholar, we all wondered. Later, we learnt that it was Don Ohadike, a senior lecturer and chair of the department of history at the University of Jos. As it turned out, Ohadike never joined the university as was anticipated. Twenty years later, I personally met Dr. Ohadike, not in Nigeria but in the United States. When I narrated to him our great expectation of his arrival at Ekpoma, he only smiled and said that he had to make some difficult choices. But what Ohadike regarded as a difficult choice – relocation to the United States – ultimately took him to the pinnacle of his scholarly career. Sojourning in the USA provided Ohadike the priceless opportunity to integrate the diaspora fully into his research on resistance. The result is an enduring intellectual legacy for peoples of African descent worldwide.

Although my task here is to comment on *Sacred Drums of Liberation*, the quintessence of Ohadike's scholarly contributions cannot totally be captured in one volume. Thus, I will not restrict my comment to this monograph. Ohadike's intellectual domains were quite transnational, cross-disciplinary, and cosmopolitan. Accordingly, his research and publications covered a wide range of topics in pre-colonial African history, contemporary African labor history, African economic history, the history of slavery and emancipation, and religion and politics in Africa and the diaspora. His publications appeared in major refereed journals on topics such as slavery and emancipation, missionary role in European colonization, the influenza pandemic and spread of cassava cultivation in Igboland, the rise of the Benin kingdom, religious conflict in Nigeria, and African resistance to European domination. As a scholar, he passionately confronted social, economic, political and psychological issues that have retarded the progress of black people in Africa and the diaspora. Ohadike was deeply committed to contributing meaningfully to Igbo studies generally and to push the frontiers of that field beyond what pioneer scholars such as Dike, Ottenberg, Anene, Ifemesia, Afigbo, Ekechi, and others accomplished. It was no surprise, therefore, that Don Ohadike was invited by Heinemann in 1996 to write the introduction to Chinua Achebe's masterpiece, *Things*

Fall Apart, a fictional prose depicting the nature and impact of European colonial intrusion into Igboland. Only eminent scholars of Ohadike's caliber deserve such an honor.

Ohadike was a man of his people, the Igbo, as exemplified by his intellectual inquiry and personal actions. Ever searching for ways to encourage Igbo studies, Ohadike organized the first international conference on Igbo studies at Cornell University in 2003 in honor of Professor Simon Ottenberg, one of the pioneers of Igbo studies. Yet, believing in the unity of Africans all over the world, Ohadike was convinced that his calling as an historian was far beyond a focus only on Anioma and Igbo resistance. Thus, as he continued to push the frontiers of Igbo studies, he also redoubled his research efforts on the African diaspora. This duality, or should I say unity, of purpose was essentially at the core of Biodun Jeyifo's eulogy affirming that "Don was 'Donatus' and he was 'Ohadike.'" Although he was born an Igbo, he identified with the plights of all Africans in Africa and in the diaspora; and though he began his intellectual life as a scholar of Igbo and continental African resistance to colonialism, he ended with pan-African studies.

Ohadike turned his research and scholarly attention to the African diaspora, joining Cornell University in the United States in 1989 to further that cause. Since then, his research work and publication became trans-Atlantic, trans-disciplinary and transnational, linking resistance movements of Africans in the continent to European colonialism to those of the diaspora in their resistance against white oppression and domination. Ohadike's commitment to this cause resulted in the publication of *Pan-African Culture of Resistance: A History of Liberation Movements in Africa and the diaspora* (2002) as well as this present work, *Sacred Drums of Liberation*, which is being published posthumously. In retrospect, Ohadike's departure from the University of Jos, and turning down Ekpoma in 1985 as anticipated, and subsequent relocation to the United States had salutary effects on black studies on a global scale.

Don Ohadike's was an authority in the field of African resistance to European colonial occupation. His painstaking research, resulting in the publication of the seminal monograph, *Ekumeku Movement: Western Igbo Resistance to the British Conquest of Nigeria, 1883-1914* (1991) revealed the tenacious resistance of the Western Igbo against British colonial incursion. This work remains a model for an indigenous resistance movement and micro historical analysis that foreshadows those of the larger, centralized kingdoms. Though specific to Western Igbo, *Ekumeku Movement* is one of the most influential studies on African resistance to European colonialism. Ohadike sheds new light into the intriguing dynamics of Igbo resistance against European colonial intrusion. Hitherto, Igbo resistance has been explained largely in terms of submission without a fight or collaboration by the disparate polities, with the exception of the well-documented resistance of the Aro, Abam and Ohafia. In some sense, Ohadike changed all that. Despite the accolades on *Ekumeku Movement*, Ohadike was aware that the work, in actuality, was the story of "European action and African reaction" and that the indigenous history of Anioma people was yet to be written. It was basically against this background that he swiftly and diligently worked on and published *Anioma: A Social History of the Western Igbo People* (1994) shortly after, focusing on the evolution, settlement and diffusion of Anioma people. With this, Ohadike did his people proud as a true *"son of the soil."*

After thoroughly reading *Sacred Drums of Liberation*, I state without any equivocation that this book is a trailblazer on black protests and resistance movements. It is well conceptualized, well researched, and well written. Works on the resistance of Africans in the continent and the diaspora are well documented, including Ohadike's own *Ekumeku Movement* and *Pan-African Resistance Culture*. However, what have been glossed over, or sometimes missing, in existing literature are the roles of music, dance, and religions in the resistance movements among peoples of African descent, and how Africans have effectively deployed these cultural traits in their resistance movements against white

xl   Sacred Drums of Liberation

domination. Fortunately, Ohadike's *Sacred Drums of Liberation*
now closes that research gap in such a refreshing fashion. Historical and sociological in both methodology and analysis, this work
is pleasantly engaging. Ohadike's love of music was a boon quite
palliative to a rather depressing story of agony and oppression of
blacks by whites. Thanks to Ohadike, readers will now appreciate
the deeper messages of *Reggae*, Rap, *Ngoma*, Samba, etc. as well
as the role of African religious beliefs in helping blacks through
the difficult eras of their history.

In general terms, Ohadike isolated two aspects of black resistance: against economic exploitation and against forced assimilation. For both struggles, the sacred drums played a significant role.
Essentially, *Sacred Drums of Liberation* explores how black people
in Africa and the diaspora used religion, music, and dance during
their struggle against European enslavement, racism, colonialism
and neo-colonial exploitation. Accordingly, "religions, music and
dance have enabled black people to survive five hundred years of
white culture of violence and economic exploitation" (p.2). The
African drum used in this context is not just an ordinary musical
instrument, "it is a communication tool, used to transmit oral traditions," and when properly performed, sacred drums may express
special feelings like joy, affection or grief (p.3).

Ambitious in its scope and content, and covering Africa and
the diaspora, *Sacred Drums of Liberation* is subdivided into eight
broad chapters. But for brevity, I have merged them in four clus-
ters. Chapters one and two examine the role of African religious
beliefs in protest movements in Africa and among blacks in the
Americas. Ohadike shows how charismatic priests and diviners
mobilized the masses against European colonization as exemplified in the case of the Maji-Maji rising in Tanzania, Nyabingi cult
in East Africa, and the Mau Mau movement in Kenya. Despite
their determinations, last-ditch religious movements were
defeated, and Ohadike argued that it was largely because the military strategies of most of the movements did not include guerrilla
tactics and attacks were not pre-planned. In the Americas, black
cultures and religious practices in Brazil, Cuba and Haiti were

used by blacks for survival and in resisting the agony of slavery. Convincingly, Ohadike argued that religious beliefs among blacks in the Americas are syntheses of the various African religions and they were linked to political mobilization and rebellion. Yet, he cautioned that "religion did not cause resistance, it was European violence and economic exploitation that did" (p.39).

Chapters three and four discuss how the music and dance of enslaved Africans became effective tools of protest against physical abuses as well as instruments of cultural resistance. Using the *Rumba* of Cuba, *Samba* of Brazil, *Steelband* of Trinidad, and *Rasta* and *Reggae* of Jamaica as case studies, Ohadike showed how they all combined African dance forms with new styles to provide a commentary on the shattered life of the erstwhile-enslaved African, to suspend the life of a slave and to resume the life of a free person, and to rehumanize the dehumanized African slaves (p.68). Readers are reminded of the deeper messages of these musical forms and dance. *Samba*, for instance, manifests itself as a secular dance, as a spiritual practice, and as oral literature. "It tells the story of slavery and oppression, of conflict and resistance" (p.69) whereas the *Steelband* music, which evolved to contest the notions of white supremacy and black inferiority became an effective form of protest against European racial prejudice and exploitation. Similarly, *Rasta* and *Reggae* identified with the plight of the dispossessed, urban, poor Jamaicans, and played an equalizing role in breaking social barriers. The central themes of their message were race pride, black unity and African redemption.

Chapter five and six focus on liberation theology, an attempt to use religion – Christianity, African religion, or Islam – to achieve freedom, equality and justice. These chapters explore the crucial roles of Islam and Christianity in the development and spread of the black culture of resistance in Africa and the diaspora. As African Muslims opposed European conquest and colonization through the jihad "for the elimination of exploitation, corruption, and tyranny," the Nation of Islam emerged among blacks in America out of the economic and political crisis of the early twentieth to fight for freedom, justice and equality.

Frustrated by the racist state structure in their efforts to achieve social equality with the other Americans, members of the Nation of Islam called for separation. Equally, the ironic role of Christianity in African communities was highlighted. While many Africans resisted Christianity, those who accepted the faith used the Bible and its lessons in their struggle against European domination. Most of the African nationalists, and pan-Africanists and civil rights advocates in the diaspora were baptized Christians. Ohadike argued that Christianity failed to achieve its intended purpose of making blacks docile through conversion. Yet, as European used Christianity "to establish relations of domination in their dealings with non-European nations so did the Africans Africanize Christianity and then used it as an instrument of resistance against European domination" (p.142). In Africa, Christian liberation theology emerged in the form of Black or Ethiopian Churches to champion the development of nationalism as Black churches in the diaspora focused the Civil Rights movement.

Finally, chapters seven and eight examine popular music of resistance in both the USA and South Africa. While locating the origins of Blues in West Africa from where Africans first transplanted it into the USA, Ohadike contended Blues actually developed out of slaves' work songs, spirituals and field hollers, and "enabled blacks in America to endure the crises of emancipation, reconstruction, and integration into the wider contemporary society of America" (p.178). The connections between five most universally popular musical form, Jazz, Blues, Rhythm and Blues (R&B), Rock, and Rap as presented in a very fascinating way. For Ohadike, all of these musical forms have their roots in Africa because Rap, Rhythm and Blues, Rock, and Jazz are derived from Blues. Like African griots from where they derived, *Rap* functions as a historical text. Rappers do not always praise; they also admonish and ridicule. Yet, Rap "is a resistant music, a child of protest" (p.180). With the exception of some capitalist driven "bad" rappers, Rap condemned white (class) exploitation and the development of the black culture of resistance and contributed to political consciousness among the powerless. Likewise, the best form of anti-colonial songs and dances which developed in South Africa ridiculed colonial taxes and labor systems. Following the discovery of gold and diamond deposits in South Africa in the mid-19th century, Europeans used all sorts of violence and intimidation to force blacks into the capitalist labor system. South African blacks came together to dance *ngoma*, a dance of resistance against the enemy; its main instrument was the base drum. Furthermore, Miriam Makeba used her music to protest racial injustice that confronted her early in life and her fellow South Africans.

Students of African history and culture recognize that sacred drums are central to most African music, dance and religious worship. However, no scholar before Ohadike had comprehensively exposed the deeper meanings of the sounds of drum especially in relation to resistance movements. From *Sacred Drums of Liberation* we see the symbiotic relationship between music and religious worship and between both and the African drums. African music is led by drums, which communicate messages full of cultural meanings. The sacred drums speak the language of the ancestors that can be regarded as texts that one can learn and write about. The texts may be about history, about the riddles of life, about real lessons from real life experiences, or about impending danger. Although Africans on the continent and in the diaspora used music to express their feeling and preserve their culture and history, they "never lost sight of the potency of religion and music in resistance" (p.5). Although long years of enslavement, colonialism, and assimilation almost destroyed them, African cultures grew more adaptable as Africans in the diaspora defended their humanity while those in the continent held on tenaciously to their cultural heritage.

In conclusion, *Sacred Drums of Liberation* is an erudite but chilling valediction to all black people worldwide. As if Ohadike had the premonition of his dignified passing, and by way of farewell address disseminated through *Sacred Drums of Liberation,* he forewarned Africans of the continent and the diaspora not to

let their guards down because it is not yet "*uhuru*".[3] As Africans in
the continent continue to celebrate their 'flag' independence and
black in the diaspora the collapse of legal segregation, Ohadike
cautioned that black people

> must be reminded that white domination has
> changed its tactics but not its basic nature, and that
> black people everywhere are still being exploited,
> no longer by the old slave and colonial masters, but
> by the new multinational corporations, the World
> Bank, and the International Monetary Fund. Hiding
> behind the pale veil of globalization, white capital-
> ists wreck havoc on unsuspecting black communities.
> Burdened with high interest payments on IMF loans
> and currency devaluation, black people in Africa
> and the Caribbean are deprived of the fruits of their
> labor. They are also left out of the current worldwide
> economic prosperity (p.224).

Furthermore, Ohadike affirmed that the failure of white people to
recognize the need for reparations for the historical injustice and
tyranny perpetrated against black people under colonialism and
slavery will continue to drive a wedge on efforts towards reconciliation and racial harmony. According to him: "On the whole,
both black and white people must be reminded that the black
culture of resistance owes its entire existence to the white culture
of domination....What matters is that as long as black people
retain the collective memory of white violence, and as long as
white people refuse to make reparations for past transgressions,
the black culture of resistance will continue to advance."(p. 225).
Indeed, it is from the last few pages of *Sacred Drums of Liberation*
that readers can truly capture the intellectual passion, philosophy
and opinions of Professor Don Ohadike. He moved his scholarly
concerns from the corridors of Igbo resistance to global issues of
freedom, racial justice, and equal opportunities for all. Evidently,
he was fiercely dedicated to all African peoples in the continent
and the diaspora, and indeed to all true lovers of mutual respect
and understanding between the peoples of the world. Though he
was very proud of his Igbo roots and identity, Don asked that his

body should be laid to rest in America. And so it was! Don was a
world man, that is, he was "Donatus" as well as "Ohadike."

Notes

1. This title is culled from Biodun Jeyifo's, "Don Ohadike, He was Here: A
   Eulogy," presented during the funeral service for Professor Don Ohadike,
   September 03, 2005, *USA-Africa Dialogue*, No. 1280, http://www.
   utexas.edu/conferences/africa/ads/1280.html

2. *Apollos O. Nwauwa* is an Associate Professor of history and Africana
   Studies at Bowling Green State University, Ohio, and interim director
   of Africana Studies Program. He specializes in modern Africa, especially
   colonial and intellectual history, and has previously taught at Bendel State
   (now Ambrose Alli) University, Ekpoma, Nigeria; Rhode Island College,
   and Brown University, both in Providence, Rhode Island. Nwauwa is the
   author of the book *Imperialism, Academe, and Nationalism: Britain and
   University Education for Africans, 1860-1960* (London: Frank Cass,
   1997). His works on the Aro of Eastern Nigeria; British Abolition of the
   Slave Trade; Edward Wilmot Blyden; the British Warrant Chief System
   in Igboland; Kenneth Onwuka Dike; colonial education; impact of the
   colonialism and the cold war on Africa; etc. have appeared in books and
   internationally refereed journals such as *Anthropos, Cahiérs D'Études
   Africaines, Africa Quarterly, Asian and African Studies, History in Africa,
   Canadian Journal of African Historical Studies, Ife Journal of History*, and
   International Journal of African Studies. Currently, Nwauwa is working
   on a book-length manuscript entitled *The Mind Game: Nigerian Univer-
   sities and the Cold War, 1960-2000*.

3. *Uhuru* is a Kiswahili word for freedom. Usage and emphasis are mine.

Introduction

RELIGIONS AND MUSIC OF RESISTANCE IN AFRICA AND THE DIASPORA—AN OVERVIEW

I have, in a separate work, shown how the history of black people in Africa was connected to the history of the black people in the Americas, and how black people as a whole waged a five hundred-year war against European domination.[1] I explained that the struggle for black liberation began on European-owned slave ships, during the Atlantic crossing, and continued in the plantations and maroon settlements, giving rise to a Pan-African culture of resistance in the Americas. I defined the Pan-African culture of resistance as a protest-based pattern of behavior—a cultural heritage--that is shared by all people of African origin.

When fully matured, the Pan-African culture of resistance became the foundation upon which the Pan-African movement and all the other black resistance movements were forged. It was the Pan-African culture of resistance that instigated slave revolts, armed insurrections, civil disobedience, protests and resistance movements throughout the Black World. Slave emancipation in the Americas, the abrogation of racial segregation in the United States, and the granting of political independence to black people in Africa, the Caribbean and elsewhere could not have been achieved without the development of the Pan-African culture of resistance. It is evident that the Pan-African culture of resistance, which owed its entire existence to the white culture of domination, fostered the survival, identity, and unity of black people. In that study I concluded that there could never have been a Pan-African movement, or a Civil Rights movement, or any independence and liberation movements in the Black World without the prior birth of a Pan-African culture of resistance.[2]

But those were only a part of the story. To complete the story I have decided to consider the roles of music and religion in the struggle for black liberation. To do so, I must state at once that blacks have used religion and music to fight all forms of oppression. Because African cultures are permeated with religious forces, blacks have never lost sight of the potency of religion in protests. Also, because music and dance are integral parts of African life, blacks have effectively used them to vent their rage. It is not surprising, therefore, that religion, music and dance have enabled black people to survive five hundred years of white culture of violence and economic exploitation. Yet the role that the sacred drums played in these struggles has not been given adequate attention.

AFRICAN SACRED DRUMS

I must, therefore, begin by briefly showing the centrality of drums—especially the sacred African drums—in setting the mood for political mobilization and war against the white culture of domination. It is important to explain that sacred drums are at the heart of most African music, dance and religious worship. Charged with supernatural forces, drums speak the language of the ancestors. To become sacred, an ordinary drum must first be consecrated in order to provide it with godlike attributes.

Every sacred drum has a name, and can be conceived as belonging to a particular clan or family unit, albeit a family of drums. During a musical performance, for example, one drum may act as the father, another as mother, and the rest as sons and daughters. Apart from belonging to particular drum families, sacred drums are part and parcel of the kinship groups to which they belong. A sacred drum cannot be treated as the property of an individual. Instead, it is a member of a lineage organization.

Like any other member of the lineage, it is treated with a certain amount of respect, and it enjoys certain rights and privileges. This explains in part why an African clan could go to war if its sacred drum was violated, seized or stolen by another clan.

Every African community has its own set of sacred drums and sacred languages, which can be understood only by those who have gained a passionate knowledge of the clan language. For example, only those that understand certain dialects of the Yoruba language can comprehend the language of the famous Yoruba talking drums. The language that sacred drums speak can be regarded as texts that one can learn to read and write. The texts may be about history, about the riddles of life, about real lessons from real life experiences, or about an impending danger. When properly performed, sacred drums may express special feelings like joy, affection or grief. It is not difficult to see that the African drum is not just a musical instrument; it is a communication tool, used to transmit oral traditions.

On some special occasions, sacred drums speak in deep-tongues, and the messages they convey may be shrouded in secrecy. Only those that have been initiated into the ancestral cults can comprehend them. Among these are drums used in divination rituals as well as those used during the installation and burial of chiefs and great people.

In addition to these functions, a sacred drum can serve as the voice of the people. No one can afford to ignore its voice when it summons the community to assemble at the town-square, or to appear at the chief's palace. The town crier's authority issues from the power invested in the sacred drum.

Sacred drums are the ties that bind music to African religious worship. At the center of most African worship is music, accompanied by sacred drums, as well as other pieces of instruments, songs and dances.

One of the preconditions that the devotees of *Santeria* religion cannot afford to ignore is the use of consecrated *batá* drums during worship. No authentic initiation ceremony can take place, even in the United States, where the religion has recently spread, without the use of *batå* drums. This is because these sacred drums speak the language of the *orishas*, and only they can induce spirit possession or, as is commonly said, summon the divinities to mount their horses.

Black people in Africa and the diaspora know that every cultural element bears its own inner meanings, that black religions and music have deeper meanings than whites can ever fully comprehend. Black people also know that drumming may summon people to a dance party, but it can also declare the right moment to start an insurrection. In the Anioma district of southern Nigeria in 1898, the Roman Catholic Father Carlo Zappa, who had acquired some knowledge of the Igbo culture, was able to report about an event that took place before the opening of hostilities. According to his diary entry, the forces of the British Royal Niger Company had entered the town of Illah, uninvited. Infuriated by the presence of these troops, Anioma warriors quickly prepared for war, and when the sacred war drums sounded their ominous beat, every one who understood the language of the ancestors knew that something was amiss. Moments later, warriors descended upon the town and razed the Roman Catholic mission houses. As Father Zappa reported the incident,

> Early on the morning of that fateful day trumpets and war *tam-tams* (drums) were heard on all sides, leaving no room for doubt as to their meaning; and the rebels poured into Illah from every side. The mission buildings were destroyed.[3]

Evidence of the use of drums to summon warriors to combat has been reported from many parts of Africa. For example, G.C.K. Gwassa has explained that in certain parts of pre-colonial Africa, the *lilunga* or *kiligondo* (war drum) was usually beaten in a certain way to warn clan members of a common danger and to summon them to war.[4] This custom was so strong in the Congo, noted John Thornton, that "dancing a war dance *(sangamento)* was often used as a synonym for 'to declare war.'"[5] This custom was reproduced during the Stono Rebellion of 1739 in South Carolina, when slaves used drums to summon other slaves from the nearby plantations and they danced before they went into action.[6] Military dancing, accompanied by elaborate drumming was, and still is, a part of the African culture of war, a form of drill and military preparation.

RELIGION, MUSIC AND DANCE

It has been over 500 years that Europeans first made contacts with sub-Saharan Africans. The meeting resulted in the Atlantic slave trade, the colonial domination of Africa, and the abusive treatment of Africans everywhere. But it was on the slave ships and plantations, as well as in the maroon settlements in the Americas that Africans first expressed their disaffection with European violence. Their response was both violent and non-violent. Whatever method they chose, they never lost sight of the potency of religion and music in resistance.

Moreover, it was religion and music that first unified the African exiles in the Americas. These Africans had come from hundreds of different nations and language groupings, where they might also have belonged to different religious affiliations. Now in the Americas they had to fall back on religion and music to help them cope with their pain and longing to return to their native Africa, where mother, father and all the ancestors were waiting. Without religion and music, the initial problem posed by language and religious differences would have been difficult to surmount. For example, blacks that sang the Negro spirituals in the United States must have come from different parts of Africa, where they might have been divided in tongue and worship. But singing and worship in America gave them a new sense of belonging to one large African family.

It is hardly remembered that African music influenced Western popular culture, and that some aspects of this popular culture served as vehicles for expressing social and political discontent. It is not difficult to show that Blues derived from African work songs, which the slaves took to the Americas. A century later Rhythm and Blues (R&B) broke off from Blues, and became the foundation upon which Rap and Hip-Hop culture would be built. Rap, as we shall see in chapter 7, has its roots in Africa and is a useful tool for conveying popular disaffection. Rock 'n Roll, though not directly associated with political protests, is, nonetheless, of interest to African studies because it is rooted in Voodoo drum beats and Black Gospel music.

Europeans may admire or abhor the choreography of African dance and music, but not all of them may fully understand the message that the artists could communicate with their bodies. European slave owners and colonial authorities that prohibited drumming and certain forms of verbal expressions did not know that Africans could transmit messages with their bodies. In Brazil, *Sambistas* (those who engage in *samba* dance) communicated with their bodies, just as black mine workers of South Africa expressed their dislike for apartheid with their gum boots dance.

Music is indispensable to African religious worship; without it, it is difficult to achieve a deep religious experience. In *Voodoo, Candomblé, Shango,* and *Kumina* worships, for example, it is difficult for devotees to experience spirit possession without the assistance of music. When performed in a protective *roda* (a ritual circle of musicians and spectators), the music becomes doubly powerful. To take the Brazilian *Capoeira,* for example, the most visible aspects of the game are its kicks and sweeps, yet it is the music that controls the game. Dominated by drums and *berimbau* (one stringed instrument) the music of *Capoeira* creates the right attitude for the game. The tempo of the music regulates the level of excitement between the players, which, if left uncontrolled, could result in painful consequences.

Black music and religion may be connected to warfare and political mobilization. Mau Mau fighters in Kenya could not ignore the potency of music and religion when they fought British colonialism in the 1940s and 1950s. They combined African religious practices with elements of Christianity as they turned Christian hymns into politically charged songs. They found in the Old Testament some usable references to "captivity under foreign masters, to wanderings in the wilderness, to suffering bravely borne, to delivery by God's hand," which enabled them to create an explosive political movement that eventually led to Kenya's national independence in 1964.[7]

Resistance movements based on religion were numerous. Some were violent; others were not. They were carried out, not only under the banner of indigenous African religions, but also under the guise of Islam and Christianity. The leaders of the religion-based resistance movements experienced divine inspiration, and they had the liberation of their people in mind. Among the better known religious affiliations, in terms of cultural resistance, are the *Nyabingi* of southern Uganda and Rwanda; the *Maji Maji* cult in Tanzania; *Santeria* in Cuba; *Shango* worship in Trinidad; the Tokoist church in Angola; the Kimbanguist church in the Congo; the Mahdist sect in the Sudan; *Candomblé* in Brazil; the Rastafarian movement in Jamaica; and the Black Church and the Nation of Islam in the United States.

Until well into the period of emancipation, the sacred African elements remained central to the slave's worldview, and most slave revolts were conditioned by the slave's prior conceptions of religion and political mobilization. Lawrence Levine has observed, for example, that many slaves in North America wore charms that they believed would make them invulnerable or invisible. African captives also believed that some charms would give them sufficient courage to shoulder tasks they normally would have avoided, or stand up to their masters, or move about freely on the plantations, or conspire to escape, or even undertake a rebellion.[8] These observations are perfectly consistent with practices in Africa where large sections of the population wore charms for similar purposes and consulted with diviners to unlock the secrets of life.

Both in Africa and in the Americas, blacks struggled to liberate themselves from European domination by military means, but the disparity in armaments and military training and organization constrained some of them to resort to other means. Music and dance readily offered themselves. This was because cultural expressions could also be used as instruments of resistance. A Brazilian *capoeirista* (one who plays Capoeira) knows

that dancing and playing could inflict much pain on an opponent if used for the desired effect. However, while many people
of African descent resorted to armed struggle, others chose music
and dance as the preferred non-violent methods of resistance. In
the United States, blacks sang Negro Spirituals and Blues to ease
their pain and to preserve their history. In Kenya, the Kikuyu
sang songs in which they reaffirmed their opposition to colonial
domination. Songs and dances enabled South African blacks to
preserve their history and re-affirm their opposition to white
domination. The South African gum boot dancers, for example,
used non-verbal communications to express their opposition to
apartheid. Also in Brazil, the Africans used *Samba* and *Capoeira*
to communicate their feelings and sustain their resistance. And
just as *Reggae* became the most popular music of resistance in
Jamaica, so did Rap become the most articulate music of protest
among black youths in the United States of America.

Whatever the purpose, it was in the process of resisting white
domination that many Africans of the diaspora re-discovered
their history, a history that had been distorted by slavery, colonialism, racial discrimination and false education. We shall see
how black artists helped to spread the black culture of resistance,
how, for instance, the Rastafarian movement symbolically linked
itself to Ethiopia, to the Mau Mau and Nyabingi protest movements in East Africa. We shall also see how the Haitian revolution
was linked to Dahomey through the practice of Voodoo, and how
the Muslim slave revolts in nineteenth century Bahia, Brazil, were
linked to the Muslim reform movements in West Africa.

It is important to remember that African music and dance
are not all about resistance. For most Africans, music simply is a
source of entertainment and a useful tool for transmitting cultural
messages. It is also a medium for expressing personal and collective feelings. Africans sing and dance at marriage ceremonies.
Hunters sing to sustain their courage during dangerous hunting
expeditions. Africans dance and sing at funeral gatherings partly
to cope with their pain or grief and partly to commune with the
spirit of the departed. Funeral ceremonies are part of the rituals

of separation and are marked by elaborate musical and dance performances.

In the United States, some runaway slaves found songs to be useful weapons. Harriet Tubman was proficient in using them. It is said that when nearing a plantation she would sing to reveal her presence to those expecting her. Earl Conrad has noted that "Often, *en route,* when companies became separated, Harriet employed songs to indicate safety or danger, to reunite her parties, or to warn them to remain separated."[9]

Whether performed or not, African-based music consists of three inter-woven components—instrumentation, singing, and dancing. Even though each of these can be performed separately, most musical performances combine the three elements. Music is useless if it cannot communicate a message. A good musical form is the one that is full of cultural meanings and is able to speak to both performers and spectators. For the African, dancing and singing are as important as instrumentation. The lyrics in African music are extremely important; what one says in a song should be packed with meaning. What one may say with one's body can also be as important as what one may say in songs. However, each musical genre and each group of artists may decide what aspects of music to emphasize. For example, *Samba* places more emphasis on dance than on lyrics. In the case of Blues, lyrics take precedence over dance, while Jazz, the most sophisticated popular music of modern times, can be performed with or without songs or dance. Wherever the emphasis may be placed, what is important is that Africans on the continent and in the diaspora use music and dance to express their feelings and to preserve their culture and history.

Songs and music, together with dance, are of special importance to Africans because of the great emphasis they place on oral and visual (as opposed to written) communications.[10] African culture as a whole is an oral culture and is governed by folklore. As was stated above, the African drum is not simply a musical instrument; it is also a communication tool, used to transmit oral traditions. When slave owners and officials in the Americas outlawed certain types of drumming and verbal expressions, blacks used dance and body movements as alternative means of communication, as illustrated by the development of *Samba* and gumboot dancing.

Dance is vital for warfare; warriors have to dance as they prepare their bodies and minds for battle. C.L.R. James has pointed out that before slaves mounted an attack during the Haitian slave revolt, they would carry out preliminary manoeuvers in dead silence. When satisfied with the prospects of victory, they would resort to one more diversionary strategy; they would sing and dance, while their priests chanted the *wanga,* as the women and children sang and danced vigorously. It was only when the dancing had reached the necessary height of excitement that the fighters would attack.[11]

Slave owners misunderstood the meanings and origins of the drumming, and as a consequence, outlawed drumming for slaves, believing that it incited slaves to rebel. What slave owners refused to acknowledge was that rebellions were caused by deepseated grievances, not by drums.

Dancing and singing are important accompaniments to traditional African religions. The power of African religion and music derive from the fact that religion for these people is not about going to heaven or hell, but about healing--healing between individuals and the supernatural forces, and healing between individuals and whole communities. When used for the purpose, singing expresses deep religious thoughts, while dancing provides the physical motions that express the various moods. A truly religious worship combines the three elements.

Africans sing and dance at religious gatherings to gain the ears and eyes of the invisible forces that they invoke. It is hard for Africans to go into spiritual possession without the help of instrumental or vocal music. Among the Shona of Zimbabwe, also among the blacks of South Africa, the *insangoma* are diviners and healers. They command much respect partly because they are believed to be possessed by ancestral spirits, and partly because they are perceived as the medium between the living and their dead ancestors. Furthermore, they are noted for their great skills in music, especially singing, for, as we have seen, music is a vital means of communication between humans and the invisible forces. Miriam Makeba of South Africa was a great singer. It is believed that the deep spirit that was later manifested in her songs could be traced back to her close relationship with her mother and grandmother who became *isangoma* later in their lives.

Like the *obeah* and the *isangoma, drummers* are respected, not only in continental Africa but also in the diaspora. As Leonard Barrett had explained in connection with the Jamaican *Kumina* cult, "the drummer is indispensable. It is he who sets the mood and controls the spirits that possess people; and it is he who controls the movements of the people under possession. The same is true of Haitian Vodun. The drummers prepare the human bodies to receive the spirit; they are the mechanism of control."[12] In Voodoo rituals, noted Michel S. Laguerre, songs help create a favorable atmosphere for possession-trance to occur.[13] In the ceremonies of possession, the linkages between Haitian and African cultures are elaborately emphasized and dramatized. They mentally enable those in trance to travel freely to and from Africa. Voodoo devotees believe that no physical boundaries can stop them from returning to their homelands. As a Voodoo song makes abundantly clear, death (for a devotee) is the same thing as making a spiritual journey from Haiti to Africa, where Voodoo spirits live.[14] This mental attachment to Africa played a crucial role in black resistance to European colonialism and slavery. It prepared the mind for resistance.

As a communication device, dance uses different types of gestures, body movements, body decorations, and even masks. Dance could serve as a form of record keeping. To the Brazilian blacks, for example, both popular and religious dances are forms of bodily writing. Dance is therefore text, a form of cultural inscription that one can learn to imprint with one's body.[15] Choreography simply means to write with the body. It is in *Samba*, perhaps, more than in any other form of African-derived dance, that the relationship between dance and communication is demonstrated. Rex Nettleford has argued that dance and music are important elements in the black culture of resistance and survival. "As a foremost creative activity," he wrote, "dance is a primary instrument of survival," not only during the period of slavery and colonialism, but also since independence." He also stated that one's body belongs to oneself, the language by which the body expresses itself does not have to be anyone else's language. And it is the exercise of the imagination that has proven to be the best guarantee for survival, from the days of slavery to the post-colonial period.[16]

Dance and music serve certain political functions; they are used as vehicles for conveying political protests, for preserving identity, for relieving the weight of oppression, for combating colonial oppression, and for sheer surviving in the face of European colonial violence. For example, in Trinidad, Calypso and Steelband music were involved in protests, in the struggle for national identity, and in agitation for political independence.[17] In Brazil, the lyrics of *Capoeira* are uplifting and full of resistant themes as is illustrated in the following *capoeiristas'* dialogue.

> Call: I was born in poverty   *naci dentro da pobreza*
> Response: but not of a poor race   *nao nace raca pobrein*[18]

This dialogue is not only uplifting, it is also intended to instill in both the players and audience a sense of self-worth. This sense of pride, insists J. Lowell Lewis, serves as a form of resistance against the poor sociopolitical conditions under which Afro-Brazilians lived both before and after emancipation. Barbara Browning has also reminded us that even the glamorous Brazilian carnival acts as a safety valve that helps let off the steam of social frustrations that might otherwise be directed toward political upheaval and change.[19] According to her, the carnival is an embodiment of ironies and cynicism. The poor participants sing songs of protest, trying to make the celebration their own glorious moment, while the carnival remains a lucrative business for the rich who control the *Samba* schools and the tourist industry. In the carnival, the poor plays rich and the meek plays powerful. Poor blacks in the ghetto dress as African royalty and those in the Rio schools try to recreate European pageantry and luxury. It is an exercise in role reversals. Thus, apart from concealing race and class differences, the carnival helps to ease tension by providing its participants with a forum to make political statements.[20] However, whereas *Samba,* as the most popular secular dance of Brazil, narrates a history of cultural contact among Africans, Europeans and indigenous Brazilians, *Capoeira* is the dance that addresses the history of racial struggle.[21]

These African-based religions and music survived five hundred years of white violence. Despite enslavement and colonial conquest, and notwithstanding the white man's attempt to destroy or appropriate them, these aspects of African cultures grew strong and adaptable. As African captives in the Americas defended their humanity, so did the Africans of the continent hold on tenaciously to their cultural heritage.

THE DANGERS AND DISAPPOINTMENTS OF ASSIMILATION

Of all the tactics that the Europeans use to subvert African cultures, especially African religions and music, none is more ingenious than the principle of assimilation. Outwardly, assimilation is harmless yet its consequences could be devastating. One of the aims of assimilation is to achieve political and cultural control by mounting a vicious attack on the victim's consciousness and self-esteem. When put in motion, the victim begins to hate the customs of his people, their language, music and religion. Now, he listens to Mozart and Beethoven, rather than Fela Kuti and Sunny Ade. And rather than visit his relatives and ancestral shrines in the countryside, he spends his vacations in Paris, London and Rome.

The oppressor, who knows what he is doing, goes even further. He divides his victims into antagonistic sects, in order to create the proper atmosphere for exploitation. In the Americas, Europeans create a social gap between house slaves and field slaves. In Africa, colonial administrators select a small crop of natives and dress them with no more than a thin layer of European table manners plus a passionate love for Europe. Thus, the house slaves in the Americas find their counterparts in the assimilated natives of continental Africa. By creating a social gap between the indigenous elite and the masses, between the house slaves and the field slaves, the oppressor produces deadly divisions within black society. These divisions are vital tools of exploitation. Without them the exploiter cannot find reliable collaborators.

Furthermore, driven by cultural arrogance and the desire to destroy African cultures, white racists recruit European Christian missionaries to assist them in this contemptible mission. Missionaries provide Western education but the school curriculum promotes white superiority and black inferiority. They ingeniously fuse secular and religious ideas, and then turn the Bible into a very powerful tool for enforcing obedience to slavery and colonial rule. Christian missionaries and colonial agents use biblical texts to frighten and demand unquestioned obedience from their African converts. The very imperialists, who are busy looting African land, art treasures and mineral deposits, admonish Africans not to break oppressive colonial laws, laws that contradict traditional African customs and notions of fair play. Combined with an overcrowded Christian religious curriculum, the colonial educational systems demand of the colonized masses impeccable honesty and submission to the very institutions that exploit and degrade them.

Now, armed with a false sense of belonging to the masters' club, many continental African "house slaves" fail to quickly realize that the preferred treatment they receive would result in painful loss of identity, self-respect, acceptance of a culture of silence, and a permanent status of inferiority. Before 1945, some of these new African zombies demonstrated a readiness to die so that their oppressors might live. In many parts of Africa during the First and Second World Wars, they collaborated with the Europeans to send African peasants into the colonial armed forces. Many native conscripts died in European conflicts that did not concern Africa.

It was only after the rise of militant nationalism in the post Second World War period that a majority of the assimilated blacks in Africa and the diaspora returned to the customs of their forefathers. One educated and partially assimilated Kenyan was later to testify that his return to his people's culture was like a religious conversion. After the necessary ritual of incorporation had been performed, he was filled with a new sense of pride and power. "I felt exalted," he wrote, "with a new spirit of power and strength. All my previous life seemed empty and meaningless. Even my education, of which I was so proud, appeared trivial and meaningless beside this splendid and terrible force which had been given me. I had been born again."[22]

Thenceforth, these "born-again" Africans began to use their knowledge of the oppressors' institutions to seek the overthrow of the monstrous colonial systems. Their close proximity to the Europeans had enabled them to understand the functioning of the oppressive colonial enterprise. No doubt, it was the assimilated blacks in Africa and the diaspora that spearheaded the movement that finally toppled colonialism and racial segregation in Africa, the Caribbean, and the United States. Europeans were disappointed; the very Africans they had tried to turn into zombies had become the most articulate and uncompromising enemies of the colonial and racist systems. From Africa came Jomo Kenyatta, Albert Luthuli, Kwame Nkrumah, Amilcar Cabral, and Nelson Mandela. From the United States came W.E.B. DuBois, Martin Luther King, Jr. and Malcolm X. And from the West Indies came Marcus Garvey, Frantz Fanon and Eric Williams. These are the names of only a tiny fraction of Western educated Africans who used their knowledge of the white man's institutions to topple colonialism and segregation laws.

Meanwhile, the vast majority of Africans refused to run around in circles between assimilation and loyalty to African customs. Convinced that culture was an indispensable tool for survival, they distanced themselves from every thing European. "The world of the white man is an established evil," warned the Tokoist church of Angola. To avoid the world of the white man is to escape a baneful world. Thus, rather than abandon their religions and music, millions of black people around the world popularized them and turned them into instruments of resistance. Black religions and music, as aspects of the black culture of resistance, were anti-slavery inasmuch as they were anti-racist. They helped to unify whole masses against their oppressors.

In the chapters that follow, we shall see how black people in Africa and the diaspora turned to religion and music during their struggle against European slavery, racism, colonialism and neo-colonial exploitation. It must be borne in mind that black resistance was not directed only against economic exploitation but also against forced assimilation. Thus, in the struggle against forced assimilation, religion and music have proved to be indispensable tools. Moreover, black religions and music are largely responsible for the preservation of African cultures, especially in the Americas where African cultures have endured five centuries of assault and misappropriation.

Notes

1. See Don C. Ohadike, *Pan-African Culture of Resistance: A History of Resistance movements in Africa and the diaspora* (Binghamton: Global Publications, 2002).

2. Ibid.

3. Don Ohadike, *The Ekumeku movement: Western Igbo Resistance to the British conquest of Nigeria, 1883-1914* (Athens; Ohio University Press, 1991), 88-9.

4. G. C. K. Gwassa, "African Methods of Warfare During the Maji Maji War 1905-1907," in Bethwell A. Ogot, (ed.) *War And Society in Africa* (London: Frank Cass, 1972): 123-48.

5. John K. Thornton, "African Dimensions of the Stono Rebellion," *The American Historical Review,* Vol. 96; No. 4 (October 1991): 1112.

6. *Ibid.,* 1110.

7. *Ibid.,* 144-5.

8. Levine, *Black Culture,* 75.

9. Earl Conrad, *Harriet Tubman: Negro Soldier and Abolitionist* (New York: International Publishers, 1942), 14.

10. Isidore Okpewho, *African Oral Literature: Backgrounds, Character, and Continuity* (Bloomington: Indiana University Press, 1992).

11. C. L. R. James, *The Black Jacobins: Toussaint L'Ouverture and the San Domingo Revolution* (New York: Vintage Books, 1963), 116-17.

12. Leonard E. Barrett, *The Sun and the Drum: African Roots in Jamaican Folk Tradition* (Kingston, Jamaica: Sangester's Book Stores 1976), 106-7.

13. Laguerre, *Voodoo Heritage,* 30.

14. *Ibid.,* 89.

15. Barbara Browning, *Samba: Resistance in Motion* (Bloomington: Indiana University Press, 1995), *xxii.*

16. Rex M. Nettleford, *Dance Jamaica: Cultural Definition and Artistic Discovery: the National Dance Theater Company of Jamaica, 1962-1983.* (New York: Grove Press, 1985), 20.

17. Stephen Stuempfle, *The Steelband movement: the Forging of a National Art in Trinidad and Tobago.* (Philadelphia: University of Pennsylvania Press, 1995).

18. Quoted in J. Lowell Lewis, *Ring of Liberation: Deceptive Discourse in Brazilian Capoeira* (Chicago: University of Chicago Press, 1992), 164.

19. Browning, *Samba,* 144.

20. *Ibid.,* 145.

21. *Ibid.,* xxii.

22. As quoted in Clough, *Mau Mau,* 99.

Chapter 1

TRADITIONAL AFRICAN RELIGIOUS BELIEFS AND ANTI-COLONIAL PROTESTS IN AFRICA

To assist them in their battle against European cultural and political violence, many blacks in Africa turned to their traditional religions and accepted magic as an integral part of warfare. To ward off bad luck and death in the battlefield, or to render harmless all bullets fired from an enemy's gun, they armed themselves with prayers, charms and amulets. Some buried strong medicines in the ground, much like modern land mines, intended to kill any enemy troops that might step on them. African traditional religions sometimes served as the vanguard of resistance against other cultures. Africans invoked religion in resistance because indigenous religions were concerned with virtually everything—war and peace, beliefs, divination, creation, medicine, history, sacred kingship, as well as performance, ceremonies, rituals, and rites of passage.

Although there are at least two thousand nations or ethnic groups in Africa, each with its own religious system, which may vary from one village or clan to another, there are certain beliefs that are common to all. Among these common beliefs are the idea of one supreme being, the notion of the existence of spirits and divinities, belief in ancestors and retributive justice, as well as belief in life after death. Moreover, until the advent of Islam and Christianity, traditional religions exerted a tremendous

influence upon the lives and thought of the peoples of Africa. It
was impossible for an individual to live outside the religion of his
community.

An important characteristic of traditional African religions
is the absence of written sacred documents. This is because, with
a few exceptions like Egypt and Ethiopia, pre-modern African
societies were illiterate. But the absence of written documents did
not mean the absence of records. Instead, their sacred manuscripts
were embodied in their music, oral history, religions, rituals, and
ceremonies, as well as in the hearts of the people, their priests,
their elders, and their chiefs. This explains why African exiles,
who did not carry any written documents when they boarded
the slave ships, were able to reproduce their traditional African
cultures in the Americas.

More importantly, because African religions have the capacity
to serve a wide range of purposes, it was possible to invoke their
assistance as the need arose. Any deity in their pantheon could
be invoked as the need arose. Among the deities concerned with
war were *ogun,* the god of war among the Yoruba, or *Amadioha*,
the god of thunder among the Igbo. Also, because, each group
had recognizable diviners or priests, it was possible to foretell the
coming of war and to make precautionary arrangements to avert
or contain it. Most diviners were charismatic figures who wielded
the power to mobilize the masses against a predictable threat.
Nanny of Jamaica and Kinjikitile Ngwale of Tanzania were charismatic diviners who succeeded in mobilizing the masses against
the European slave owners and colonial invaders.

Perhaps it was in East Africa, more than in any other part
of the continent, that traditional African religious belief systems
and charismatic religious leadership encouraged the formation
of wide spread alliances against Europeans. Materials collected
from different parts of East Africa confirm that male and female
prophets foretold the coming of the Europeans and urged their
people to prepare themselves for war. The Usuku of Uganda,
wrote J. B. Webster, lived in Adacar, Ngariam. One of their
priests was Okadaro and had messengers all over the north. The

messengers foretold the coming of war and advised the Usuku on battle tactics. They provided the soil with which the soldiers smeared themselves before setting off for war.[1]

Prophets and spirit cults instigated many rebellions in East and Central Africa. Among the more popular were the Nyabingi cult of southwestern Uganda, the Maji Maji cult of Tanzania, and the spirit cults of the Shona of the Zambezi Valley. Among the better known prophets and prophetesses were Maluma, the Tonga priest of Malawi; Onyango Dande, the founder of the Mumbo cult of Kenya; and Kinjikitile Ngwale, the founder of the Maji Maji cult of Tanzania.

Priestesses instigated and led wars of resistance in East Africa. In 1911, the priestess, Siofume, mobilized the Akimbo of eastern Kenya against the British, and in the Congo, it was the cult priestess, Maria Nkoie, who led the Africans in a protracted war against the Europeans. Maria provided her followers with charms, believed to render them immune to European gun shots, and she kept the Europeans busy in the battlefields for five long years (1916 till 1921). One thing common to all these religion-based resistance movements was their success in "arousing mass excitement." They appealed to a wider unity than had been achieved in the past, noted Terence Ranger, and were not afraid to challenge the secular authorities,[2] and, according to Iliffe, they often spread to areas lying beyond the center of the initial rising.[3] Although most of the religiously inspired movements were invariably suppressed, the flames of liberty they often lit burned on. One of the religion-based protests of the early colonial period was the Maji Maji rising.

THE MAJI MAJI RISING IN TANZANIA

Starting from the coast, the Germans fought inland and imposed themselves on the various Tanzanian groups whom they forced to work on cotton plantations. The Germans also extracted taxes and tributes from the peasants, beat them, and then forced them to construct roads. The peasants were not united and had to endure untold hardships until Kinjikitile Ngwale, the priest of a religious cult, offered them the magic water, *maji*. Kinjikitile was the priest of the god, Hongo, believed to be a huge snake that lived in rivers or lakes. The peasants treated Kinjikitile with extreme reverence because they believed that Hongo had possessed him. To be possessed by Hongo meant that one's body had been transformed into the abode of the god.[4]

Acting as the god's surrogate, Kinjikitile imposed new regulations and prohibitions upon his followers. To accept membership in the movement was to agree to enter a new society under new laws and loyalties. The reward included immunity from bullets and resurrection after death to enter a golden age.[5]

When the news of this magic water reached the people's ears, they flocked to Kinjikitile's home to obtain it. Kinjikitile also sent his subordinate priests to distant places to distribute the water, and many that drank it could not resist the urge to fight. According to one source,

> The Maji was not in fact literally "drunk" as the word itself implies. Instead a leaf or preferably a feather was used to sprinkle the medicine on each warrior's forehead, chest, knees, feet, elbows, and back. Anyone who had the maji sprinkled in this way was regarded as having "drunk" it.[6]

The members of the Maji Maji movement opposed not only the Europeans and their oppressive colonial administrative system, but also economic imperialism. Thus, even though the uprising that ensued was on the surface a reaction to German imperialism, it was also directed against traders who had established themselves in southeastern Tanzania, exploiting the peasants and laborers.[7]

The psychic influence of religion in the Tanzanian uprising is particularly interesting. Kinjikitile Ngwale assured his followers that war with the white man would definitely break out. He told them that the white man would leave, and that the entire country would be liberated. He prepared them for war; he promised them protection against European weapons, and he offered them leadership and unity. "But for the time being," he cautioned, "go and work for [the white man]. If he orders you to cultivate cotton or to dig his road, or to carry his load, do as he requires. [Meanwhile] Go and remain quiet. When I am ready, I will declare the war."[8] The peasants went home and quietly counted the moon as it came and went. By mid-1905 no orders had come, and their patience faded. They recalled that the priest had told them that he would declare war against the Germans, asking, "Why then is he delaying? When will the Europeans go? After all, we have already received the medicine and we are brave men. Why should we wait? How do we start the war? How do we make the Germans angry? Let us go and uproot their cotton so that war may [start]."[9]

The peasants went into the cotton fields and uprooted the plants, thereby starting the war. The resulting conflict spread from Ngarambe to Kibata, then to Kichi, to Uzaramo, to Uluguru, and to Ugundu, involving over twenty ethnic groups, occupying over 10,000 square miles. Never had so many African communities in East Africa come together to battle a common enemy.

The Tanzanian masses were mistaken, however. They started the war before Kinjikitile was ready. This was a tragic case of disobedience, which Gwassa described as "a fundamental conflict or disequilibrium between ideology *(maji)* and practical realities and the respective leadership. Thereafter *maji maji* could never expect to have centralized leadership."[10] Although the Tanzanian warriors fought courageously, they were already doomed to lose the war because they failed to heed the prophet's warning. This emphasizes the importance of obedience, discipline, and leadership to success in any revolutionary activity. In the short-run, therefore, the Maji Maji rising was a failed revolution. In the long run, however, it formed a vital link in the chain of violence that characterized Euro-African relationships that hastened the collapse of white rule in East Africa.

It should be understood that if a prophetic leader instructed his (or her) followers to act in a certain manner and they obeyed and yet suffered a defeat, the blame was leveled against the prophet or the spirits that he represented, and there might be mass desertion. This was the case in 1908 among the Gusii of Kenya when the prophetess, Muraa, urged the people to resist the British. She had provided them with the necessary protective medicine against bullets and had urged them to go into action. The Gusii, relying on the magical powers provided by Muraa, confronted the better armed British troops but suffered defeat and humiliation.[11] They had their villages totally demolished, their crops burned and their livestock taken away. Gusii chiefs were rounded up and forced into an unconditional surrender. Enraged by what they considered a disgraceful defeat and a betrayal, the Gusii composed songs that ridiculed the priestess.[12] Also in Tanzania, many Africans blamed the prophet, Kinjikitile Ngwale, for preparing them to fight a war that ended in defeat. The elders of Matumbi sang this song:

> The swindle of Kinjikitile
> He deceived people
> To go to Ngarambe
> To drink the maji.[13]

Although religion played an important role in unifying and instigating resistance and war against Europeans, in accounting for the defeat of the *Maji Maji*, one must consider not only the role of religion in inspiring resistance, but also the nature of the military strategy that was employed. Unlike the maroon[14] and Ekumeku[15] fighters, the Tanzanian insurgents did not make use of guerrilla tactics, nor did they plan their attacks properly. Iliffe described the Maji Maji rebellion as following a "kaleidoscopic pattern." In most of the armed confrontations between the Maji Maji fighters and German soldiers, he said, the insurgents would simply group together and venture out to attack the first available European target. Neither their attacks nor the strategies they employed were pre-planned. Iliffe described the progression of an attack as follows:

> The men of a locality hear that rebellion has broken out elsewhere. They congregate into a band, leaders and spokesmen emerge, and the property of notable local enemies is destroyed, and the enemies, if available, are killed. If they escape the area, they are rarely pursued. The band may coalesce with another and march jointly on a more prominent provincial center, where the same process is repeated. Often the coalition dissolves and the men return home.[16]

These methods were totally different from those of the maroons and Ekumeku, whose attacks were pre-planned, and who, upon a signal, would launch an offensive, usually in complete silence. The maroon and Ekumeku fighters also ensured that their locations remained concealed, which in turn gave their military activities the added advantage of surprise. Be that as it may, in those days of endless anti-colonial wars, only strong leaders, religious or secular, could have gained the co-operation of the masses for unified political actions. There were many grievances; courage and gallantry were never lacking; what was in short supply was modern weaponry.

THE NYABINGI CULT

The cult of Nyabingi instigated many uprisings in early colonial East Africa. The primary objective of cult members was to unify the Africans against the Germans, British and Belgians who, at the end of the nineteenth century, were scrambling for territories in Uganda, Burundi, and Rwanda. To resist these European powers, the leaders of the Nyabingi cult resorted to counter violence, using their religion to unify their followers. Like the Maji Maji cult, the Nyabingi spirit cult was able to unify a large number of previously antagonistic groups. The cult was very effective in arousing mass excitement and unity.

There are several explanations of the origins of the Nyabingi cult. One of them states that Nyabingi was a princess who had died a sudden and violent death. Her restless spirit possessed mediums or prophets, called *mugirwa,* through whom she demanded obedience, gifts, and reverence. She was sometimes referred to as "she who possesses many" and it was generally believed that misfortune visited those who doubted her power. Another explanation is that Nyabingi was the princess Kitami who was killed and therefore deprived of her right to succeed to the throne of Mpororo. She was immortalized after her death and possessed *mugirwa* or prophets who carried out her orders.[17]

In pre-European times, the Nyabingi cult fulfilled certain political objectives. In the Rwanda kingdom, for example, the cult stood in opposition to the existing ruling classes. The oppressed, using the Nyabingi spirit as an active instrument of resistance, periodically raided, pillaged, and murdered those that oppressed them, claiming that they merely obeyed the orders of Nyabingi. On the other hand, whereas the repressed tried to use Nyabingi to secure their freedom, in Mpororo kingdom, the rulers tried to use the same cult to unify and impose themselves upon the masses. However, threatened by European encroachment at the turn of the century, the focus of cult activity had to be redefined.[18] The previously antagonistic groups sometimes unified themselves under the Nyabingi cult.

Nyabingi adherents carried out several sporadic rebellions under different leaders. In the Rwanda territory, Muhumusa led the first resistance to German occupation.[19] She declared herself the liberator of the Africans and instigated many uprisings against British rule in southern Uganda. It was under her that the Nyabingi cult first became a militant, anti-European movement. Muhumusa prepared her followers for war and promised them victory over the Europeans. She assured the Africans that bullets would not harm them, and that if guns were fired at them, the bullets would turn into water. In 1911, as the British advanced into southern Uganda, Muhumusa burned and pillaged the settlements of those who professed friendship with the British. Some Kiga, disappointed that the British could not protect them, joined Muhumusa.

Another important Nyabingi-inspired uprising took place in 1914. This uprising was led by Ndungutsi, and was in reaction to heavy taxes imposed on the Africans. The First World War had just broken out and, as part of their war measures, the British forced many African communities to pay all sorts of levies, fines and taxes. The hardships caused by these conditions in World War I, together with forced taxes and levies, helped to fuel discontent. Furthermore, the allied forces were at war with the Germans, and poor Africans, who had nothing to gain from European quarrels, were forced to participate in the conflict. In an attempt to break free from European control as well as from unnecessary suffering and death, cult leaders spread rebellion.

The uprising that broke out was eventually suppressed, but in 1916, it resurfaced with Ndochibiri as the leader. This outbreak, which lasted until 1917, was also known as the Nyakishenyi rebellion. It emanated from mounting anti-European feelings. On the surface, the rebellion was against Abdulla, a British agent, but underneath it was a challenge to British colonial authority.[20]

Large-scale fighting that saw roughly 1400 Africans in arms marked the Nyakishenyi rebellion of 1916-17. Although they were responding to diverse grievances, these rebels were united under the banner of religion. The Nyakishenyi rebellion is another example of the ability of traditional African religions to assemble large numbers of people in resistance to European rule.

There also were rebellions in 1919 and 1928. The 1919 rebellion was largely over the outbreak of influenza and meningitis epidemics, while the 1928 rebellion was over the imposition of an official language, harsh taxation, excessive demands for labor, and the alienation of local chiefs in administrative practices and structures.[21] The tactics of the 1928 rebellion were not as effective as those used in earlier decades. As the followers of the Nyabingi cult developed a better understanding of the workings of the European colonial administration, they gave up the more violent aspects of their resistance though they never abandoned their opposition to European domination.

The culture of resistance that the Nyabingi cult fostered sometimes experienced periods of dormancy, but it never died out completely. The Nyabingi continued to mobilize large masses of people for political action throughout the colonial period. Because it was founded on strong traditional African beliefs in spirit possession, the organization never ran out of leaders. If a leader was killed or captured, another person could claim that he or she had been possessed by the Nyabingi spirit and would immediately be accepted as a new leader. To be possessed by Nyabingi was to be chosen by Nyabingi.

Mass appeal for the Nyabingi cult declined as Christianity spread, thanks to the Christian missionaries. It also declined under pressure from the colonial governments' decrees. For example, in Uganda, British authorities treated Nyabingi sympathizers as enemies of the colonial administration. Many people embraced Christianity to avoid indiscriminate arrests and punishment. Through this and similar tactics, the British succeeded in confining Nyabingi cult activity to remote districts. Although Nyabingi's participation in active political protest against the British declined after 1928, it thrived in the minds of the people who sometimes feared its power more than they feared the authority of the British courts. Most of the post-Second World War followers of Nyabingi accepted the principle of avoiding British authority rather than confronting it. Thus, even though many Africans were not actively involved in cult activities, they remained sympathetic to their basic message.

THE MAU MAU MOVEMENT IN KENYA

The role of African traditional religions in resistance is further illustrated by the organization of the Mau Mau Movement in Kenya. The Mau Mau uprising can be traced to the protest of some African peasants who started a political movement in 1945 and sustained it with traditional belief systems. The political turbulence they set in motion brought political independence to Kenya in 1964.

The Mau Mau uprising was a reaction to many repressive colonial policies. The colonial administration ushered in a period of land and labor crisis in Kenya when it seized African lands and introduced squatterdom rather than a fair wage labor system. Because of their desire to amass "cheap, adequate and controllable supply of labour," European settlers persuaded the British colonial administration to introduce a number of offensive land and labor regulations.[22] The grand design was to curtail the amount of land available for the Africans and then to drive them into a controlled wage labor market as their only means of survival. Africans had to seek wage labor to earn the money with which to pay colonial taxes. On top of this, the colonial administrators denied them access to alternative means of making money; they were prohibited from growing the most profitable cash crops such as coffee and sisal, and in the highlands only whites were permitted to grow maize.[23] Many dispossessed African youths fled to the cities in search of wage labor. In due course, the overcrowded cities became the breeding grounds for urban misery, discontent and protest. The most devastated by European enterprise in Kenya were the Gikuyu people, and it was they who eventually launched the Mau Mau uprising.

More than any thing else, it was land confiscation that desta-bilized the Kikuyu community the most. For up till the time of the arrival of the Europeans, the Kikuyu pursued their agricul-tural life with all their energy. They grew crops and grazed their animals. They traded the surplus with the traveling Muslims and the neighboring Masai. Wealth was measured in land, sheep, goats and cattle.[24] Most of their cultural activities revolved around land, a crucial determining factor for the size of family units and the overall population.

Land confiscation resulted in land shortages, and was the most vexing issue that the Africans wished to discuss. For example, in 1934, after the government had destroyed the crops and houses of the Africans, it confiscated their livestock and land in the Tigoni-Limuru area, and forcibly relocated them in Olen-guruone.[25] In due course, the colonial government sold the stolen land to newly arrived settlers from Europe. The harassment of the Africans was endless. Ten years after their resettlement in Olen-guruone, the Kikuyu were again compelled to move on to other locations because white settlers wanted their lands. The Africans,

who were being uprooted from their ancestral lands, were systematically being pushed into the reserves or coerced into accepting the life of squatters on the very land that originally belonged
to their fathers.

These land and labor crises were compounded by many other
grievances, too many to be listed here. Among the often forgotten, yet very disruptive, was the introduction of Christianity,
which conflicted sharply with traditional customs. Christianity
disrupted the traditional family structures when it insisted on
monogamy instead of polygamy. Polygamy had enabled households to maintain a stable family life and to divide the tedious
household and agricultural tasks among its members. On top of
this, the missionaries mounted an attack on the age-long custom
of female circumcision or clitoridectomy. The conflict it sparked
accelerated the erosion of the stability of community life.

Furthermore, many Kenyans who admired the ostentatious
life style of the Europeans soon found out that they could only
take part in it as servants.[26] Tensions heightened when European
settlers schemed to take over the country from the British government as other settlers had done in South Africa, Zimbabwe, and
other parts of the world.[27] Eventually, the landless populations,
who at that point despised life more than death, decided to fight.
The unrest that erupted after the Second World War naturally
fed into the evolving Kenyan nationalism.

THE MAU MAU RELIGIOUS CEREMONIES: OATHING

Although Frank Furedi recognized the important role that
oathing played in sustaining the Mau Mau movement, he has
warned against distractions by what he described as "the exotic
features of the movement," and the "enduring fascination with
rituals and oaths," which characterized the movement.[28] Furedi
is right in sounding these words of caution, for it was a common
practice among earlier writers, especially British writers, to avoid
the real issues and to dwell upon the rituals of the oathing ceremonies. Furedi's warning notwithstanding, I will, in the pages
that follow, revisit the oathing aspects of the movement because

they help to illustrate the roles of religious belief systems in black resistance movements. However, like Furedi, I must caution against offensive Eurocentric views about African religious practices.

Among the more abusive of the British commentators was John C. Carothers who, in *The Psychology of the Mau Mau*, described the Mau Mau ceremonies as "peculiarly obscene and bestial," which resulted from "the spontaneous instinct of a primitive people" whose life was dominated by a "forest psychology."[29] He also claimed that the Mau Mau broke out when "relatively sophisticated egotists" tried to exploit some real or fancied grievances for their own political ends.[30] Dr. L. S. B. Leakey, an official of the colonial government of Kenya, declared: "I am sure that it was this religion, of which the oathing ceremony formed only a small part, that was the force which was turning thousands of peace-loving Kikuyu into murderous fanatics."[31] Another British apologist, Margery Perham, claimed that "The Kikuyu had lost only a small proportion of land to European settlement. But a loss, which was spatially unimportant, was, in the circumstances, psychologically oppressive. . . . The Africans were too much dominated by the land issue to recognize that European development had created many new opportunities for employment. This is not surprising."[32]

The biases of these British commentators are clear. Dr. Leakey stated that the oathing ceremony formed only a small part of the religion, yet he and other colonial detractors tried to make too much of it. Furthermore, Margery Perham's biased claim is instantly exposed if one places it side by side with the personal experience of a Kikuyu, Josiah Mwangi Kariuku, to whose own book Perham wrote a foreword. According to Kariuku, "My parents had left their home in Chinga in the Nyeri Native Reserve the year before to become 'squatters' on the farm of a European. . . . Squatters in European farms in the White Highlands were given a small piece of land to cultivate and allowed to pasture a specified number of cattle or goats. In return they were expected to be available, with members of their family, to do regular or seasonable jobs for the farmer. The wages were extremely low and the system had all the social disadvantages found in any feudal relationship."[33]

What Perham did not disclose is that the Europeans seized the Africans' land and then hounded them into artificially created reserves. And because life was so intolerable in the reserves, they were forced to squat on European farms where they were treated as serfs and servants on their own land. Although Perham stated that Africans were paid wages, she did not disclose that those wages were so miserable that the Africans preferred to stay away from the farms or migrate to regions where wages were "fair." For the same amount of work done, an African received, on the average, only one fifth the pay of a white man. Robert B. Edgerton has confirmed that "as early as 1907, Kikuyu walked more than three hundred miles to Mombassa where wages were twice those offered in the Highlands. But white farmers were not interested in paying high wages."[34] Instead, they preferred to force Africans into the labor market by cutting the amount of land available to them. Because wages were abysmally low and the Kikuyu were not allowed to grow the more profitable crops, they could not raise enough money to pay colonial taxes or pay for the education of their children.[35]

Of course, Margery Perham, John Carothers, Louis S. B. Leakey and the other British writers of that period could not have faced the truth objectively. They were out to deceive and entertain Europeans who were obsessed with the assumed barbarity of the Africans. In any case, most people in Britain believed that the British policy in Kenya was fair. To these British detractors, the oathing ceremony of the Mau Mau movement was repulsive to an extreme. They failed to point out that in virtually every part of the world, including Western Europe and the United States, different types of oaths promoted bonds of solidarity. Politicians, policemen, and other public officials in Western Europe took oaths of allegiance to the nation as part of their induction process to office. Even boy scouts and members of the Ku Klux Klan (KKK) took oaths of allegiance.

One of the earliest responses of the Kikuyu to these missionary and colonial abuses took the form of petitions to the government; they asked the government to return the stolen land, but for this they were roundly rebuked. Convinced that the Europeans had no plans to return the land, or embark on a program of administrative reform, the Kikuyu decided to curtail their reliance on European institutions. Some abandoned white-run churches and formed their own African churches, where they worshipped the God that made them in His own image. The formation of these break-away churches was important, but more important was the fact that it afforded them the opportunity to resist forced assimilation. Their return to the religion of their fathers was a reaffirmation of their rejection of the imposed European religious worldview. Some Gikuyu wanted schools for the education of their children. By the 1930s, Peter Koinange, had built the Kenya Teachers college for the training of African teachers.[36] At the same time, militants began to take oaths of solidarity, swearing to fight the white man to the bitter end.

The Kikuyu oath taking was not different from a pledge of allegiance to one's nation, or the act of swearing by a sacred object, as was customary in virtually every part of the world. The Kikuyu took their oaths very seriously because they were, like many other Africans, very conscious of the consequences of breaking traditional oaths.

In the 1940s and 1950s, the Kikuyu took the Mau Mau oaths very seriously because of the very tense political situation of the period. It must not be forgotten that protest against autocratic colonial regimes had to be planned in secret. For example, the organizers of the Ekumeku movement in southern Nigeria observed this code of secrecy and carried out their activities with so much silence that they were nicknamed "The League of the Silent Ones."[37] Such precautions, according to Furedi, were "characteristic of rural protests," and not of "any natural secretiveness but to a sense of survival."[38]

H. K. Wachanga, a former Mau Mau fighter, lamented the tendency among foreigners to underestimate the importance of the various oaths of the Kikuyu people. Writing in the *Swords of Kirinyaga,* he stated that taking an oath was the special Kikuyu way of binding people together. Although there were different traditional oaths, such as those for witchcraft, paternity and theft, battle and land oaths took precedence over all others during the era of the Mau Mau uprising.[39]

The Mau Mau insurgents derived much of their sustenance from the warrior and solidarity oaths, however. The solidarity oath united the Mau Mau combatants and Kikuyu society in the struggle for national liberation. The warrior oath bound warriors to each other, and discouraged flight when confronted by the enemy.

The vanguards of the anti-colonial movement were the members of the Kikuyu Central Association (KCA). The KCA had been formed in 1919 partly as a political organization and partly as a cultural association, but in the 1930s, it took on the philosophy of a secret society and was largely responsible for spreading the oath-taking rituals. To ensure that its members were loyal to the cause, they were given new types of battle and solidarity oaths, which some observers have described as the KCA oaths. Although the battle oath was used frequently during the pre-colonial times, it had fallen into disuse in the early colonial period only to be re-introduced in the 1930s, when the British indulged in the disturbing habit of land seizure. Wachanga recalled that when the displaced peasants and squatters at Olen-guruone re-introduced this ancient oath, "they rediscovered a unity which had almost been forgotten."[40]

It is believed that by 1946, the entire population of Olen-guruone had taken the oath of unity. From Olenguruone, oath-taking diffused into Nakuru, Elburgon, Naivash Laikipia, Uasin Gishe and beyond, where KCA activists were busy administering it on both their supporters and their squatters. By late 1946 the Mau Mau had become a full-blown resistance movement.

Alarmed by rumors about these oathing ceremonies and the attendant unrest, the colonial government drew up a counter-insurgency program. It declared a state of emergency, relocated many people and sentenced a large number of Africans to prison. Jomo Kenyatta was arrested on October 20, 1952 and was charged with managing the Mau Mau. Rather than try to inquire into the fundamental causes of unrest, the colonial government resorted to a military action against the insurgents. To avoid arrest and relocation, many Africans ran away, some to the Mau hills from where they launched military attacks on the government, the white settlers, and all the other enemies of the Africans.

Apart from the oathing ceremonies, the political militancy of some priests and prophets of the African traditional religions sustained the Mau Mau rebellion. The Kikuyu people believed that their God, Ngai, spoke to them through their high priests. "Ngai," they believed, "passed on information about impending enemy attacks, the best time and places to strike back, what taboos would be necessary, and what supernatural actions could be undertaken to weaken or confuse the enemy."[41]

Prophets shouldered difficult tasks because of the nature of the Mau Mau enterprise. They administered oaths, presided over initiation ceremonies, foretold the future, nursed the ill and the wounded, and then protected the people against witchcraft or sorcery.[42] Only the prophets, with the help of Ngai, could have performed these difficult tasks in those difficult times.

Of course, the Mau Mau insurgents could not have functioned effectively from their forest and mountain bases without their secular leaders. Among the civil leaders were Stanley Mathenge, Dedan Kimathi, and General China. The main responsibilities of these men were numerous; they provided their followers with arms, ammunition and food. They were the first to take the Mau Mau oaths, and in due course, administered them on new members.[43]

A third group that was indispensable to the Mau Mau enterprise consisted of sympathizers in the urban centers, the vast majority of whom were unemployed. They were what one may describe as Frantz Fanon's urban spearhead of a revolution. In a region that was rife with discontent, it was not difficult to find sympathizers; what was difficult to ensure was that all oath takers would be reliable. As might be expected, a few unreliable persons joined the movement and exposed its methods. A leading Mau Mau activist, who was in charge of the oathing ceremonies at Ngata, was betrayed and imprisoned. He later recalled: "On Ngata farm we made the mistake of oathing people who could not keep secret. They were men who were too close with the Europeans."[44] Apart from betrayals, colonial government agents and spies infiltrated the Mau Mau.

Betrayals and infiltration, notwithstanding, the Mau Mau leaders found willing urban workers and trade union leaders ready to take the oath of solidarity. These oath-takers were mostly non-combatants. The initiate, repeating certain words after an administrator, made a series of vows. After each vow the candidate was reminded that the oath would kill him (or her) if he proved unreliable or betrayed his people.[45] A version of the vows made by non-combatant oath-takers is reproduced below. (The initiate substitutes "I" for "you," and "my" for "your"):

1. If you ever disagree with your nation or sell it, may you die of this oath.
2. If a member of this Society ever calls you in the night and you refuse to open your hut to him, may you die of this oath.
3. If you ever leave a member of this society in trouble, may you die of this oath.
4. If you ever report a member of this society to the government, may you die of this oath.

Kariuku has disclosed that the Mau Mau fighters made no distinction between the African and European enemies of the country. He was required to repeat these words at the time of his initiation:

> I speak the truth and vow before our God
> And before our people of Africa
> That I shall never betray our country

That I shall never betray anybody of this movement
          to the enemy
Whether the enemy be European or African
And if I do this
May this oath kill me, etc.

I speak the truth and vow before our God
That if I am called to go and fight the enemy
Or to kill the enemy – I shall go
Even if the enemy be my father or mother, my
          brother or sister
And if I refuse
May this oath kill me, etc.[46]

Many oath takers described oath taking as a religious experience. They claimed to emerge from the ceremony with strong feelings of satisfaction and commitment as if going through a religious conversion. Kariuki jubilantly stated:

> Afterwards in the maize I felt exalted with a new spirit of power and strength. All my previous life seemed empty and meaningless. Even my education, of which I was so proud, appeared trivial and meaningless beside this splendid and terrible force which had been given me. I had been born again.[47]

The Mau Mau fighters combined elements of traditional African religions with Christianity and created an explosive revolutionary situation. As already stated, they turned Christian hymns into politically meaningful songs. They even saw the Old Testament as a useful source of inspiration.[48]

The Mau Mau entered into the phase of armed resistance in 1952 and its organizers had to introduce more sophisticated oathing that would be sufficiently strong to contain the escalated military situation. They introduced the *Batuni* or platoon oath, which was administered on young squatters of warrior age in the Nakuru District. This oath committed those who took it to fight the enemies of the Mau Mau. This move, commented Furedi, was

seen as a first step in preparing themselves for armed confrontation and a first step in participating in future revolts.[49]

The Mau Mau movement turned out to be one of the most
active anti-colonial movements in Africa. Based on guerrilla
warfare and religion, the organization disrupted the functioning
of colonialism in Kenya. Although the movement was eventually
suppressed, the resistant ideology it fostered remained a force
to be reckoned with. European settlers and their African sympathizers did not forget quickly the fear and pain that the Mau
Mau caused them. On the eve of Kenya's independence, Jomo
Kenyatta, who had been jailed on the false allegation that he
managed the Mau Mau movement, was released from prison and
was appointed the first African Prime Minister of the country.

On the whole, one must not overlook the role that religion
played, as a powerful unifier, in this struggle for Kenyan national
liberation. Perhaps, without oaths, prophets and rituals the
Mau Mau movement might not have been launched or Kenya
liberated from the shackles of British colonialism on December
12, 1963. Perhaps European rule would have lingered on there
for one or more decades as happened in Mozambique, Angola,
Guinea (Bissau), Zimbabwe, Namibia and South Africa.

Above all, it is important to remember that the Mau Mau
was not formally organized with a hierarchy of control. Like
most associations formed by acephalous communities, noted
Furedi, it was "essentially an ad hoc response to changing conditions." Communication was based on a network of informal ties
rather than a formal system. The oathing ceremonies, and those
who administered the oaths, played a crucial role in spreading
this influence and maintaining the "informal ties," which were
based on the ideology of the movement. Economic insecurity,
land hunger, frustration and racial oppression sparked spontaneous anti-European sentiments.[50]

Although oathing played a crucial role in the Mau Mau
movement, students of African history are advised not to place
too much emphasis on the ritual before the widespread social and
political consciousness and unity of purpose that they helped to

engender. "It was not the oath," wrote Furedi, "that drove squatters into battle but a determination to fight. Behind the ritual lay an entirely secular purpose."[51] The same could have been said of the Haitian Voodoo, Ugandan Nyabingi, and Tanzanian Maji Maji movements. Students must not lose sight of the fact that religion did not cause resistance, it was European violence and economic exploitation that did. All that religion did was to unify the oppressed and instill in them a new sense of purpose. As Robert Egerton has reminded us, "the Mau Mau was an epic of sacrifice, cruelty, and courage. This struggle between black Africans and white minority rule was the first to take place in modern Africa, but it was followed by others."[52]

Notes

1. J. B. Webster, "The Civil War in Usuku" in Bethwell A. Ogot, *War and Society in Africa* (London: F. Cass, 1972): 46.

2. T. O. Ranger, "Connections between Primary Resistance Movements and Modern Mass Nationalism in East and Central Africa," parts 1 and 2, *Journal of African History*, 9 nos. 3 and 4 (1968): 451-52.

3. John Iliffe, "The Organization of the Maji Maji rebellion," *Journal of African History*, 8, no 3 (1967): 512.

4. G. C. K. Gwassa, "African Methods of Warfare During the Maji Maji War, 1905-1907" in Ogot (ed.), *War and Society in Africa*, 127.

5. Ranger, "Connections," 450.

6. O. B. Mapunda and G. P. Mpangara, *The Maji Maji war in Ungoni* (Nairobi East Africa Pub. House 1969), 12.

7. Arnold J. Temu, "Tanzanian Societies and Colonial Invasion 1875-907," in *Tanzania Under Colonial Rule*. Ed. H. Y. Kaniki (London, 1969): 241.

8. Gwassa, "African Methods of Warfare, 136.

9. G. C. K. Gwassa, and Iliffe, John (eds.), *Records of the Maji Maji Rising* (Nairobi East African Publishing House 1967, 14.

10. Gwassa, "African Methods of Warfare", 136-37.

11. A. Ogot Bethwell and William Ochieng, "Mumboism--An Anti-colonial Movement" in Ogot (ed.) War *and Society in Africa,* 161.

12. *Ibid.,* 160-61.

13. Gwassa and Iliffe, *Records of the Maji Maji Rising,* 28.

14 See Richard Price, *Maroon Societies: Rebel Slave Communities in the Americas.* Baltimore: The John Hopkins University Press 1979.

15. See Don C. Ohadike, *The Ekumeku Movement: Western Igbo Resistance to the British Conquest of Nigeria, 1883-1914.* Athens: Ohio Univ. Press, 1991.

16. Iliffe, "The Organization of the Maji Maji rebellion," 500.

17. Elizabeth Hopkins, "The Nyabingi Cult of Southwestern Uganda," in Robert Rotberg and Ali Mazrui (eds). *Protest and Power in Black Africa* (New York, Oxford University Press, 1970): 263.

18. *Ibid.,* 267.

19. *Ibid.,* 273.

20. *Ibid.,* 289.

21. *Ibid.,* 300-320.

22. Tabitha M. Kanogo, *Squatters and the Roots of Mau Mau, 1905-63* (Athens: Ohio University Press, 1987), 35-6.

23. Robert B. Edgerton, *Mau Mau: An African Crucible* (New York: Free Press, 1989), 14.

24. Jomo Kenyatta, *Facing Mount Kenya* (New York: Vintage Books, 1965), 75

25. H. K. Wachanga, *The Swords of Kirinyaga: the Fight for Land and Freedom* (Kampala: East African Literature Bureau, 1975), 4.

26. Margery Perham, Foreword to Josiah Mwangi Kariuku, *"Mau Mau" Detainee: Account by a Kenyan African of his Experiences in Detention Camps 1953-60* (Oxford: Oxford University Press, 1964), 17.

27. *Ibid.,* 17.

28. Frank Furedi, *The Mau Mau in Perspective* (Athens: Ohio University Press, 1989), 8.

29. John Colin Carothers, *The Psychology of Mau Mau* (Nairobi: printed by the Government Printer, 1954), 4.

30. *Ibid.,* 15.

31. L. S. B. Leakey, *Defeating the Mau Mau* (London: Methuen, 1954), 43.
32. Perham, Foreword to Kariuku, *"Mau Mau" Detainee,* 17.
33. Kariuku, *"Mau Mau" Detainee,* 27-8.
34. Edgerton, *Mau Mau,* 14.
35. (Krenshaw, 1997, 167).
36. (Rosenstiel, 1953, 425).
37. Ohadike, *The Ekumeku Movement,* 13-14.
38. Furedi, *The Mau Mau in Perspective,* 8.
39. Wachanga, *The Swords of Kirinyaga,* 2.
40. *Ibid.,* 4.
41. Edgerton, *Mau Mau,* 120.
42. *Ibid.,* 121.
43. Furedi, *The Mau Mau in Perspective,* 113.
44. Quoted in *Ibid.,* 106.
45. Marshall S. Clough, *Mau Mau Memoirs: History, Memory, and Politics,* (Boulder Colo.: Lynne Rienner, 1998), 98.
46. Kariuku, *"Mau Mau" Detainee,* 56-7.
47. As quoted in Clough, *Mau Mau,* 99.
48. *Ibid.,* 144-5.
49. Furedi, *The Mau Mau in Perspective,* 112-13.
50. *Ibid.,* 140.
51. *Ibid.,* 141.
52. Edgerton, *Mau Mau,* x.

Chapter 2

FROM AFRICA TO THE AMERICAS: TRADITIONAL AFRICAN RELIGIONS AND PROTEST IN BRAZIL, CUBA, AND HAITI

Yoruba, Ashanti, Igbo, Dahomean and Congolese religions and music have had a profound impact on the black cultures of Brazil, Cuba, Haiti and Trinidad. This is true if one thinks of Voodoo in Haiti, *Santeria* and *Rumba* in Cuba, or *Candomblé, Samba*, and *Capoeira* in Brazil, or even *Shango* worship and *Calypso* in Trinidad.

If African captives arrived in the Americas without any cultures, as some Western writers have claimed, how then could they have reproduced African cultural practices in the Americas? There is no doubt that Africans experienced some difficulties in reproducing their cultures in the Americas, but the problem had more to do with the impediments that their captors deliberately placed before them than by their inability to recreate their ancient African cultures.

Separated from Africa and from the white society that held him captive, an enslaved African just brought into the hostile environment of American society could not survive without African religions. This is largely because religion integrated him into the black community, especially with those who had some knowledge of the curative powers of medicinal herbs. African religions, as vital elements of African cultures, were the real tie that bound individuals to their communities, ancestors, gods and goddesses. We have abundant evidence of the linkages between religious practices in Africa and the Americas. For example, Haitian Voodoo was only an extension of Dahomean Vudou, just as *Chango* (or *Shango)* worship in Trinidad is an extension of the *Sango* practice in Nigeria. We also have enough evidence to confirm that African religions in the Americas are syntheses of the various African religions and that the new religious practices were linked to political mobilization and rebellions.

The clearest evidence of linkages between African religions and New World adaptations could be found in maroon settlements. Elements of African religions in maroon religious practices were evident in the use of cowries, charms and poison. As in Africa, the traditional medicine men and women played important roles in rituals, medicine, politics, and governance. The inhabitants of maroon villages recognized the ritual roles of women, exemplified by the fact that maroon women, like women in Africa, occupied very important politico-religious positions because of the belief that they possessed special magical powers, such as being more susceptible to ritual trance.[1] Both in Africa and the diaspora, women often led religious congregations.

A runaway's departure from a plantation and his or her incorporation into a maroon settlement was not considered complete before he or she had been born again into the traditional African religions. In many *quilombos* of Brazil almost every black person engaged in African traditional religious practices, their previous contacts with Christianity notwithstanding. In Palmares and elsewhere, there was a tendency toward "tribal regression," a phenomenon which Roger Bastide has described as a kind of return to Africa, a form of reversion to African thought.[2] This entailed re-teaching African culture, ceremonies, and rituals to Africans who had recently escaped from the plantations.

Also in the plantations, slaves believed that there were medicines that could reveal if a person would be whipped. They believed that some medicines could actually neutralize a master's decision to flog them. For precautionary purposes, slaves often carried voodoo or hoodoo leather bags, which they believed would render the whip harmless or keep them from being flogged. Such bags were handed down from generation to generation.[3] One other type of slave resistance was the use of poison. The fear and reality of poisoning were common. Newspapers carried accounts of death, often ascribing them to the "Negro disease," the slaveholders' euphemism for death by poisoning.[4]

Many blacks believed that the souls of relatives who died in the Americas returned to Africa. Death was not always treated as an end to a person's life but the beginning of a necessary journey back home to Africa. The evidence is borne in the fact that funeral offerings usually included foodstuff intended for the use of the deceased during his or her journey. Here we have historical evidence of the origin of Pan-African feelings that became clearer as time went on. In the nineteenth and twentieth centuries many Africans abroad wanted to be repatriated, not in the next world, but in the here and now.

There is no doubt that Africans in the Americas encountered some initial problems when they tried to reproduce their African cultures. They had come from different geographical areas-- Angola, the Congo, the Bight of Biafra, the Slave Coast, the Gold Coast, and the Upper Guinea Zone, as well as their vast hinter-lands.[5] On arrival in the Americas, these Africans were confined to plantations, or what I have chosen to describe as miniature "slave villages." In Brazil and in the Caribbean, the large planta-tions had between 100 and 200 slaves, while on the plantations of the southern United States, the average slave population was slightly over 20. Moreover, it was a common practice to ship slaves first to the Caribbean and then to the southern United States. As a result, slaves on the plantations in the southern United States were more ethnically mixed than were slaves on the plantations in the Caribbean.

Because language is an indispensable vehicle for transmit-ting cultural values, one of the initial obstacles that a slave had to deal with was the language problem. An Akan slave's neighbors may have been Bakongo, Bameleke, Chokwe, Ndembu, Fulani, Igala, Igbo, Ibibio, Hausa, Hutu, Mandinga, Nupe, Ovimbudu,

Shona, Thonga, Tiv, Venda, Yoruba, or Zulu. In such a settlement, it would have been difficult for each slave to speak his or
her native tongue or practice his or her individual religion. In due
course, many blacks would have forfeited their own languages
and religious practices. Nevertheless, it was easier to overcome
the religious problem than the language problem largely because
African traditional religious beliefs are basically similar--they are
generally tolerant of other belief systems and they all are rooted
in the belief in one supreme-being. Africans at home and abroad
believed that one must not forget one's creator and ancestors.
Consequently, they communed with them every day through
prayers, proverbs, sacrifices and incantations. The desire to stay
in touch with the supreme being and the invisible forces created
a strong bond of unity between the Africans in the Americas and
their native Africa. No matter their pain and anguish, African
exiles never forgot their original homelands in Africa, even if
they never set foot on them. This attitude was one of the strongest energies that kept African cultures alive in the Americas.

Invariably, however, many African languages and religions
would have merged with others completely. Voodoo, for instance,
is a synthesis of more than eight different African religions. In
Surinam, the Africans there spoke a language that was a synthesis
of six African and three European languages.

Accordingly, the survival of any religion would have
depended on its resilience and the individuals' concentration
levels from particular ethnic groups in the slave communities
concerned. For instance, the Yoruba religion survived in the
Americas partly because of the concentration of Yoruba in many
slave societies, partly because of the resilience of their religion,
and partly because the Yoruba were among the last batch of slaves
to be imported into the Americas. Perhaps no one has explained
this phenomenon more lucidly than Voeks when he wrote: "...in
spite of the wide variety of religious traditions brought to Bahia
[in Brazil], it was the cosmology of the Yoruba, a spiritual universe circumscribed by the *orixas,* that had the greatest impact on
Afro-Brazilian religion." Voeks went on to explain that some of

the other African ethnic groups abandoned their own spiritual vision in favor of the Yoruba. Voeks warned that even though the reasons for the dominance of the Yoruba have not been fully explored, it must have stemmed "in part from the geographic movements of the slave trade," and from the fact that the last wave of African immigrants was predominantly Yoruba. Thus, the religious dominance of the Yoruba must have resulted, not only from their numerical superiority, but also from their possession of a rich and complex religious system. This religious system had, according to Voeks, "a rigidly defined social structure, a highly portable animism, one that was tied less to object and place than were the beliefs of the other African groups."[6]

The concentration of people from particular ethnic groups on the plantations also affected the survival rates of African religions in the Americas. This explains the emergence of such African-derived religions as Voodoo in Haiti, Candomblé in Brazil, and Santeria in Cuba. On the other hand, in the United States, where slave population per plantation was relatively small, and where slaves were drawn from diverse African regions, the Black Church evolved as the dominant religious affiliation.

Despite the inconsistencies, however, blacks in the Americas managed to resolve the crisis of religious and ethnic identities by adopting an attitude that tended towards mutual cultural accommodation. Each batch of newcomers was inserted into a new black cultural melting pot. In due course, they produced a new African or black consciousness which, in the United States, for instance, was sufficiently different, yet basically similar to the old African cultures and identities, especially with regard to religious belief systems and ideas of warfare and political mobilization. "The African component of the earlier slave cultures was so overwhelming," wrote Mechal Sobel, "that, with growing awareness of it, it has become impossible to explain black religion in [the United States of] America without exploring continuities with African understandings."[7]

SANTERIA

The continuities that Levin wrote about are evident in Cuban religious culture of Santeria, which is rooted in Yoruba religion. The linkages between Santeria and Yoruba religious practices can be found in the concepts of Olorun, orisa, and Ifa divination. One cannot effectively discuss Santeria without first grappling with the theological foundations of Yoruba religion and society. To begin with, one must understand that Yoruba culture and society are a perfect blend of history and religion. The dozen or so Yoruba sub-groups claim descent from a putative founding father that they refer to as Oba Oduduwa. Unlike many African groups, the Yoruba are urban dwellers, and one of their earliest urban centers was Ile-Ife, the home of hundreds of *orishas* or deities.

Like all other African communities, however, the Yoruba believe in the existence of a supreme being whom they call *Olodumare, Olorun,* and *Olofin-Orun.* The word *olorun* can be translated as owner of the sky, while *Olofin-Orun* can be treated as supreme sovereign ruler who is in heaven. (Idowu, 36). *Olorun* or *Olodumare* has variously been represented as the king of the cosmos, the creator of heaven and earth, the Supreme Being who keeps the universe in motion, the Supreme and Eternal Being, and the Lord of Life. The world and all that is in it owe their existence to Him (Sawyer, 40). No one can see *Olodumare* for he resides far away in the heavens, yet He is everywhere at the same time. Temples for His worship are unnecessary because men cannot confine Him to one place. He sees and cares for all that He creates. His power is infinite; He judges men and women according to their deeds. No one knows His mind. Consequently it is fruitless for humans to approach Him directly. To reach Him, one must seek the help of the lesser deities, messengers or intermediaries. There are 201 or 401 or 1001 of such intermediaries, but for the purposes of this discussion, we will visit only seven of them, namely, *Obatala, Orunmila, Esu, Ogun, Sango, Yemonja,* and *Osun.*

Obatala

According to a popular Yoruba myth of creation, *Obatala* is the foremost among the *orisas* or divine entities. *Obatala* is said to be present when the world was created. And it was to him that *Olodomare* relegated the actual task of molding humans out of clay or earth. This task was restricted to the sculpturing of man's material body or *ara*. After man was molded, *Olodumare* breathed life *(emi)* into him. This explains why *Obatala* is described as the maker of the body, the giver of forms, and the god of creation and wisdom. (Hallgren, 28). Among other things, *Obatala* was the source of fertility.

Orunmila

Orunmila or *Ifa* is depicted as the god of divination. He is conceived both as a divine entity and a divination system. *Orunmila*, like *Obatala,* was present when each person was created in heaven and was then presented with his or her own destiny. *Orunmila,* therefore, is believed to know the fate of men as well as *Olodumare's* plans for them. (Hallgren 29-30). However, because humans had the tendency to forget their destinies when they entered the world, *Olodumare* sent *Orunmila* to guide them, lest they went astray. But this was by no means an easy task for *Orunmila* because humans could not commune directly with him. He therefore appointed *Ifa* diviners or *babalawo*, as his mouthpieces and officiating priests through whom he could pass on divine instructions. This chain of communication is borne out clearly in a Yoruba expression that was coined during the colonial period: *sofun oga ko sofun oyinbo* (speak to the headman so that he may speak to the boss).

Ifa diviners or *babalawo* are the messengers of *Orunmila*. These messengers can unlock the secrets of life. With their vast knowledge of the ancestors and the will of the gods, *babalawo* help humans navigate the difficult paths of life. But only those who seek can benefits from their vast knowledge.

Not every man can qualify as *babalawo,* however. Training is tedious and may last for fifteen years. It involves training in a mystery system that is accompanied by elaborate rites of passage. Once successfully completed, the initiate receives the power to divine. The knowledge to understand the secrets that link humanity with the past, the present and the future are contained in secret *odu,* a set of stories or poems, that provide information concerning a person's or even a community's destiny. There are sixteen possible situations and sixteen variations in each situation, resulting in a total of 256 possible interpretations. Each of these 256 permutations is attached to a number of verses and stories that can be read only by the *babalawo,* the priest of *Orunmila,* who uses the *Ifa* oracle to interpret messages.

Thus, because a *babalawo* can accurately interpret the *ifa odu,* he is the best suited to help an individual make right judgements or grapple with difficult situations. It is expected of a man to seek the advice of a *babalawo* or *Ifa* diviner before choosing a wife or a vocation. A man or woman may consult a *babalawo* to determine the best time to embark on a journey, or even to find out when to appease an irate god or ancestor. Some people may approach a *babalawo* to help them deal with threatening family problems. A council of *babalawo* can also help a community choose a rightful king, or offer advice on how to avert a famine, flood, epidemic or war. To ignore the advice of a *babalawo* is to invite the wrath, not only of *Orunmila,* but also that of *Olodumare.*

Esu

Esu is another prominent *orisa* among the Yoruba group of divinities. He is perceived as an embodiment of good and evil, a destructive and yet dynamic deity. (Hallgren 31). Esu has been described in many other ways: troublemaker, rascal, "trickster," the source of all evil, he who disturbs, provokes, and exerts bad influences on people.

Influenced by these negative images, the early Christian missionaries to work among the Yoruba people compared *Esu* with the Devil or Satan of the Judeo-Christian traditions. Yet *Esu* is not the equivalent of the Biblical Satan, whose primary preoccupation is to seek the downfall of both man and God. Unlike the Satan, *Esu* does not seek to dethrone *Olodumare.* Instead he acts both as the messenger of *Olodumare* and the protector of those who live according to the laws handed down by the ancestors. Although *Esu* symbolized that which is both evil and good, his powers could be harnessed for positive ends. Like a watchdog, *Esu* keeps unwelcome guests away from homes and villages. Almost every house has an image of *Esu* placed at its entrance. Daily prayers, libations and sacrifices are offered in return for his protection.

Yoruba people have a deep reverence for *Esu,* "the divine trickster and the keeper of the gates associated with the crossroads and the messenger of Olodumare."[8] *Esu* is not only the keeper of the gates associated with the crossroads; he is also a principal messenger of *Olodumare.* He observes everything that occurs and then reports them to *Olodumare.* One cannot ignore his powers, nor can any one risk provoking his wrath. Yet his benevolent nature is constantly being reaffirmed. Sacrifices between *Ifá* and *Olodumare* must of necessity pass through him. He punishes those who ignore prescribed sacrifices. (Hallgren, 31)

Esu may tempt people but the purpose is not to cause them pain. He uses temptations to search their mind, to show them their inherent weaknesses, and to encourage them to improve their conducts. *Esu* also uses the information he gathers from his tests to set up a code of morality and piety for humanity as whole.

Further more, *Esu* is said to be the keeper of the *ase* which is a "copy of the divine authority and power with which *Olodumare* created the universe and maintained its physical laws." This book is very important because without it all the other divinities cannot effectively discharge their duties. Thus, before the commencement of certain rituals, supplicants first request *Esu* to give *ase* to the divinity being invoked.

Ogun

Ogun has been described as the god of iron and war. It was he who came down from heaven at the time of creation and cut paths through the forest with an iron cutlass so that the other deities and, in due course, all Yoruba people could move through them with ease. It was *Ogun* who gave the people farming and hunting instruments of iron so that they might be able to grow edible crops and kill wild animals. Because of this, *Ogun* is recognized as the patron of farmers and hunters. Furthermore, because *Ogun* gave the Yoruba people the instruments of warfare he is the patron of the warriors. Sacrifices are offered to *Ogun* either to secure his protection or to ward off his anger, or even to enlist his cooperation in the event of an inter-group strife.

Iron tools are used as instruments of divination because of the recognition of the ritual potency of iron. Blacksmiths are highly respected, not only because of their close association with the power of *Ogun,* but also because iron tools are indispensable to the survival of Yoruba communities. Any one who swears in the name of *Ogun* takes his oath seriously. Despite modernization and industrialization, the power of *Ogun* has increased. Today, *Ogun* is associated with everything made of metal, such as trains, trucks, cars, bicycles, and even air-crafts. A journey in an aircraft, a train, a car, or even on a scooter, usually begins with a prayer for *Ogun's* protection.

Sango

Sango is depicted as the god of thunder and lightening. The priests of *Sango* are said to wield the power to send thunderbolts and fire down from the heavens. *Sango* worshippers sing praise songs about his power, claiming at the same time that he has the power to "kill the liar" and "strike the stupid to the ground." The shrines of *Sango* can be found in virtually every Yoruba town. Each shrine contains a representation of *Sango* in human form. The bitter kola is *Sango's* most preferred offering. It is believed that *Sango* possesses people, protects his followers and gives long life to warriors.

Among the other deities that require brief mention here, especially since they feature prominently in *Santeria* worship, are *Yemonja, Olokun, Osun* and *Oya.* These four deities are associated with water, fertility and motherhood. *Yemonja* is depicted as the goddess of salt water or the sea. *Osun* is a river goddess, and *Oya* is identified as the goddess of whirlwind and fierce weather.[9]

These and other Yoruba deities formed the basis of *Santeria* belief system. African captives went to Cuba with the knowledge of these deities and tried to recreate them. They succeeded in doing so to the extent that the reality of "New World" slavery could permit. But it is not their success or otherwise in recreating Yoruba traditions in Cuba that concerns us here, rather it is their success in using them to resist forced acculturation or assimilation. Their continued attachment to their African religious worldview enabled these African captives in Cuba to affirm their rejection of imposed European religious worldview. By identifying their deities with certain Christian saints, they demonstrated a wonderful ability to improvise. By naming their deities after Catholic saints, they deceived their captors into believing that they were in communion with Roman Catholic saints. Thus, the major Yoruba deities found equivalent saints, on account of which the entire religious practice took the name of *Santeria,* meaning, "the way of the saints." The true devotees became *santeros* or *santera,* meaning, men or women who have "made the saint." The vast majority of flock simply remained faithful to the religion, for not every one could achieve sainthood.

All these were made possible by two patterns of behavior exhibited by both the Spaniards and African captives in Cuba. The Spaniards indulged in the fetish of saint worship, to the same degree that the Africans held tenaciously to the worship of their deities. The Spaniards told tales of the wonders that saints performed just like the Africans believed that their deities equally performed wonderful and supernatural feats. Unfortunately, while the Spaniards in Cuba could almost freely express their religious views and indulge in the veneration of the saints, Afro-Cubans were restricted from indulging in the public veneration of their deities. The church and the colonial authorities claimed the right to regulate the moral and ethical behavior of their slaves. To the church, it was a religious obligation to expose all slaves to the gospel and to punish severely those who continued to follow the traditions of their fathers. For the African captives in Cuba, the decision to disguise their deities as Roman Catholic saints was an act of solemn expediency.

The transformation from a purely Yoruba religion to *Santeria* took place almost entirely in the *cabildos* or clubs. These were places that blacks gathered for relaxation, but also used the occasion to communicate their feelings or comment on their struggles. For it was customary to allow the Africans to congregate after work for rest and relaxation.[10] The church and the state allowed the establishment of *cabildos* because they helped to reduce social tensions that might otherwise build up. Some *cabildos* were, in fact, located within church premises and were supervised by the Catholic priests. It is not surprising that the *cabildos* would be the most important centers for the development of *Santeria*. But how could *Santeria* have thrived under the watchful eyes of the clergy?

A perfect condition for disguise was created when the clergy insisted that it reserved the right to control the *cabildos*. The Africans, who wanted to worship their own gods, tried to manipulate the protective arms of the *cabildos* to their own advantage. The conflict of interest that ensued created both the necessity and opportunity to disguise African divinities as Roman Catholic saints. Consequently, several select Yoruba divinities were named after the saints that conjured up similar sentiments. For example, *Ogun* became associated with Saint Peter, while *Shango* was disguised as Santa Barbara. In order to avoid suspicion, the worship of the *orishas* incorporated certain elements of Catholic worship such as the burning of candles and incense. Thus, it was in the *cabildos* that the initial contact between the *orishas* and the saints were made.[11]

It is important to point out, however, that *Santeria* was not just a syncretic blending of elements of Yoruba traditions and Roman Catholicism. Instead, as *Santeria* developed it incorporated elements of other African traditional religions as well as certain indigenous Cuban belief systems. Furthermore, even though *Santeria* could be described generally as a syncretic blending of Yoruba and Roman Catholic practices, it is more

African than European. This explains why the saints do not posses devotees. Instead, it is the African divinities that send them into trance. Likewise, it is not Roman Catholic devotional hymns that invoke possession. Instead, it is the sacred African drums and vocal chanting that create the right atmosphere for the right *orishas* to "mount their horses."

Be that as it may, *Santeria* provided Afro-Cubans the opportunity to express their protest against European domination by non-violent means. Rather than confront their oppressors with arms, these Africans of the diaspora chose the path of non-violent confrontation. In the long run they won the battle, not only for physical survival from the stifling effects of "New World" slavery, but also against deculturation and cultural petrifaction. The religious practice of *Santeria* not only triumphed in Cuba, it also spread to many parts of the Caribbean, South America and the United States. Today, *Santeria* communities can be found in New York City, Boston, Los Angeles, and many other American cities.

AFRICAN RELIGIONS OF RESISTANCE IN BRAZIL

Brazil has the largest black population in the Americas. Today, according to some estimates, 60 million blacks live in that country. It is doubtful, however, that these 60 million people see themselves as blacks. Equally unique, though of a questionable validity, is that out of the 1.5 million slaves estimated to have lived in Brazil in the nineteenth century, about 90 percent were of Yoruba origin. It is conceivable that many Afro-Brazilians claim Yoruba origin when they no longer remember the exact ethnic group they hailed from.

Be that as it may, the Yorubas were among the last batch of African immigrants to arrive in Brazil in the nineteenth century. Moreover, slavery was abolished in Brazil in 1888, barely twenty years after slave imports to that country were stopped. All of these factors contributed to the large concentration of Yoruba speaking people in Brazil.

Furthermore, the high concentration of Yoruba immigrants is largely responsible for the survival of the Yoruba religion in Brazil. Before the abolition of slavery, the Africans of Brazil coped with their hardships by resorting to various forms of religious practices. *Santidade* and *Candomblé* enabled them to advance the African culture of resistance. However, while the followers of *Santidade* adopted the strategy of violent resistance,[12] *Candomblé* worshippers accepted the principle of non-violent resistance.

Candomblé

Candomblé is the religion of the *orishas* or *orixas*, the supernatural forces who serve as "the earthly ambassadors of *Olorun* [the creator of all things] who are directly linked to the everyday world of mortals."[13] Slaves and freedmen founded the first houses of *Candomblé* in Brazil in the early nineteenth century. Three freed African women--Iya Deta, Iya Kala, and Iya Nasso--erected the first *Candomblé* houses of worship in 1830.[14] The Brazilian City of Salvador in Bahia is the spiritual headquarters of *Candomblé*. Throughout the nineteenth century, *Candomblé* adherents maintained contacts with continental African royal houses through visits and recourse to spiritual training.[15] *Candomblé* is not only a community of devotees; it is also a dance for communication with spirits. *Candomblé* dances are performed in sacred spaces. When performed in this manner, the sacred space creates the conditions necessary for spirit possession.

Candomblé is not only about religion. It is also about medicine and healing. It gives its followers access to ancient African divination systems and, like most African-derived religions, *Candomblé* is not concerned with individual salvation and the hereafter, but about coping with earthly problems and achieving good health and prosperity for individuals and the wider community. Since its inception, the religion has armed its practitioners with the necessary tools for preserving their cultural heritage and for improving their well being. Women head many Candomblé houses.

Candomblé is a religion of peace, yet it is a resistant religion. Unlike *Santidade* worshippers who frequently raided plantations and cities, and unlike Voodoo devotees who organized a successful violent revolution under the banner of their religion, *Candomblé* adherents contented themselves with non-violent resistance. Despite slavery and colonialism, *Candomblé* prepared the Africans for a spiritual escape from slavery and white domination. As Voeks has explained,

> Empowered perhaps by manumission, Africans and their descendants were actively sowing the seeds of religious rebellion, a collective resistance to the spiritual and cultural hegemony imposed by the ruling class. These early houses of African worship offered perhaps the only viable alternative to the European social and religious order, to which slaves and freedmen had little or no access.[16]

One interesting commentary about *Candomblé* is its appropriation of certain elements of Roman Catholicism. At the time of its formation, the religious practice had to be masked under the guise of Roman Catholicism for fear of official reprimands and retribution. The countless *orixas* took on the names of Christian saints. On *Candomblé* altars and temples were placed the sculptures and paintings of Catholic saints, each of them representing a corresponding force in the Yoruba pantheon. "For most of the faithful, wrote Voeks, "the images and the legends of the African *orixas* and the European saints have become hopelessly tangled. A dreamy depiction of a voluptuous and porcelain white Virgin Mary passes without notice for the maternal African goddess Yemanja."[17] Thus, in colonial Brazil, *Candomblé* became an important tool in every day negation of the forces of slavery and colonialism. Candomblé gatherings were, therefore, useful centers of resistance activities, serving, at the same time, as potential centers of friction between slaves and freedmen. The practice of *Candomblé* kept the free populations so uneasy that ordinances had to be passed to forbid its activities. From the early nineteenth century until the very recent past, explained Joseph Murphy, *Candomblé* devotees were periodically harassed and suppressed. Yet, when they did not pose a threat as centers of insurrection, they offered an alternative world, where the memory of freedom continued to be expressed powerfully through the practice of *Candomble'*.[18] The memory of freedom lost and a commitment to freedom to be regained, "made for a remarkable continuity with the traditions of their ancestors and nurtured in Afo-Bahians a force for resistance to the brutal system of oppression that they endured."[19] Though physically removed from their native Africa, the practice of *Candomblé* enabled these Africans of the diaspora to preserve their heritage. Through music, dance and worship, they strengthened their spiritual ties with their ancestors and forged a distinct Afro-Brazilian identity.

VOODOO AND THE HAITIAN REVOLUTION

Traditional African religious beliefs and practices were evident in the Haitian revolution. To survive the harsh environment of Haitian slavery, where mortality was excessively high, African captives quickly learned to maintain sanity and, eventually, to overthrow the slave system, through the practice of Voodoo. Carolyn Fick described Voodoo as "a unique blend of retained Africanisms and New World adaptations." She also stated that during the Haitian revolution, the religious practice "provided a medium for the political organization of the slaves, as well as an ideological force, both of which contributed directly to the success of what became a virtual . . . attack on plantations across the province."[20] Mederie Louis Moreau de St. Mery, a Martiniquean traveler, stated in 1797 that Arada blacks were "the true followers" of Voodoo.[21] His and several other accounts seem to agree that the practice was imported from Whydah in the region of Dahomey.[22]

New World Voodoo was not an exact copy of Dahomean Voodoo, but it certainly was a structure into which many elements of different African religious practices were grafted. For instance, Haitian Voodoo practice involved the invocation of the gods, appeals to the omniscient, omnipotent "Good Lord beyond the clouds," and the vow of secrecy, all of which are found in most traditional African religions.[23] Also, according to Fick, "Voodoo as generally practiced in Saint Domingo (and especially its linguistic diversity) constituted, in effect, a broad synthesis of the various religious beliefs and practices of all the African nations forming the slave population."[24] One of the most famous hymns, "chanted in unison for the initiation of a neo-phyte," is Congolese in origin.[25] Thus, even though Voodoo in Saint Domingo eventually acquired its distinct characteristics, the most important contribution of Dahomey to its sustenance was the provision of a "substructure within which the religious, cultural, and linguistic traditions of the diverse African nations successively found a place and effectively contributed to its evolution."[26] Thus, Voodoo, as we know it, is a synthesis of more than eight different African religions. These shared religious experiences were not only at the center of their culture and society, but they also provided them with a bond of unity. If, therefore, one speaks of Voodoo in its widest sense, commented Joseph Murphy, then all the African-derived elements of Haitian religion might be considered Voodoo.[27]

Some of the primary functions of Voodoo were to protect its practitioners from the terrible powers of the slave holders, provide an organizational tool for resistance, facilitate clandestine meetings for those involved in secret plots against their masters, and create a network of communication between slaves of different plantations.[28] Elaborating on these functions, Jean Fauchard cited the case of the Voodoo gatherings that took place after a religious ceremony at Bois-Caiman on the eve of the Haitian revolution. During the ceremony, wrote Fauchard,

> Maroons, under the pretext of the dance, organized the rebellion, established necessary liaisons with the work gangs, distributed arms and issued passwords. Thus it is in this sense that this popular religion which in itself rested on no precise ideal of liberty can be linked with all slave resistance and with the struggle for liberty.[29]

Fauchard insisted that "secret Voodoo rites provided singularly effective means of action and facilitated important secret meetings and a network of communications among various work gangs." It was those rituals and meetings that eventually created an atmosphere of panic favorable to rebellions.[30] Encouraged by the echoes of the French revolution, maroons who had practiced their voodoo rituals faithfully turned their cult into a "powerful expression of their demand for liberation."[31] First, under the auspices of Voodoo, slaves gathered at Morne-rouge to discuss sensitive political issues. They agreed to rise up in arms and sealed their agreement with a blood pact during a ritual ceremony at Bois-Caiman. The ritual involved the symbolic drinking of blood, "that committed the participants to utmost secrecy, solidarity, and a vow to revenge."[32] To this day, insists Murphy, Voodoo has remained a potent force for organizing the disenfranchised majority of Haitian society . . . and has remained a critical force against external authority, particularly when that authority has come from imperial powers, be they French, American, or Roman."[33]

How does one explain the origins of Voodoo? No one knows exactly but Voodoo or any of its variants simply mean "spirit." In its original form, Voodoo was an all-powerful being among the Ardra pantheon. Below this spirit were lesser deities known as *lwa,* with whom the devotees communed through rituals and ceremonies. One became united to Voodoo through the *lwa.* A devotee cannot be a "member" of Voodoo; he or she can only be a servant of the *lwa.* Nor can a person choose to join a Voodoo community; one only responds to a call from a *lwa.*[34]

Voodoo can also be described as "a belief system of the symbiotic interdependence of humans and spirits," expressed in songs and rituals.[35] In the Voodoo belief system, the *lwas* were overseeing spirits. Voodoo rituals were founded on the principle of physical and spiritual possession by the *lwas.* Each person is said to have a specific *lwa* that he or she must find (through physical and spiritual possession) to achieve a spiritual balance. In Voodoo rituals, noted Michel S. Laguerre, songs and music help create a favorable atmosphere for possession-trance to occur.[36] In the ceremonies of possession, the linkages between Haitian and African cultures are elaborately emphasized and dramatized. They mentally enable those in trance to travel freely to and from Africa. Voodoo or Voodoo devotees believe that no physical boundaries can stop them from returning to their homelands. As a Voodoo song makes abundantly clear, death (for a devotee) is the same thing as making a spiritual journey from Haiti to Africa, where Voodoo spirits live.[37] Death also meant freedom—freedom from slavery and humiliation. This spiritual connection with Africa played a crucial role in black resistance to European colonialism and slavery. It prepared the mind for resistance.

Fearing uprisings and the influence of Voodoo on slaves, colonial authorities in Haiti passed laws which, on pain of death, proscribed meetings during night or day (especially in the absence of a Catholic priest), congregations of any type, drumming and singing, and any "fetishes" that could be used for magic.[38] These prohibitions notwithstanding, Haitian blacks prepared for war, using different methods to conceal their plan. They also used various incantations, ceremonies and dances to render themselves invincible to European guns.

The fears of the whites were founded, however. The air was permeated with panic as a number of blacks proclaimed themselves prophets and aroused mass followings. A black man named Hyacinth is said to have gone from one plantation to the other in the Western province, claiming that he was divinely inspired. There was also Romaine, a prophetess, who, like Hyacinth, succeeded in strengthening her authority by claiming divine attributes. Mackandal was a voodoo practitioner who thought of exterminating the white population through poisoning. His plan was exposed and he was captured and burned alive. Christoph thought differently, but his idea was not considered constructive enough. Boukman, a High Priest and the headman of a plantation, organized a revolution, using Voodoo as a symbol of unity. He gathered a large following, several thousand strong, and hoped to use it to massacre the whites. None of these moves had any lasting effects except to alarm the whites and give them enough reasons to intensify their sadistic behaviors.

The foremost leader of the Haitian revolution was Toussaint L'Ouverture. He was raised in the harsh climate of New World slavery, where slavery was so harsh that all that slaves did was dream dreams of freedom, and when they did not dream dreams, they sang songs, vowing to kill all their oppressors. "We swear to destroy the whites and all they possess," they sang, "[and] let us die rather than fail to keep this vow."[39] In this statement, one can find the highest expression of the black culture of resistance.

Many of the leaders and instigators of the Haitian revolution were voodoo practitioners or men and women who had an intimate knowledge of the potency of medicine and religion in revolutionary movements. Toussaint L'Ouverture, though a Roman Catholic, had an excellent knowledge of the curative properties of herbs.[40]

Most of the blacks who first joined the Haitian revolutionaries were native-born Africans. The quest for freedom found its energy and outlet in religious practice; thus, Voodoo became a valuable tool for a successful revolution. The actions of the revolutionaries suited well the desire of an oppressed people yearning for freedom from the yoke of their oppressors.[41]

CONCLUSIONS

We must give credit to these Africans for preserving African religions in the Americas. These Africans, even those who lived in the maroon settlements in the far bush, threatened the stability of colonial society in several ways. They were lively religious centers for slaves and free blacks. Africans of all social classes sought spiritual and material remedies for their problems in maroon settlements. The continued practice of African traditional religions offended the Catholic Church as well as slave owners and colonial authorities. Both in Africa and the Americas, Europeans found the refusal by the Africans to give up their religions offensive, but more galling to their sensibility was the African's use of their religion to fight European domination.

Notes

1   Roger Bastide, "The Other Quilombos," in Richard Price, (ed.), *Maroon Societies: Rebel Slave Communities in the Americas* (Baltimore: The John Hopkins University Press 1979), 196.

2. *Ibid.,* 195.

3. Lawrence W. Levine, *Black culture and Black Consciousness: Afro-American folk thought from Slavery to Freedom* (New York: Oxford University Press, 1977), 72.

4. Gary Okihiro (ed.) *In Resistance: Studies in African, Caribbean, and Afro-American History* (Amherst: The University of Massachusetts Press, 1986), 16.

5. See Map.

6. Robert A. Voeks, *Sacred Leaves of Candomblé: African Magic, Medicine, and Religion in Brazil* (Austin: University of Texas Press, 1997), 52.

7. Mechal Sobel, *Trabelin On: The Slave Journey to an Afro-Baptist Faith* (West Port: Greenwood Press, 1979), xix.

8. Anthony B. Pinn, *Varieties of African American Religious Experience,* (Minneapolis, Fortress Press, 1998), 58.

9. *Ibid,* 60-61

10. Yvonne Daniel, *Rumba: Dance and Social Change in Contemporary Cuba* (Bloomington: Indiana University Press, 1995).

11. Anthony B. Pinn, Varieties of African Religious Experience (Minneapolis Fortress Press, 1998), 67.

12. Stuart B. Schwartz, "The Mocambo: Slave Resistance in Colonial Bahia," in Price, *Maroon Societies,* 215-6.

13. Voeks, *Sacred Leaves of Candomblé,* 54.

14. *Ibid.,* 51.

15. Joseph M. Murphy, *Working the Spirit: Ceremonies of the African diaspora* (Boston: Beacon Press, 1994), 44.

16. Voeks, *Sacred Leaves of Candomblé,* 52.

17. *Ibid.,* 61.

18. Murphy, *Working the Spirit,* 47.

19. *Ibid.,* 47.

20. Carolyn E. Fick, *The Making of Haiti: The Saint Domingue Revolution From Below* (Knoxville: University of Tennessee Press, 1990), 94.

21. As quoted in Murphy, *Working the Spirit,* 15.

22 . Dahomey is now known as the Benin Republic.

23. Fick, *The Making of Haiti,* 241.

24. *Ibid.,* 57.

25. *Ibid.,* 57.

26. *Ibid.,* 58.

27. Murphy, *Working the Spirit,* 15.

28. Fick, *The Making of Haiti,* passim.

29. Jean Fauchard, *The Haitian Maroons: Liberty or Death* (New York: Edward W. Blyden Press, 1981), 224.

30. *Ibid., 224.*

31. Vittorio Lanternari, *The Religions of the Oppressed: A Study of Modern Messianic Cults* (New York: New American Library, 1965), 140.

32. Carolyn E. Fick, *The Making of Haiti: The Saint Domingue Revolution From Below,* 94.

33. Murphy, *Working the Spirit,* 14.

34. *Ibid.,* 19.

35. Vera Rubin, Foreword to Michel S. Laguerre, *Voodoo Heritage* (Beverly Hills: Sage, 1980), 12.

36. Laguerre, *Voodoo Heritage,* 30.

37. *Ibid.,* 89.

38. Leslie Desmangles, *The Faces of the Gods: Voodoo and Roman Catholicism in Haiti* (Chapel Hill: University of North Carolina Press, 1992), 26.

39. James, *The Black Jacobins,* 18.

40. *Ibid.,* 19-20.

41. Lanternari, *The Religions of the Oppressed,* 141.

Chapter 3

RUMBA, SAMBA, CAPOEIRA AND STEELBAND MUSIC OF RESISTANCE IN CUBA, BRAZIL, AND TRINIDAD

RUMBA **IN CUBA**

The continuities in African cultures are evident, not only in the Cuban religious culture of Santeria but also in the dance form known as *Rumba*. Blacks in Cuba have danced *Rumba* for over two hundred years. *Rumba* is a secular form of music and dance that expresses love, personal freedom and political empowerment. Its origins go back to the period of slavery, yet it is now a contemporary Cuban dance.

During the days of slavery Africans danced and sang to cope with the anguish of captivity and white racism. No system of slavery can be described as mild, but in comparative terms, however, one can describe slavery in Cuba as ranging from mild to extremely harsh. On the coffee and tobacco plantations, slaves were treated fairly because production did not require great capital investment, nor was work very demanding.[1] Labor conditions were different on the sugar cane plantations. The industry was highly capitalized and it employed over 50 per cent of all Cuban slaves. As described in chapter two, owners thought it was cheaper to work slaves to death in a relatively short time and import new ones than to treat them humanely and care for them in their old age. The excessive rush to amass profit called for extreme brutality and regimentation. "The crucial role of labor in sugar production," observed Franklin W. Knight, "led to the wretched conditions of the slaves in the plantations."[2]

Until the right moment for escape or rebellion was considered, enslaved Africans in Cuba occupied their thoughts with music and dance.[3] Singing and dancing enabled them to conceal their rage and uplift their spirits. Whenever they gathered in their slave quarters or in the major settlements, these places became centers for singing and dancing, or more appropriately, centers for non-violent protests.

Rumba was used in Cuba, not only as a tool of protest against physical abuses, but also as an instrument of cultural resistance. The prime objectives of the Spanish authorities and slave owners was to destroy African cultures.

The basic steps of *Rumba* were imported from Western Africa and were further developed by slaves in Cuba. *Rumba* succeeded in combining African dance forms with elements of Cuban influences. It matured during the second half of the nineteenth century in places where free blacks gathered for relaxation. Most of such gatherings took place in the *cabildos* or clubs, which were a common feature of nineteenth century Cuba. As discussed in chapter 2, it was customary to allow blacks to congregate after work for rest and relaxation at the *cabildos* or clubs.[4] The *cabildos* were run by blacks but were supervised by the church and the state. The authorities reasoned that providing blacks with some facilities for relaxation and entertainment, would minimize the social tension that might build up. *Cabildos,* on the other hand, provided suitable center, not only for recreation and relaxation, but also for the reconstitution of their shattered African heritage. As Anthony B. Pinn has explained, "On one level, these clubs allowed for an outlet that reduced the push toward rebellion and, on another, they allowed for the preservation of cultural memory based upon maintenance of particular *naciøns* or African "national" identities."[5] But this was not all that took place in the *cabildos*. *Santeria* worship developed in the *cabildos*. Likewise, it was in the *cabildos* that *Rumba* acquired its most important characteristics.

Some writers believe that *Rumba* did not come from Yor-ubaland but from several dances which originated from western Central-Africa among the Bakongo, Luanda and Luba, and was later infiltrated by non-African steps.[6] While recognizing some elements of Congo dance in *Rumba*, Peter Lamarche Manuel insists that "*Rumba* is a distinctly Cuban creation, not a reten-tion of an old African genre."[7] One can also argue that *Rumba* was an African dance form that was modified by the realities of life in the plantation.

A close look at the music and dance steps of *Rumba* reveals its original African roots. Like most African-derived dances, *Rumba* is unstructured. As Peter Lamarche Manuel has explained, *Rumba's* guiding principle is improvisation; the lead vocalist improvises as the conga players tap their fast beat. *Rumba's* songs are composed on the spot, and could be about love, politics, cockfights, or neighborhood events.[8] This could be said of most African derived music such as *Calypso*.

Rumba has been described as a spontaneous, free-for-all dance that does not call for explicit male and female partners.[9] Although *Rumba* is also performed for entertainment, Afro-Cubans believed that to dance *Rumba* was to identify with one's African roots. Fur-thermore, in their harsh and isolated foreign environment, *Rumba* helped Afro-Cubans to retain a feeling of oneness.

As an uplifting dance, *Rumba* is a commentary on the shat-tered life of the erstwhile-enslaved African. It separates the dehu-manized African slave from the rehumanized free African. To dance *Rumba* is to suspend the life of a slave and to resume the life of a free person. As Daniel explained, *Rumba* time means: for the moment, work is over, play is at hand. "Relaxation and release are the content of the moment, the space, and the event."[10]

Daniel also explored two aspects of New World slavery that were often overlooked by scholars. First, she demonstrated that slavery distorted gender relations among enslaved Africans. She then showed how *Rumba* helped to temporarily correct these distorted relationships. Whereas in Africa there were clear-cut gender divisions of roles and expectations such that the roles of men complemented those of women. In the New World during slavery the roles of the two sexes were hardly complementary. Both men and women were treated as mere tools of production, exploited and worked to death whenever slaveholders felt it was necessary. Not true in other parts of Africa, but under the conditions of New World slavery, these protective and supportive roles were almost completely taken away. Third, black female slaves, having been reduced to the status of unprotected beings, were brutalized and compelled to work, even in old age and during periods of illness and advanced pregnancy. Fourth, whereas in Africa romance and sex often went hand in hand, in the New World, slavery often took romance away from sexual acts. Many female slaves were raped by their masters, overseers and headmen, or forced to have sex for breeding purposes. Under these circumstances, the feeling of love and affection that characterized male and female relationships in civilized societies did not apply on the plantations.

One of the historic roles that *Rumba* set itself out to play was to rehumanize the dehumanized African slaves. As Daniel explained, "Manhood, associated with males seeking and protecting females, is at the center of Cuban cultural value." Also, "The human need for a sense of well-being and security directs both men and women toward affection, love, sex, freedom, and spontaneity, and Cuban men seek these things from women generally."[11] *Rumba* gave males the opportunity to play the protective role symbolically that slavery denied them. For women, *Rumba* also provided them with momentary feelings of protection that slavery denied them. Dancing *Rumba* made women feel that they could still be sexually and passionately desired. It made them feel that they were women who could be won, not by force, but through sweet songs and dance, which symbolized protection against physical abuses. "In genteel mannerisms of respect, cordiality, and admiration, male *Rumba* dancers assess themselves as strong, benevolent protectors of women and children."[12] That is to say *Rumba* allowed men to resume their protective role and women to enjoy the feeling of comfort and security that was often violated during slavery and colonialism. *Rumba* also helped alleviate the burden of slavery and acted as a form of resistance against the dehumanizing tendencies of New World slavery and colonialism.

Long after emancipation, and long after the declaration of independence by Cubans, Afro-Cubans continued to dance *Rumba*. They danced *Rumba* because it embodied the history of the whole black race and its struggles against white domination. By refusing to give up *Rumba* for Spanish dance forms, Afro-Cubans demonstrated that they had the right to choose. The Cuban government had no alternative than to accept *Rumba* as a national dance and to use it to convey its anti-racist ideals and programs. The government also used *Rumba* to forge national unity and to publicize its attachment to the working masses, more than with the elite and the aristocracy, more with Africa than with Europe.[13] Today, all Cubans (black, brown and white) do the *Rumba*.

SAMBA **IN BRAZIL**

While *Rumba* was developing in Cuba, *Samba,* another African-derived dance form, was evolving in Brazil. *Samba* can be described as the Brazilian national dance. Superficially, it paints the picture of a nation of happy people, but beneath the surface it is racial, cultural, and political suppression that finds an outlet through body movements. According to Barbara Browning, *Samba* manifests itself in three major forms, namely, as a secular dance, as a spiritual practice, and as oral literature. As an oral literature, it narrates a story, the story of cultural contacts among Africans, native Brazilians, and Europeans. It tells the story of slavery and oppression, of conflict and resistance. It is graceful yet elusive. It inverts and conceals the meanings of things, yet it is both an art and an expression of political culture. *Samba* enables the practitioner to understand the intricacies of contemporary society, and yet "it is resistance in motion." It is in opposition to forced acculturation. It is a dance that rejects all forms of slavery and colonial domination.[14]

Browning explains further, that to dance *Samba* is to speak with the feet, with the hips, and the joints. It is to send out messages without words. Its historical mission is to recount the story of the colonization of Brazil, the suppression of indigenous peoples and cultures, and the enslavement of African peoples, which lasted longer in Brazil than in any other nation of the New World.[15] Slavery was abolished in Brazil in 1888, but for Afro-Brazilians, it merely meant the substitution of one form of slavery with another. To conceal the accounts of the importation of Africans and the cruelty with which they were held down, the Brazilian authorities destroyed relevant historical documents, supposedly to erase the shame of slavery and to build a non-racial society. What they failed to realize, however, was that the destruction of the text could not abolish the slave story.[16]

The Brazilian authorities tried to close the book but the book remained open. They tried to gag the people by legislating against free speech, but they were ignorant of the fact that the body could communicate what the mouth could not utter. They destroyed historical records and left a breach in the narrative of the history of Brazilian blacks. The authorities tried to plug the orifice with false notions of Brazilian race equality. They declared racism illegal, but many blacks refused to accept that Brazil was a non-racist country. Afro-Brazilians wondered how their history and collective memory could be so easily erased with a mere stroke of the pen. They insisted that slavery had not ended in Brazil, and that all they got was abolition on paper.[17]

Samba can be perceived as a secular dance that is strongly tied to religion. This assertion can be understood only if one perceives that the Brazilian and Congolese worlds are cut into two—the sacred and the profane.[18] *Samba,* explains Browning, is a secular dance but it is an entrance through which the profane enters the sacred space. *Samba* is also an attempt to break down the barriers that separate the sacred from the secular. Derived from Congo-Angolan dance forms, *Samba* is characterized by the circles that the dancers form as they perform. The circle of dancers might move counter-clockwise, as in *Samba de Candom-*

blé or in a stationary circle, as in the *Samba de roda.* The dancers stand and clap and recite, one after the other. Then, a dancer receives a divine spirit. She moves to the center of the circle and is no longer a dancer but a goddess. Each goddess presents a particular choreography. Alternatively, the *roda* is fixed and the *caboclo* spirit comes down and *Sambas.*[19] The circle or *roda* represents the boundaries of the African religious community. It is a divine circle that can be inclusive or exclusive. According to Browning, the *roda* of *Samba* is the embodiment of shattered cultures of the Africans and of the indigenous or native Brazilians reconstituted, first into concentric circles, some representing religious notions, others violence and anger, yet intent on healing spiritual and political wounds. The language that *Samba* speaks is one of resistance. It is a text that narrates what cannot be put into words; it is a language that is spoken with the body.[20]

CAPOEIRA IN BRAZIL

Capoeira has been described as a fighting game performed to percussive and stringed musical instruments. It is another Kongo-derived dance.[21] The *berimbau,* a stringed bow-like instrument common in Angola, Namibia and Botswana, is the primary instrument used. Other instruments used are drums and tambourines. Most *Capoeira* games are played in a *roda,* a circle of musicians, singers, players, and spectators. Originally used for entertainment in Africa, *Capoeira* became in Brazil became a martial art used to defend the maroon villages, also known as *quilombos.*

Outside the *quilombos,* the Brazilian authorities prohibited *Capoeira,* but slaves turned the *roda* into "a useful protective circle" for training in the art of *Capoeira.* The game took place in a *roda* or ritual circle of musicians, players and spectators to evade detection by the slave owners and law enforcement officers. If an overseer or a police officer approached, the rhythm of the percussion changed and the *capoeiristas* disguised their dance as *Samba.*[22] The sudden switch from *Capoeira* to *Samba* was possible because of the close association between the two.

The warning could be *Aviso* or *Cavalaria*. The first was a general warning, and the second specifically signified the approach of mounted "cavalry" corps, used in the cities to catch *capoeiristas* and other potentially dangerous persons. The warning beat and the accompanying lyrics of *Cavalaria* are said to imitate the hoof beats of horses.[23]

It is not clear when *Capoeira* was first converted from a mere dance to a martial art. But it is believed that this transition took place, not in the plantations, but in the *quilombos* or maroon villages. Brazil was a thriving Portuguese colony. Between 1624 and 1654, the Dutch raided towns and plantations along the northeastern coast of Brazil. African captives took advantage of the raids to escape into the interior and to form a number of independent maroon villages called *quilombos*.[24] The largest of them was Palmares, which attracted more than 20,000 inhabitants, among whom were Indians and whites. It was in these *quilombos* that Africans of various ethnic groups formed a bond of unity and developed a rich African-based culture.

To escape into the bush and form settlements was one thing, but to defend them against destruction was another. The maroons had no guns to fight the Portuguese and the Dutch, who ventured far into the interior to recapture runaways. Even Palmares, the largest and boldest of all the *quilombos*,[25] lasted only sixty-seven years. To survive in the far interior without guns, the maroons had to develop new fighting methods. They adopted guerrilla tactics and then transformed *Capoeira* into a martial art of unity and defense against re-enslavement.

In addition to defending their communities, many runaways often banded together to raid plantations and towns, not only for livestock and food, but also to free family members and to urge others to escape.[26] These violent maroon activities affected colonial legal and military policies in parts of Bahia, Minas Gerais, and Palmares.[27] There were large communities of runaways in Bahia because its geography and ecology encouraged escape. Unlike Palmares and many other maroon settlements that were located in the far interior, Bahia's *mocambos* thrived in areas inaccessible to colonial troops yet near large urban centers. The settlement's proximity to large population centers, the boldness and ingenuity of its inhabitants, and the political insecurity it posed annoyed colonial authorities.[28]

Meanwhile, from the *quilombos, Capoeira* filtered into the plantations and towns of colonial Brazil. Fearing that *Capoeira* might have had a hand in encouraging these violent raids, the authorities mounted a campaign against it. The art was banned in Bahia and other places, and *capoeiristas* were persecuted.

The abolition of slavery in Brazil did not halt the development of *Capoeira,* nor did it bring the persecution of *capoeiristas* to a sudden stop. Emancipation left most blacks at the bottom rungs of Brazilian society. It also created a horde of *lumpenproletariat* that crowded slums and *favelas.* Many of these job-less people organized themselves into gangs of criminals. A few served as bodyguards for politicians. The dissatisfied *capoeiristas* turned their art into a collective force for the disruption of the oppressive colonial system. The government lashed. It put in motion more austere laws against the practitioners of *Capoeira.* For example, any person who was identified as a *capoeirista* ran the risk of being imprisoned or deported. Yet the *capoeiristas* refused to abandon their art. For them it was a weapon of survival. They played *Capoeira* in secret places, in the back allies, until the mid-twentieth century when the realities of the modern world forced the Brazilian authorities to legalize *Capoeira.* Today, there are schools for the teaching of *Capoeira,* not only in Brazil, but also in the United States and other countries.

Capoeira is an art, a martial art. It is a game, a fight, and a dance, all combined into one. *Capoeira* is a dialogue, a conversation between two players. This conversation or game of *Capoeira* (*jogo de Capoeira*) takes place in a *roda. Capoeiristas,* who are engaged in their ritualized combat, must observe the rules and proper manners of the art. Two players enter the circle; their focus remains on each other; they pivot either clockwise or counter-clockwise; they kick and sweep in apparent near misses; they spin in loops together in a series of near misses, but never take their focus away from their opponent.[29] Each player attempts to confuse his opponent by employing one deceptive move after another. Using only their feet, they try to score a *queda,* or fall, by knocking their opponents down.[30] One of the game's attractions is the physical grace with which *capoeiristas* engage each other.

The most visible aspects of the game are its kicks and acrobatics, yet the soul of the game is embodied in its music. The most recognized instrument is the berimbau, a one-stringed instrument that produces a soft drone-like sound. It is the music that sets the tone for the game; it creates the proper atmosphere for combat. Its songs and rhythm heighten the level of interaction or tone of conversation between the players. It also calms them down if the players become too excited. The songs of *Capoeira* are composed on the spot are usually about history, real life experiences, and impending dangers. *Capoeira* songs are permeated with riddles. They could also be about great masters of the game. The most remembered is Mestre Bimba, one of the icons of the art. Several Capoeria schools are named after Mestre Bimba. A published account stated that Mestre Bimba challenged the masters of all the other schools of martial art to public combat and defeated all of them. His style became the standard to be emulated.[31] He was well known and beloved by most Afro-Brazilians, and despite his fame, he never turned his back to the religion of his people, for he was a stout follower of the *Candomblé* faith.

Barbara Browning described *Capoeira* as a game of ambiguities, an art that conceals the intents of its practitioners. Its strategy, she explained, is founded on irony—saying or doing one thing and meaning another.[32] Though the contestants may appear to be playing, they take their game very seriously. *Capoeira* can be played purely for entertainment, in which case, it could be described as a truly theatrical act in which the participants use the occasion to express various complex emotions.[33] Whatever the emotion might be, it is the movements in *Capoeira* that animate the soul of the game.

As a martial act, *Capoeira* was fabricated not just for entertainment, but also for attack and defense. It was fashioned specifically to take the sting out of European violence. Its kicks were intended to enable escaping or rebelling slaves, whose hands might be shackled, to accomplish their escape. The scissors technique might have been created specifically as a means of disarming a slave owner or guard carrying a gun.

The principle of *Capoeira* was also based on the culture of refusal, a refusal to wear the shackles of humiliation and oppression. To be trained in the art of *Capoeira* was to be knowledgeable about one's African heritage. It was to reaffirm African values, unity and nationalism. The songs of *Capoeira,* most of which were Congolese in origin, excited the emotions of those who heard them and invoked their spirituality. For slaves hoping to escape to the independent black communities or *quilombos,* *Capoeira* provided the ultimate diversion and self-defense.[34] For those already in the *quilombos,* it prepared their minds and bodies for resistance against re-enslavement. It also endowed its practitioners with a sense of discipline and moral fortitude. A *capoierista* learned to conceal his apprehensions, his rage and intentions through seemingly harmless playful dances and acrobatic displays. The *capoierista* keeps the oppressor ignorant of the real intentions of his moves. The oppressor is left to believe that dancing and playing are harmless. But the *capoeirista* knows that dance and play can also be deadly weapons of resistance. *Capoeira* underscores the fact that resistance is defense in action. "*Capoeira* has always been a fight," wrote Browning. "Calling it a game or a dance has never detracted from the fact that Africans in Brazil developed it with the potential to disarm whites, whether through literal blows or through the subtle art of seeming to be in meaningless motion while actually reinforcing a circle of cultural and political race consciousness."[35]

Every move of the game has hidden meanings. "*Capoeira's* defensive moves," cautioned Browning, "are not so much blocks or even counter-attacks as they are ironic negations of the offense."[36] Also Lewis has warned that any move can function either as attack or defense, or even as both simultaneously.[37] For instance, in one of the *esquiva* moves, or escape moves, the player turns his back at the last moment of the opponent's strike, faking an escape from it, and then immediately strikes back. These moves were intended to encourage a *capoeirista* to deceive his opponent (or oppressor) into thinking that he is submissive and cowardly when he turned his back in fear, giving the *capoeirista* the opportunity to strike back when the oppressor least expected it. Such an attack was more effective when the oppressor had been manipulated into a defenseless position. The broader lesson was to try to expose the weakness of one's enemies while protecting one's position.[38]

One of the most basic and common kicks of *Capoeira* is called the blessing. The Afro-Brazilian slave was aware that the very same slave owner that gave him (or her) his daily Christian blessing could flog him the next day.[39] Thus, the name "the blessing" became a deceptive way of referring to the kick by masking it in a religious overtone. It could mean, "never trust any one," for behind every friendly gesture lies "a potential kick in the gut."[40] Meanwhile, the unsuspecting slave owner, hearing the expression, blessing or benediction, might mistake it for a harmless religious act.

Even the music of *Capoeira* is illusive. Its songs generally express the game's ambiguity. The lyrics of the songs of *Capoeira* disguise the basic meaning of the game, which, according to Browning, is not about the struggle between positive and negative forces but rather about what may be "negative, painful, or malicious within the ostensibly positive, whole and benignant." The riddles of the game, insists Browning, are "the no in the yes, the big in the little, the earth in the sky [and] the fight in the dance."[41]

To play *Capoeira* was to strive to achieve liberty under the cover of secrecy. It was to break down barriers that restrained enslaved Africans in Brazil from expressing their culture or regaining their freedom. As a master disguise, *Capoeira* was the fight in the dance, the dance in the fight. The real intentions of *Capoeira* had to be disguised, always. *Capoeira* prepared the minds and bodies of Afro-Brazilians for physical combat that might be required when escaping from the plantations or when defending existing *quilombos*. To play *Capoeira* was to resist white domination and to deflate the political pressure that was forcefully brought to bear upon the minds of Africans in Brazil during slavery. It was also to preserve African identity, to reinforce black consciousness, and to re-write the history of Afro-Brazilians that had been distorted or partially destroyed under white domination. Till this day, *Capoeira* instills self-esteem in its practitioners, keeps them physically and mentally fit, and enables them to retain consciousness of their African heritage. Certainly, *Capoeira,* during the days of its early development, was not art for art's sake. It was art for survival.

THE STEELBAND MUSIC OF TRINIDAD

The poor and oppressed people of Trinidad left their marks on the annals of Black History when they invented Steelband music. Their major musical instruments, which were fashioned out of discarded containers, especially oil tin and barrels, testify to their imagination and ingenuity. Blinded by their own prejudices, government officials and the members of the upper classes denounced Steelband music, describing it as noise. And just as the Brazilian elite looked down upon the practice of *Capoeira* in the nineteenth century because of the social standing of its practitioners, so did the elite of Trinidad treat the Steelband musicians (or panmen), describing them as undesirables.[42] The panmen were also treated as subversive. Consequently, they became the scapegoats of the demonstrations, riots, and social unrest that characterized post-world-War agitation for political independence in Trinidad in the 1940s and 1950s.[43] As Afro-Cubans and Afro-Brazilians sang and danced against the slave and colonial systems, so did the Steelband musicians of Trinidad continue to drum against the dominating upper classes in government.

The panmen struggled for recognition in the eyes of the officials and in the eyes of history. They fought against the image that portrayed them as criminals. They used their music to contest the notions of white supremacy and black inferiority. In particular, they fought against the assumed inferiority of black music. This struggle was an important one in Trinidad where the notions of European cultural superiority had been institutionalized since the days of slavery.

In the midst of the struggle for freedom of expression emerged a small body of progressive intellectuals who sided with the panmen, proclaiming their music "a worthy form of musical expression" that had to be encouraged. Among such progressives were Albert Gomes, Eric Connor, Beryl McBurinie, Jack Kelshall, and Eric Williams. These men were quick to realize that steelband music was an indigenous art form that could serve as a potential symbol of national identity in Trinidad. A local historian and the head of the government's Education Extension Services, C.R. Ottley, wrote in a newspaper that steelband was a form of cultural expression that should be encouraged. "I am convinced, "he wrote," that with proper organisation, the steel bands can be used as a means of bringing a change of social attitude to the young men in them."[44]

Impressed by this and other comments, a majority of the people of Trinidad began to accept Steelband music as a culturally meaningful musical form. By the early 1950s, the Steelband Movement had spread into non-black communities and was destined to become entangled with class negotiations and agitations for political independence.[45] The People's National Movement, led by Eric Williams, championed the cause of the Steelband movement in as much as the Steelband movement popularized Eric Williams and the People's National Movement. On August 31, 1962, Trinidad became an independent nation.[46]

In sum, Steelband music, which was invented by the poor and oppressed members of the Trinidadian community, created an atmosphere of awareness that reinforced the struggle for national identity. These struggles for identity then fed into the battle for freedom and helped the people of Trinidad to preserve the black culture of resistance. The steelband music has remained one of Trinidad's foremost art forms, an art form that was born out of a struggle for black identity and racial equality. The steelband exemplifies African initiative, inventiveness and adaptability.

Notes

1. Franklin W. Knight, *Slave Society in Cuba during the Nineteenth Century* (Madison: University of Wisconsin Press, 1970), 63-7.
2. *Ibid.,* 69.
3. Edward Thorpe, *Black Dance* (Woodstock: Overlook Press, 1990), 1-31.
4. Yvonne Daniel, *Rumba: Dance and Social Change in Contemporary Cuba* (Bloomington: Indiana University Press, 1995).
5. Anthony B. Pinn, *Varieties of African Religious Experience* (Minneapolis Fortress Press, 1998), 67.
6. Daniel, *Rumba Dance,* 17.
7. Peter Lamarche Manuel, *Caribbean Currents: Caribbean Music from Rumba to Reggae* (Philadelphia: Temple University Press, 1995), 24.
8. *Ibid.,* 25.
9. Daniel, *Rumba Dance,* 64.
10. *Ibid,* 114.
11. *Ibid.,* 122-3.
12. *Ibid.,* 123.
13. *Ibid.,* 118.
14. Browning, *passim.*
15. *Ibid.,* 2.
16. *Ibid.,* 3.
17. *Ibid., passim.*
18. See the section on the Tokoist Movement in chapter 6.
19. Browning, *Samba.,* 26.
20. Browning, *Samba, passim.*
21. *Ibid.,* 29.
22. *Ibid.,* 29.
23. Lewis, *Ring of Liberation,* 150-51.
24. Kenneth Dossar, "*Capoeira* Angola: An Ancestral Connection." In American Visions. August 1988.
25. Palmares attracted many refugees. Its residents sometimes came downfrom the mountains to trade or raid plantations for livestock and foodstuffs. They also ventured to free slaves. The colonial authorities sent many expeditions against the nation of Palmares but were turned back by the rebel slaves.

26. Dossar, "Capoeira," 104.

27. Stuart B. Schwartz, *Slaves, Peasants and Rebels: Reconsidering Brazilian Slavery* (Urbana: University of Illinois Press, 1992), 103.

28. Joås José Reis, *Slave Rebellion in Brazil: The Muslim Uprising of 1835 in Bahia* (Baltimore: Johns Hopkins University Press, 1993), 44.

29. Browning, *Samba,* 88-9.

30. Lewis, *Ring of Liberation,* 89.

31. Nestor Capoeira, *The Little Capoeira Manual* (Berkeley: North Atlantic Books, 1995), 78-88.

32. Browning, *Samba,* 93.

33. Lewis, *Ring of Liberation*, 95.

34. Browning, *Samba,* 94.

35. *Ibid.,* 100.

36. *Ibid.,* 122.

37. Lewis, *Ring of Liberation.*, 98.

38. See International *Capoeira* Angola Foundation.

39. *Ibid.,* 30.

40. *Ibid.,* 30-2. Browning, *Samba,* 121-2.

41. Browning, *Samba,* 108.

42. Lewis, *Ring of Liberation,* 46.

43. Stephen Stuempfle, *The Steelband Movement: the Forging of a National Art in Trinidad and Tobago* (Philadelphia: University of Pennsylvania Press, 1995), 62.

44. As quoted in *Ibid.,* 88.

45. *Ibid.* 121.

46. *Ibid.,* 116-18.

Chapter 4

FROM KUMINA TO BLACK ZIONISM THEN TO RASTA AND REGGAE IN JAMAICA

Jamaica's social history is unique because it shows transitions from traditional African religions to Christianity, and then to Rastafarianism and *Reggae*, each of them producing its own unique form of resistance against white domination. The foundations of these historical events were laid during the first 150 years of British rule in Jamaica, when the slaves were forbidden to learn to read the Bible. This policy was totally different from practices in the neighboring Spanish, French and Portuguese colonies where slaves were promptly exposed to the Bible message. During this long period, and until the mid-nineteenth century, blacks in Jamaica stuck to their traditional African religions in which the *Obeah* and *Myal* priests held sway in matters of religion, ritual and healing.

Most Jamaicans perceived the *Obeahman* (or *Obeahwoman*) as a person who exercised evil influence on society. On the other hand, they looked upon the *Myalman* (or *Myalwoman)* as a person who wielded the power to cast away evil spells inflicted upon individuals by the former.[1] The competitive activities of the *Obeahman* and *Myalman* resulted in a religious cult known as *Kumina,* an ancestor possession cult in which "hidden secrets, witchcraft and bad medicine were detected and exposed." For example, when an individual was troubled as a result of the

assumed evil acts of an *Obeahman,* the troubled individual would
be taken to a *Kumina* shrine to seek help. Under the supervision
of a *Myalman,* the patient was made to go through a spirit-possession ritual believed to induce the necessary healing. This possession ritual or crisis in *Kumina* is known as *myal.* According to
Leonard Barrett, it is at this stage, "that the spirit of an ancestor
actually takes control of the dancer's body . . . and the dancer
loses control of speech and faculties and is actually the ancestor."[2]
But the *Myalman,* despite, or rather, because of the beneficial
nature of his vocation, could not function effectively within the
prevailing evil institution of slavery. The *Myalman* was, therefore, obliged to join hands with the *Obeahman* to fight the evil
magic of the white masters.[3] With their energies combined, the
Obeahman and the *Myalman* instigated the formation of secret
societies, which became centers of secret plotting and rebellion.
They provided slaves with necessary charms and medicines for
protection and the tools to attack slave-owners and the plantation system. Nanny of Jamaica was one such person. She was an
obeahwoman, a warrior and a military strategist who wrecked
havoc on slave owners and their mercenaries during the First
Maroon war (1734-39).

The combined powers of the *Obeahman* and *Myalman*
remained in sway until the mid-nineteenth century. In 1831-
32, for example, Myalists played a vital role in the last Jamaican
slave rebellion. *Myalism* or *Kumina* continued to influence the
society but after the Emancipation Proclamation of 1834, it had
to deal with new threats; it would thenceforth fight, not only
former slave-owners and colonial government officials, but also
the Anglican Church and the Christian missionaries. In the
end, it incorporated elements of Christianity and the result was
Pukumina or *Pokomania.* As we shall presently see, *Pukumina*
is a syncretic blending of African traditional religious practices
with elements of Christian faith. In this regard, *Pukumina*
could be compared to *Santeria.* But first, how was this blending
achieved?

The blending of the Jamaican version of African religious practices with elements of Christianity had, in fact, been in train for quite some time. As early as 1791, *Kumina* or *Myalism* had incorporated aspects of Baptist rituals that were brought into the Caribbean by the United Empire Loyalists who had fled the United States during the American War of Independence. *Myalists* had no problem accepting two aspects of the Baptist rituals, namely, possession by the Holy Spirit and Baptism in large bodies of water, as John the Baptist did in the Holy Bible. The Myalists found no contradictions in the idea of possession by the Holy Spirit because spirit-possession was an integral part of the *Kumina* healing ritual. Similarly, Baptism by emersion presented no problems because even in far away Africa, rivers, lakes, and the sea were thought to be dwelling places of spirits. For example, *Yamanja* or *Iya Lokun* was and still is the Yoruba goddess of the sea. Kinjikitile Ngwale, the priest of the Maji Maji cult in Tanzania was believed to have been possessed by the spirit, *Hongo,* who dwelt in lakes. And in South Africa, the Zulu believed in the existence of a river monster known as *Inkanyaba*. Periodic offerings and sacrifices were made to it in order to ward off its wrath. In the southern Nigerian town of Igbuzo, no citizen of this place fished in river Obashi because they believed that the fish of the river were the children of the goddess of the river. To the Africans of Jamaica, therefore, to be buried with Christ in baptism, in a large body of water, was equivalent to receiving the spirit of an African ancestor. This partly explains why the *Myalists* promptly accepted but reinterpreted the Baptist doctrines of possession by the Holy Spirit and baptism by emersion.

Despite their attempts to adjust to new ideas coming from abroad, blacks in Jamaica had to deal with the realities of American slavery which, as we have seen, was an established evil and the source of much pain. One of its prime tactics was to destroy the cultures of African captives. It is therefore baffling that the British, though recognizing that the success of the slave system in Jamaica depended largely on the extent to which they could erase the culture of Africans, initially refused to indoctrinate the

Africans into the Christian religion. And, even though there had been some isolated cases of conversion to Christianity in Jamaica, it was only in 1815 that the Church of England began to expand its religious teachings there.

The abolition of slavery in 1834 was accompanied by a period of persecution, worsened by outbreaks of epidemics, food shortages, and violent protests. By the 1840s, *Myalism* had almost been driven underground by the Jamaican colonial government only to emerge in the 1860s as Revivalism.[4] Revivalism exhibited many *Myal* elements like dancing, drumming, and spirit possession. This religious movement, known as "The Great Revival" or "The Great Awakening," swept through the West Indies, giving rise to the formation of many Black Christian denominations.[5] The age of Black Zionist Revivalism had come.

Meanwhile in Jamaica, since blacks could not suddenly give up their traditional African beliefs, they blended them with the missionaries' Bible teachings, resulting in the emergence of over 200 Afro-Christian cults, sometimes referred to as *Pukumina* or *Pokomania*. According to Barrett, "The word *Pukumina* [or *Pocomania*] refers to the brand of Jamaican religion that is a syncretism of Kumina and Christianity. This special brand of Jamaican religion is believed to have emerged out of the 1860 revival which swept the island a generation after the emancipation of the slaves."[6]

Whether one wishes to call them Zionist sects or *Pukumina* cults, certain things are clear. Traditional African modes of worship were evident in the revival style of worship. These included shouts, spirit possession, music and dance. Though accepting the basic teachings of Christ, the Zionist preachers placed much emphasis on the Old Testament, while drawing from ancient African traditions. It would appear that the blending of African traditions and ritual dances with such biblical characters as the archangels, Michael, Gabriel, Moses, Jesus and the Holy Ghost, often induced collective possession experience. The Zionists indulged in an elaborate rite of baptism, which, according to Ivor Morrish, was "a sort of rite of passage similar to African initiation ceremonies."[7] The Zionists saw great similarities between the suffering of blacks in Jamaica and the plight of the children of Israel in bondage. They also believed that the oppressed Africans would regain their humanity through spiritual redemption.

RASTAFARIANISM

The Rastafarian movement developed in Jamaica under these circumstances. Jamaicans' strong attachment to Africa and their solemn passion for independence in matters of religion found expressions in the Rastafarian movement. Rastafarianism is a movement that seeks to establish its own separate identity. Yet it owes its roots partly to African traditions, partly to the West Indian Zionist or *Pocomania* movement, and partly to the World wide social upheavals of the first three decades of the twentieth century. These upheavals were marked by labor unrest as well as repressive colonial policies against striking sugar-cane workers. Disillusioned with the harsh treatment they received, many workers detached themselves mentally from the wider society by forming a social movement. Thenceforth, this movement became identified with the dispossessed, urban, poor Jamaicans. That was the Rastafarian movement.

Viewed differently, Rastafarianism can be described, not as a religion, but as a way of life for certain West Indians whose ances-tors had endured centuries of degradation and repression. Yet the movement was founded on syncretistic belief systems that blended biblical messages with traditional African social thought. In other words, the movement has its roots in the distant past, not in the early twentieth century, as it is often claimed. As we have seen, its roots go back to the days of slavery when the *Obeahman* and the *Myalman* combined their forces to resist the evil magic of the white man. It is because of this that Horace Campbell declared that the Rastafarian movement carries with it "a continuity of resistance and confrontation with white racism."[8] Ivor Morrish, dwelling on the political dimensions of the Rastafarian move-ment, stated that it is "as much a politico-religious movement as a cult, and whilst its forms are religious its purposes are mainly political."⁹ Although these claims are contestable, their implications are obvious.

Connections with Africa

The Rastafarian movement has strong connections with Africa. First, there is the connection with the early east and central African resistance movements against European conquest and colonial rule in Africa, as exemplified by the Nyabingi movement. Second, there was the connection between the Rastafarian deep-seated fascination with the ruling house of Ethiopia. However, whereas Rasta's connections with Ethiopia are fairly well understood, some of us are not so clear about its connections with the Nyambigi resistance movement in eastern and central Africa.

In chapter 1, I have shown how the members of the Nyabingi cult stood against the autocratic and exploitative tendencies of the aristocracy. And when the Europeans descended upon the Africans at the onset of colonial rule, the Africans rallied around the Nyabingi leaders and waged a protracted war against the Europeans. This ideology of resistance to all forms of exploitation and intimidation that the Nyabingi adherents exhibited can still be found among the Rastafarians of today. The Rastafarian culture of resistance is not only similar to the Nyabingi opposition to aristocratic and anti-colonial tendencies, it is derived from it. In a sense, one can say that the rastafarian culture of resistance is a continuation of the Nyabingi culture of resistance against white exploitation of the black man..

Closely following the Nyabingi outbreak was the crowning of Emperor Haile Selassie of Ethiopia in 1930. Perhaps, it was this coronation that gave the Rastafarian movement its most enduring strength. Some Jamaicans who had been fascinated by the linkages between the legendary biblical lineage of King Solomon and the Royal House of Ethiopia had also looked forward to the fulfillment of Marcus Garvey's prophesy that a Black King would be crowned in Ethiopia. To these Jamaicans, the crowning of Ras Tafari as emperor of Ethiopia in 1930 was the fulfillment of a prophecy. For did the Bible not state that "Princes shall come out of Egypt: Ethiopia shall soon stretch her hands to God?" Did the Bible not also state: "And he had on his vesture and on his thigh a name written, King of Kings and Lord of Lords?"[10] And was Ras Tafari not crowned with the title, King of Kings and Lord of Lords, Conquering Lion of Judah? To the Rastafarians of Jamaica, Emperor Haile Selassie was the leader of their movement. He was also a messiah, a redeemer and God himself. Certainly, this Rastafarian belief is similar to the Christian belief that Jesus Christ, the son of Mary and her husband, Joseph, a carpenter, is a prophet, a redeemer, the Son of God, and God Himself. Christians who may be critical of other people's beliefs may well revisit the foundations of their own faith.

It is equally important to remind ourselves that the term Ethiopia was not, in ancient times, restricted to the modern country of Ethiopia. Instead, it was a term that was used to describe the entire continent that we now call Africa. Modern Ethiopia was once part of the Kingdom of Axum, which was later called Abyssinia, before it was changed to Ethiopia. When, therefore, we read in the Holy Bible about the Ethiopian Eunoch, it was about a black man who could have come from any part of the African continent. What is important to us is that with the resurgence of African solidarity and the back-to-Africa movement in the nineteenth and early twentieth century, many Africans of the diaspora became excited about the term Ethiopia and their linkages with it. Many churches and religious affiliations were formed at this time and were referred to as Ethiopian churches. These churches were born out of protest against the racial practices of predominantly white churches. The Rastafarian movement can be regarded as one of the church movements that resulted from that protest.

Meanwhile, black opposition to white racism was given a new lease of life when the Ethiopian army, under their great leaders, Emperor Menelik and his wife, Titus, defeated an invading Italian army at Adwa in 1896. This victory over the Italians, reinforced the Biblical stories about the might of Ethiopia, and kindled a passion for Ethiopia among many Africans in the diaspora. In fact, Ethiopia's victory over Italy stimulated the formation of the Pan-African movement in 1900.

Marcus Garvey was a Jamaican, and one of the most famous Pan-Africanists. He was also a proponent of the back-to-Africa movement and an admirer of every thing Ethiopia. As early as 1918, he had begun to prophesy the crowning of a black king in Ethiopia. This was important because by this time the European colonial adventurers in Africa had deposed, killed or exiled most african kings. Then in 1930, the son of Ras (king) Makennen, who had helped Emperor Menelik in the successful war against Italy in 1896, was crowned the new Emperor of Ethiopia. At his coronation, the new Emperor assumed the name Ras Tafari. Like Emperor Menelik, Ras Tafari conceived a vision of Ethiopian modernization, with a strong central government, a national army, an enviable educational system, as well as a modern network of communications infrastructure of roads and airports.

Black people around the world were thrilled about the stories that came out of Ethiopia, especially the crowning of Ras Tafari. But hardly did they take into account the growing political ambition of Italy and Benito Mussolini's designs on Ethiopia. In 1935 Mussolini attacked Ethiopia, even though Ethiopia was a member of the League of Nations. Now living in exile in England, Emperor Haile Selassie became a figure around who militant Africans anchored their hope. Black nationalists were appalled that rather than help the Emperor of Ethiopia drive the Italians out of his country, European power continued to supply Italy with military hardware. This unconscionable action of the League of Nations increased African solidarity and gave the Pan-African culture of resistance a great boost. Emperor Haile Selassie returned to his country after five years in exile to the joy of Africans at home and abroad. The Rastafarians of Jamaica were particularly jubilant; their fascination for Ethiopia soared. The Emperor responded favorably and visited Jamaica. He also encouraged all Rastafarians to visit Ethiopia and settle there if they so wished. Many did. To this day, the Rastafarian bond with Ethiopia has remained strong.

The Rastafarians draw much of their inspiration from the political and religious thought of Marcus Garvey, especially from those aspects that dwell on the repatriation of all dissatisfied blacks to Africa. Rastafarians are familiar with certain prophecies that Marcus Garvey had made. One such prophecy stated that a king shall be crowned in Ethiopia and that that king would be Jah. When, therefore, Haile Selassie was crowned the Emperor of Ethiopia some Jamaicans interpreted his spectacular coronation as proof that the expected Messiah had indeed come. "The splendor of the coronation ceremonies," wrote Lewis F. William, "rekindled a passion for Africa in the psyches of many Jamaican blacks whose cultural identity had been eroded under the class and racial segmentation that was taking place on the island."[11]

The Rastafarian philosophy armed the downtrodden masses with the necessary ideology to confront their oppressors. In particular, the masses were fascinated by the movement's connections with Africa, which reinforced their own appeal for black identity. However, rather than confront their exploiters violently, they opted for more subtle forms of resistance. Virtually everything that the Rastafarians did enraged the dominant ruling classes of Jamaica. The acceptance of Emperor Haile Selassie as the head of their congregation signified a refusal to conform to the Christian belief systems of the upper classes. Their habit of smoking marijuana in public, as well as their hairstyle, offended the upper classes.

Rastafarianism promoted black consciousness and the necessary will to oppose white domination. The teachings of the Rastafarians liberated the minds of the Jamaican working poor. As a part of their rejection of mainstream ideology, the Rastafarians of Jamaica set up their own separate communities wherever they could. By so doing, they hoped to recreate an African lifestyle that emphasized communalism and religious toleration. In the very heart of the ghettos of Kingston, they formed a community, which went by the name of "Dung Hill" or "Addis Ababa."

Infuriated by the perceived subversive activities of the Rastafarians, the upper classes lashed back. The Rastafarians could never be conquered, however. They regrouped in ghettoes known as *Burru* (derived, perhaps, from the Yoruba word for wicked or bad or worthless), and developed what has been described as the *Burru* culture. It was in the *Burru,* and within the context of Burru culture, that the Rastafarians revived the resistant folk music from the days of slavery, turning it into a musical form we now call *Reggae.* "You can never conquer Rasta," *Reggae* artists sang, immortalizing their victory over the forces of oppression.

The authorities intensified their repressive activities, increasing the social gap that separated the Rastafarians from the upper classes. Yet, the Rastafarians refused to be violent. They invited scholars from the University of the West Indies to observe their activities. A report published after a thorough investigation confirmed that the "Ras Tafari cult is unique, but it is not seditious. Its adherents have and should have the freedom to preach it."[12] This investigation spurred scholarly research on the Rastafarian movement, which also produced positive results.

Thus in Jamaica, Rasta (and *Reggae*) played an equalizing role. It was through them that the social barriers of the West Indian communities were broken down. Before 1950 those social barriers were wide and deep and were reinforced by race and class antagonism. By the 1960s, Rasta and *Reggae* had captured the sympathy of the middle-class, as well as those of university students, staff and faculty. For it was in 1960 that a national hearing was conducted with a view to determine the needs of the Rastafarians. Scholars from the University of the West Indies were also requested to study the doctrines of the Rastafarian movement and submit their recommendations to the Prime Minister. Their recommendations were positive. Among other things, they called for an end to police brutality, the provision of affordable housing for the poor, and the recognition of the Rastafarian movement as a branch of the Ethiopian Orthodox Coptic Church.[13] Although these recommendations were intended to ease the Rastafarians' plight, they also affected the image of *Reggae* musicians. Thus, the middle and upper classes, which had treated them as outcasts and subversives, began to come around.

The dissipation of suspicion and misunderstanding was quickly followed by a general acceptance of the Rastafarian way of life.[14] Some members of the middle and upper classes began to wear dreadlocks. A few politicians used the admonitions of the Rastafarians to promote black unity and to re-Africanize many blacks whose worldviews had been distorted by slavery and British colonialism.

Walter Rodney considered the Rastafarian movement "a major force in the effort towards freeing and mobilizing black minds . . ."[15] Though a syncretic religion, its Pan-African ideals give it a unique standing among other African-based religious movements. Rooted in the ideas of African unity, African redemption, and a return to Africa, Rastafarians display a sense of collective identity and a feeling of belonging to a common African ancestry.

Rastafarians, who are mostly self-employed or chronically unemployed, have every reason to believe that Jamaica is one step from hell. Corrupted by hundreds of years of association with "Babylon," the country is nothing but an "outpost of oppression for the black man."[16] To the Rastas, a return to Ethiopia, a land reserved for the chosen people of Jah, is an ideal to be pursued. This identification with Africa may be a reaction against Western domination,[17] yet it is an expression of the concept of Negritude, which, in its original formulation, is more than a return to Africa; it is to bring about the renewal of African personality.

Rastafarians promote Jamaican national pride and identity, which had been seriously eroded by European domination, on the one hand, and by Jamaicans' own sense of despair and subservience to British ideas. The deculturation of Black Jamaicans was particularly severe, especially among the elite who emulated unquestionably the English way of life, "sometimes even beyond the standards of the English themselves."[18] The colonial educational system had turned them into little English men and women; they had learned more about England and their queens than they ever learned about Africa and its civilizations. Furthermore, as Tracy Nicholas has pointed out, Jamaicans "were taught to despise and fear everything reminiscent of their African heritage."[19] The Rastafarians were convinced, therefore, that this tragic incomprehension could be corrected with a proper education, which must include a thorough knowledge of Africa. They argued that racial pride could only issue from knowing where they came from. Jamaicans must therefore reject Western cultures and avoid all European-centered ideas and teachings because they were detrimental to black redemption and advancement. Black people must learn about their history for, as Bob Marley has put it, "If you know where you're coming from, then you wouldn't have to ask me who the hell I think I am."[20] Some of the principal aims of the Rastafarian movement were to purge Jamaicans of their inferiority complex, instill self-pride in them, and create a bond of unity between them and their African brothers and sisters.

REGGAE IN JAMAICA

It is in the course of resistance that many Africans of the diaspora re-constitute their history, a history that had been battered by slavery and colonialism. In the West Indies, the songs of *Reggae* afford many blacks an opportunity to appreciate the exuberance of their African roots. *Reggae* may be treated as music for entertainment, but it evolved out of the Pan-African culture of resistance. It is the product of the Jamaicans' syncretic, resistant beliefs. It is also an embodiment of Pan-African consciousness that deals with many social and political issues that disturb West Indian communities and black people around the world. *Reggae* artists narrate the story of slavery and economic exploitation of the poor. They insist that Jamaica is poor, not because its people do not work hard, but because the United States and the other capitalist countries take away the fruits of their labor. As the spokespersons of the ordinary people, *Reggae* artists expose all forms of social injustice, especially of white domination, capitalist exploitation, police brutality, corruption and political intimidation.

Reggae is linked, directly and indirectly, to the Rastafarian movement. Like Rasta, *Reggae* is the product of the race consciousness and race solidarity that had been growing throughout the Black World since the days of slavery and colonialism. *Reggae* artists also draw from a certain verse of the Bible, which states, "The singers as well as the players of the instruments shall be there."[21] Rastafarians who perform *Reggae* music see themselves as heirs to this biblical prophecy.[22] *Reggae* artists denounce Babylon (the Biblical land of captivity). They preach redemption, act as apostles of hope, and champion the cause of the downtrodden.

Many *Reggae* practitioners are Rastafarians but it would be wrong to equate Rasta with *Reggae*. *Reggae*, as an art form, had its own independent origins and development, which some writers have traced back to other musical forms like *Mento, Ska,* Rhythm and Blues, and then Rock Steady. *Reggae*, also known as "music fit for a king," is at the same time music for common folk. It is the end product of the blending of various African rhythms with West Indian *Ska,* Rhythm and Blues, and Rock Steady. This blending is believed to have been completed in 1968, in the slums of West Kingston Jamaica. Though a West Indian based musical form, *Reggae* has retained its African derived work songs that are laced with lyrics that are part singing, "antiphonal call-response chanting, and the repetition of single short musical phrases." (Stephen Davis and Peter Simon, *Reggae Bloodlines: In Search of The Music and culture of Jamaica* (New York: Anchor Press, 1979, 9)

By the late 1950s, the most popular music played on government owned radio stations of Jamaica was foreign. This was so because Jamaica had been bombarded by foreign cultures, especially from Miami and New Orleans, on the one hand, and from Britain and Canada, on the other hand. "To educated Jamaicans," wrote Stephen Davis and Peter Simon, "anything British, American or Canadian was vastly superior to anything home grown." (page 14) This colonial mentality could be attributed to the inherited colonial educational system and to Jamaicans' own inferiority complex, born out of centuries of slavery and colonialism. By the early 1960s, Rhythm and Blues, also being imported from the United States, had virtually displaced all other forms of music in Jamaica.

However, with the attainment of political independence in 1962, a strong wind of change began to blow across the country. Even music would feel this wind of change. The first signs of changing times was signaled by the emergence of *Ska,* "a unique Jamaican jazz culture where the melody of horns fused with drums in a free form of music which was mellifluous and rebellious." (Campbell, *Rasta and Resistance: From Marcus Garvey to Walter Rodney* (African World Press, 1987, 126). Unlike its forerunner, *mento,* which was nothing more than "a depoliticized, bad imitation of the riotous calypso of Trinidad," Ska's tunes contained rebellious verses, on account of which the music was shunned by the government owned radio stations. Once unleashed, the government could neither gag the Skatalites, nor could it stifle the desire of the masses to indulge themselves with this type of home made music. Thanks to the so-called sound-system man who some years back had developed the practice of setting up "sound-systems" or music turn-tables in someone's backyard or on street corners, to entertain the public. The sound-system man enabled the people to bypass the government owned radio stations and listen to the very type of music they preferred.

As *Ska* waxed in popularity, so did it transform its nature. By 1966, it had evolved into a new form of music known as *Rock Steady. Rock Steady* might have earned its name from its emphasis on its steady, slower beat, but, unlike *Ska,* which sometimes sang about love, Rock Steady exposed such troubling social evils as police brutality, hunger, and unemployment. (Davis and Simon, 16). Even Rock Steady was to be overtaken in 1968 by yet a newer, slower and more militant musical form—*Reggae.*

More than *Mento, Ska* and *Rock Steady,* it was *Reggae* that really resurrected all the anger that black Jamaicans had nursed against the evils of slavery and colonialism. From 1968 onwards, many Rastafarians, who had been vocal against colonialism, began to use *Reggae* to transmit their own messages.[23] For, it so happened that many Rastafarians were musicians and many Jamaican musicians were Rastafarians. Nonetheless, in the midst of mixed identities, *Reggae* music eventually carved out its own separate identity. What it could not shed, however, was the use of African instruments, especially the African drum. More than any thing else, it was the African drum that strongly anchored *Reggae* to its African roots. Nor could *Reggae* free itself completely from the religious symbolism of the Rasta belief systems. Often, even when a *Reggae* singer is not a professed Rastafarian, he still transmits the Rasta message on a conscious and unconscious level at once.[24]

The humble beginnings of *Reggae* created some of its teething problems as well as bringing it into conflict with the members of the middle and upper classes. *Reggae* was fashioned in the West Kingston slums. The innovators that created it came from the oppressed lower classes. Sometimes described as "Rude Boys," they were men in the age bracket 14-30. Some of them were born in Kingston, but a large number of them had recently fled the rural areas and crowded in the urban centers. For the most part, they had no skills and could not find regular jobs. They roamed the streets and sometimes lived a life of debauchery. Some of them turned to music for livelihood, and in due course, used it to expose and denounce the evils of society.

The members of the middle and upper classes, on the other hand, could not ignore these developments. First, the influx of workless youths into the cities created a feeling of insecurity. Second, the music that the "Rude Boys" preferred to play or listen to was offensive to them. These upper classes, which were the main subjects of attack in *Reggae* songs, lashed back. They sent the police and other law enforcement agents against *Reggae* artists who, along with the Rastafarians, suffered persecution. It was only in the 1970s that these misunderstandings were addressed in the manner described earlier.

Meanwhile, *Reggae* artists continued to denounce corruption and exploitation. They sometimes used verses from the Bible to preach their own brand of deliverance. They encouraged resistance against Western capitalism and exploitation. They believed that as God delivered Daniel from the lions' den, so would Jah free blacks from the strangle hold of Western capitalism. Like Rastafarians, *Reggae* artists depicted European society as Biblical Babylon and Africa as Zion. The central themes of their message were race pride, black unity and African redemption.

Reggae artists were internationalists, but their nationality transcended the narrow Jamaican nationality. For them, Jamaican nationality was synonymous with the wider African nationality. They believed that independence for Jamaica was useless without the total liberation of Africa.

Reggae artists emphasized the need for positive action in the struggle for liberation. The anguish that black people suffered in "Babylon" could be halted only through a meaningful revolution. In his song, "Revolution," Bob Marley warned that there could be no meaningful political change without revolutionary struggle. For Marley, however, revolutions did not necessarily have to involve bloodshed. Nor are all those who speak of revolutionary change necessarily violent people. Of course, Bob Marley was a peace-loving man. In his song, "Get up Stand up," Marley encouraged the oppressed to stand up and fight for their rights. Standing and fighting for one's rights do not have to involve violence. In 1955, Rosa Parks fought for her rights in the United States, on an Alabama bus, not even by standing up, but by sitting down. Also in India, Gandhi fought for India's independence by peaceful means. We must not, therefore, be unduly excited whenever we hear the words "fight," "struggle" and "revolution."

Early *Reggae* artists were among the first Jamaicans to rise above the narrow social stratification that divided Jamaica into white, black and brown. Bob Marley, who later became the uncrowned King of *Reggae*, was the child of an English man and a black Jamaican woman. But rather than seek white privilege, as some brown Jamaicans of his day would have done, Bob Marley sought refuge among his mother's people. When he denounced "Babylon," his attacks were directed, not against white people as such, but against all those who operated systems of oppression, be they white, black, brown or Indian. Marley witnessed the great changes that came to Jamaica in the post-World War II period.

He saw Jamaica achieve political independence but he was dismayed by the persecution of Rastafarians and the "Rude Boys" by the authorities. He witnessed the rapid changes that occurred in the music scene. The successive changes from *Mento* to *Ska,* and then to Rhythm and Blues, Rock Steady and *Reggae* fired his own musical ingenuity. He lived through all the conflicts that bedeviled Jamaica during those trying decades.

Marley was a "Rude boy" himself. Born in St Ann's Bay in 1944, he became an apprentice welder at a tender age. He managed to combine his vocational training with song writing. Although he later achieved a meteoric flight to local and international stardom, Marley never turned his eyes away from the suffering masses among whom he had been raised. Nor did he shy away from the prospects of bringing peace and reconciliation to the Jamaican community that had been torn apart by civil strife. Marley once invited the leaders of the two rival political parties, Edward Seaga and Norman Manley to his concert. He persuaded them to come on the stage. And he made them shake hands. The effect was unprecedented. It sent a salutary message across the country. Everywhere, people spoke of peace, forgiveness and reconciliation. In due course, some politicians had their own *Reggae* songs composed for them. This is interesting because, until then, the upper classes that listened to Beethoven and Mozart had treated *Reggae* as music for the wretched of the earth, for outcasts and the people without class. This is understandable because the word, *Reggae,* derived from the term "regular people," or ordinary people, bearing in mind that in Jamaica the word regular also means ordinary.

Bob Marley's music captured the ears of the white world as well. His music tours abroad helped diffuse racial tensions between whites and blacks. By the 1970s, everybody did the *Reggae*. Yet, Bob Marley never betrayed his people. He continued to sing about the days of slavery, about colonialism, about hunger and about injustices that the poor were subjected to. His messages reached the ears of the downtrodden peoples of the world. They loved him and his songs because he too came from the lowest rungs of the social ladder, the grass-roots society.

Reggae artists believed that the world would be changed if people saw the light. Music, they said, could be a source of light. They therefore sang songs that praised uprightness and condemned the evil path. They ridiculed politicians who fooled the people (Never trust a politician to grant you a favor: They will always want to control you forever). They despised leaders who stuffed their bellies while the masses starved ("Them Belly Full. . . But We Hungry). They sang with derision about preachers who deceived their congregations ("Preacher man don't tell me heaven is under the earth, I know you don't know what life is really worth"). They sang about African redemption and African unity and the virtues of struggle for freedom.[25]

As back-to-Africa black nationalists, *Reggae* artists sang about their longing to return to the land of their ancestors. Their songs told stories about the trials and tribulations they suffered in the land of captivity. Bob Marley sang:

> Open your eyes and look within
> Are you satisfied with the life you're living?
> We know where we're going; we know where we're
> from
> We're leaving Babylon; we're going to the father-
> land.[26]

For many blacks of the African diaspora, who did not know enough of their history, Bob Marley reminded them that they were Buffalo Soldiers, stolen from Africa, and taken to America.

Reggae artists were among the first musicians to realize that the independence, which the former colonial masters were conceding to black countries in Africa and the Caribbean, was useless as long as it was not accompanied by a complete liberation of the mind. They admonished blacks to emancipate themselves from mental slavery because only they could free themselves from the colonial mentality. They urged the West Indian black communities to accept Africa, not Europe, as their reference point. This was necessary because the inherited colonial school curriculum placed too much emphasis on European rather than African and Caribbean studies. To many *Reggae* artists, a return to Africa was a matter of necessity, not of convenience.[27]

The early *Reggae* artists therefore endeavored to promote race consciousness through music. Although their songs were concerned with the everyday experiences of ordinary people, a sizable number of them emanated from the speeches and exhortations of well-known political figures. *Reggae* artists used Marcus Garvey's admonitions to deliver their own messages. "There will be a false leader," Marcus Mosiah Garvey said, "and this leader, whoever he shall be, shall be stoned with stones." *Reggae* artists sang about controversial political issues that explain white-black misunderstanding and the framing of blacks for crimes they did not commit. A good example was Bob Marley's "I Shot the Sheriff." By turning the speeches of black political leaders into songs, *Reggae* artists made it possible for very important political messages to reach wider audiences. A good example was Emperor Haile Selassie's speech of 1968 in which he declared:

> Until the philosophy which holds one race superior and another inferior is finally and permanently discredited and abandoned; until there are no longer first and second class citizens of any nation; until the color of a man's skin is of no more significance than the color of his eyes; until the basic human rights are guaranteed to all without regard to race; until that day the dream of everlasting peace and world citizenship and the rule of international morality will remain but a fleeting illusion to be pursued but never attained; and until the ignoble and unhappy regimes that hold our brothers in Angola, in Mozambique and in South Africa in subhuman bondage have been toppled and destroyed; until bigotry and prejudice and malicious and inhuman self-interest have been replaced by understanding and tolerance and goodwill; until all Africans stand and speak as free human beings, equal in the eyes of the Almighty; until that

day, the African continent shall not know peace. We
Africans will fight, if necessary, and we know that we
shall win, as we are confident in the victory of good
over evil.[28]

Many African-centered voices in Africa and the diaspora echoed
Haile Selassie's message but Bob Marley turned it into a song,
emphasizing that "until the philosophy which holds one race
superior and another inferior is finally and permanently discred-
ited and abandoned everywhere, there will be war."[29] Certainly,
many more people heard this message, not from the Emperor of
Ethiopia, but from the "King of *Reggae*." In fact, the whole soci-
ology of *Reggae* can be written around Marley's musical work.

Marley believed in the power of music, not just music
for music's sake, but music as a tool for cultural resistance. He
believed that the world would be changed through love and
music. The oppressed would be awakened to political action
through positive musical vibrations. The evil forces of repression
would be dislodged by the positive power of songs and music.
Seemingly powerless people would tear down colonialism and
its systems of exploitation and repression. These sentiments are
captured in his song, "Small Ax," part of which goes:

> If you are a big tree
> We are the small ax
> Sharpened to cut you down

Although Marley believed that music could change the world,
he warned, nonetheless, that counter-violence must not be
ruled out. Likewise, even though he believed in peace, he was
convinced that there could be no meaningful political change
without a revolutionary struggle.

Despite his mistrust for politicians, preachers, and other
agents of deceit and oppression, Marley still had confidence that
in the end, there would be "One World, One Love." Although
Marley appeared to be a spokesperson of the Rastafarians of
Jamaica, in fact, he was a spokesperson of the oppressed people

of the world. However, his greatest concern was for the people of African origins, the most oppressed of all humans. Most of his songs stressed peace and African unity.

As Horace Campbell has testified, *Reggae* songs appeal to the poor and struggling people. The poor want to hear that their suffering is only temporary and that soon everything will be all right. Similarly, those engaged in wars of resistance against oppressive regimes welcome songs that assure support and victory. When guerrilla fighters in Zimbabwe heard Bob Marley sing "Africa A Liberate Zimbabwe" they appropriated it.[30]

Reggae and Rasta played an equalizing role in Jamaica. It was through Rasta and *Reggae* that the social barriers of the West Indian communities were broken down. The middle and upper classes, which had treated them as outcasts and subversives, began to imitate aspects of their life style; they began to wear dreadlocks, which they had previously detested. Not only did these middle and upper class people learn to appreciate *Reggae*, but they also appropriated it, promoted it, and used it as an instrument for forging cultural and national identity.

It is amazing how the members of the upper classes (both white and black) use African works of art to forge national identities. We have already seen how the upper classes in Cuba used *Rumba* to forge national identity. In Brazil the upper classes use *Samba* to fabricate a Brazilian national identity. In Jamaica, *Reggae* is the tie that binds the people. *Reggae* artists, along with the Rastafarians, have acted as agents of change.

Notes

1. Leonard E. Barrett, *The Sun and the Drum: African Roots in Jamaican Folk Tradition* (Kingston, Jamaica: Sangster's Book Stores, 1976) 69.
2. *Ibid.,* 25.
3. *Ibid.,* 70.
4. Margaret Crahan and Franklin W. Knight. *Africa and the Caribbean: the Legacies of a Link* (Baltimore: Johns Hopkins Univ. Press, 1979).

5. Ivor Morrish, *Obeah, Christ and Rastaman: Jamaica and its Religion* (Greenwood: The Attic Press, 1982).

6. Barrett, *The Sun and the Drum,* 27.

7. Morrish, *Obeah, Christ and Rastaman*, 56.

8. Campbell, *Rasta and Resistance*, 1.

9. Morrish, *Obeah, Christ, and Rastaman,* 68.

10. Revelation 19:16.

11. William F. Lewis, *Soul Rebels: The Rastafari* (Prospect Heights: Waveland Press, 1993), 1.

12. *Ibid.,* 9.

13. For a detailed study of the movement see, for instance, Leonard E. Barrett, *The Rastafarians: A Study in Messianic Cultism in Jamaica* (Rio Piedras, Puerto Rico: Institute of Caribbean Studies, 1968); Barry Chevannes, *Rastafarai: Roots and Ideology* (Syracuse, Syracuse University Press, 1994); Barry Chevannes, *Rastafari and other African Caribbean Worldviews* (Houndmills, Macmillan, 1995).

14. Louis, *Soul Rebels,* 10.

15. As quoted in Campbell, *Rasta and Resistance,* 129.

16. Tracey Nicholas, *Rastafari: A way of Life* (New York: Anchor Books, 1979), 33.

17. Morrish, *Obeah, Christ, and Rastaman,* 68.

18. Barrett, *The Sun and the Drum,* 71.

19. Nicholas, *Rastafari,* 28.

20. Bob Marley and the Wailers, "Confrontation," Island Records, 1983).

21. Psalm 37:7.

22. Erna Brodber and Edward J. Greene, *Reggae and Cultural Identity in Jamaica,* Working Papers on Caribbean Society, (Institute of Social and Economic Research, Mona Campus, Kingston, Jamaica. (University of the West Indies, 1981), 13.

23. *Ibid.,* 26.

24. *Ibid.*

25. Horace Campbell, *Rasta and Resistance: From Marcus Garvey to Walter Rodney* (Trenton, NJ: Africa World Press, 1987).

26. Bob Marley and the Wailers, "Exodus." Produced by Bob Marley and the Wailers, Distributed by Island Recording Inc. New York.

27. Brodber and Greene, *Reggae and Cultural Identity,* 26.

28. Speech by Emperor Haile Selassie I. February 28, 1968.

29. Bob Marley and the Wailers, "War." Produced by Bob Marley and the Wailers, Distributed by Island Recording Inc. New York.

30. Campbell, *Rasta and Resistance,* 144.

Chapter 5

BLACK JIHADISTS: ISLAMIC RESISTANCE TO EURO-PEAN DOMINATION IN AFRICA, BRAZIL, AND THE UNITED STATES

J ust as the traditional African religions unified different groups of black people in Africa and the Diaspora against white domination, so did Islam act as an integrating force for similar ends. Muslim communities preferred to have no dealings at all with European Christians, known as infidels. In the United States, the Nation of Islam chose to remain separate from white society.

Muslims sometimes resorted to violence when it became obvious to them that Europeans would not leave them alone. For example, when Frederick Lugard forced himself upon the Muslim emirates of what later became part of modern Nigeria, and then proposed to establish trade with them, the Sultan of Sokoto emphatically rejected the idea. In a letter he wrote to Frederick Lugard in 1902, Sultan Attahiru stated:

> From us to you. I do not consent that any one from you should ever dwell with us. I will never agree with you. I will have nothing ever to do with you. Between us and you there are no dealings except as between [Muslims] and Unbelievers, War, as God Almighty has enjoined on us. There is no power or strength save in God on high.[1]

In the early nineteenth century there were several slave revolts in Brazil that were thought to have been religious in nature because they were led by Muslims. In North, West and East Africa, Muslims opposed European imperialism.

Muslims opposed the presence of European imperial agents because, by definition, they were unbelievers or *kafirs*. *Kafir* implies both religious disbelief and "obstruction in the creation of a just and egalitarian society free from all forms of exploitation and oppression."[2] In other words, a person who seeks to dominate and oppress the weak and obstruct the creation of a just society no matter what his professed religion is a *kafir*. Certainly, by this definition, Frederick Lugard as well as Generals Faidherbe, Gallieni, Gordon and the other European colonial agents that waged war on weak African village communities were *kafirs*, not only because they were unbelievers, but also because they had gone to Africa to dominate, oppress, and create unjust societies.

On the other hand, African Muslims who opposed the European conquest and the colonization of Africa acted consistently with the principles of Islamic liberation theology, which was rooted in the concept of *tawhid* or unity with God. *Tawhid* implies not only unity with God but also unity of mankind in all respects. It cannot tolerate any form of discrimination, whether based on race, religion, caste or class.[3] As we have seen, the European invaders of Africa in the nineteenth and twentieth centuries established systems of inequality and discrimination based on race, religion, and class. Since the societies they established were unjust, Muslim masses were enjoined to wage *jihad* against them until they were defeated and then expelled.

The concept of *jihad* in Islam literally means struggle. The purpose of a *jihad* in the context of Islamic liberation theology is to wage a struggle *(jihad)* for the elimination of exploitation, corruption and tyranny.[4] When properly applied, a *jihad* is not a senseless act of aggression; it is an attempt to replace injustice with justice and to build an egalitarian society. In North Africa, for example, Muslims united themselves under the banner of Islam and under the leadership of their *caliphs, mahdis, emirs* and *mallams* as they declared a *jihad* against the French who, in 1832, tried to impose a tyrannical regime upon them. Throughout the period of struggle for the liberation of Algeria and Morocco, Muslim leaders created a structure that was held together by a strong sentiment for Islam in which the *emir* appeared "as the instrument of God gathering the community of the faithful in a holy war against Christianity."[5] To the Muslims, therefore, war against European domination was part of an ongoing battle between the abode of Islam *(dar al-islam)* and the abode of war *(dar el-harb)*.[6]

With the foregoing in mind, it is easy to see why black Muslims would resist European domination. As Engineer has pointed out, Islam, as compared to other religions, has much greater potential for developing a liberation theology. Its revolutionary potential is tied up with the origins of Islam itself. At the time of its formation in Mecca, social tension was developing between the dominating wealthy class and the repressed poor. Prophet Mohammad condemned the actions of the rich, warning them of the dangerous consequences that would follow if they failed to spend their wealth in the way of Allah. The Prophet also warned them that their power was useless unless it benefited society, for the only power that did not oppress others was the power of God. Any power that did not emanate from God oppressed others and could not contribute to the development of a just society.[7]

Such revolutionary injunctions appealed to the poor and the downtrodden. It is no surprise that among those who joined the Prophet Mohammad in the beginning of his struggle were mainly young and poor people. Bilial (an African from Ethiopia), together with many slaves and other oppressed sections of Mecca, joined the struggle "as they saw the possibility of their liberation through his mission."[8]

Although the Prophet was concerned primarily with the survival of the new religion, his utterances initiated a revolutionary movement that would enable the oppressed of Mecca and future generations of Muslims everywhere to confront their oppressors. By denouncing oppression, exploitation and injustice, the new religious movement provided guidelines for the establishment of just and egalitarian societies here and now on earth. Thus, when

European adventurers encroached on Muslim territories, they came face to face with societies that had developed their own attitudes and standards for dealing with external threats. These attitudes ranged from direct military confrontations to avoidance or accommodation. For example, although Muslims opposed European colonial domination and the spread of Western culture, yet for commercial and diplomatic reasons, they allowed European traders, explorers and diplomats to reside in Muslim territories as persons "seeking and receiving protection." Their treatment was based on the *sharia* (Islamic law), which allowed *musta' min* (holders of *aman,* i.e., self-conduct) to reside in *Dar al-islam* (Muslim territory) and carry on with their usual business.[9]

These sentiments were also intricately tied to the question of how best to protect the religion of Islam itself. Although required to declare a *jihad* (struggle) against the enemies of Islam, in order to protect their right to worship, Muslims were encouraged to undertake a *hijra* (flight) from a land dominated by infidels if a successful *jihad* could not be accomplished. This withdrawal from a land dominated by the enemies of Islam is at the heart of the religion; even the Prophet of Allah had to resort to this when he fled from Mecca to Medina. In later centuries, this sentiment may have been stretched to include a total separation of the domain of Islam from the domain of unbelief, or simply, a reluctance to tolerate the presence of rival faiths.

The assumed reluctance of Muslims to tolerate the presence of other religions may have derived from the Islamic principle that *Dar al-Islam* (Muslim territory) and *Dar al-harb* (a land of unbelievers on which war by Muslims is obligatory) could not co-exist. As an exclusionist religion, wrote William Montgomery Watt, Islam was skeptical of mixing with other religions, and the Koran warned Muslims against fraternizing with *harbi* (unbelievers or persons from *Dar al-harb*). Believing in the self-sufficiency of their religion, many Muslims maintained that any knowledge not sanctioned by the Koran was unnecessary or dangerous. They considered secularism and Westernization particularly dangerous because of their perceived corrupting nature.[10]

These principles might have been strongly adhered to in previous centuries but have been weakened by the political and economic realities of twentieth-century globalization. Today, many Muslim countries like Turkey, Jordan and Qatar have incorporated several non-Islamic practices into their economic and political systems, and have no good reasons to avoid non-Muslims. In fact, Muslims have no reason whatsoever to avoid non-Muslims, for in the Koran it is asked: Say: "Why do you dispute with us about God when He is equally your Lord and our Lord?"[11] It is further affirmed in the Koran:

> We believe in God and what has been sent down to us, and what had been revealed to Abraham, Ishmael, and Isaac, and Jacob, and their progeny, and that given to Moses and Christ, and all other prophets by the Lord. We make no distinction [between one and another] among them, and we submit to Him.[12]

In other words, Muslims are enjoined to avoid any form of discrimination that is based even on religion. Instead, an individual should be judged by his or her actions, for, according to the Koran, "To us belong our actions, to you yours . . . ."[13]

Indeed, modern Islamic opposition to non-Muslims seem to derive, not necessarily from religious differences, but from what the Muslims perceive as the disruption of Muslim society by outsiders. For instance, during the scramble for Africa in the late nineteenth century, many Muslims were disturbed, not by the mere presence of Christians in their territories, but by European imperial ambition. Just as the Pope would have felt disturbed if Muslims erected mosques in Rome, so did many Muslim clerics feel when Christian missionaries began to build churches in Muslim territories. Likewise, just as the Queen of England would have felt if Muslims began to build military barracks in Liverpool, Birmingham and Manchester, so did the Sultan of Sokoto feel when Christians from Europe began to build military barracks in the emirates of Ilorin, Kontagora and Kano. In any case, it would appear that it was the Christian missionaries' attack on Islam, as well as European colonial imposition, that made Muslims more aware of the value of their own religion and more determined to protect it.[14]

Until the turn of the twentieth century, however, the principles of avoidance and confrontation guided Muslim societies as they dealt with Western European imperialists. When Muslims failed to halt a European invasion, they tried to avoid assimilation into Western culture. They also stood against European slavery and colonialism. In Brazil, Muslims also opposed European slavery. In the United States, they fought against white racism and economic exploitation. In Africa, they resisted colonial invasion. Even when Muslims agreed to work within imposed colonial structures, they made sure that the friendship they professed was "from the mouth and not from the heart." Throughout Africa, oppressed Muslims never stopped thinking of re-establishing the true Islamic community *(umma),* nor would they give up their commitment to the general principle of *jihad.*

Against this background must be placed European attitudes toward Muslims, for the whole desire to conquer, enslave and dominate Africa was instigated by European Christian attitudes towards Muslims. As far as Africa, south of the Sahara, is concerned, it all began in 1454, when Pope Nicholas V, in his Papal Bull, *Romanus Pontifex,* gave the Portuguese the right to occupy all the lands of the misbelievers that might be discovered along the west coast of Africa. The declaration was in keeping with "a wider expansive movement on the part of Christian Europe, aimed mainly against Islam."[15] Once initiated, some of the primary objectives were to bring down the power of Islam, to destroy the assumed monopoly of African and Asian trade by Muslims, and to convert the local people (including Muslims) to Christianity. These objectives were put to test as soon as the Portuguese adventurers rounded the Cape of Good Hope and entered the Indian Ocean. The Portuguese destroyed Kilwa in 1505 and then went on to attack several Swahili trading cities on the Indian Ocean. By 1550 they had virtually eliminated Muslim traders from the other African ports, as well as from their lucrative gold trade in the Zambezi Valley. Having accomplished this, they imported Christian missionaries to convert the people of the Zambezi region and its capital city, Muenemutapa.[16] However, these early conversion attempts failed disastrously.

The first European adventurers in Africa went armed with the sentiments of conquest and conversion. As Mervyn Hiskett has noted:

> Whether these Europeans came to trade or to convert the local people, they all shared a similar attitude toward Islam. They accepted the assumption of the Christians of their day, that the world was divided into Christian believers and the rest who were mis-believers or downright infidels. They were wholly uncritical of their approach to their own beliefs and never doubted for one moment that Christianity was the true faith, believing all other religions, including Islam, to be false.[17]

As will be explained shortly, Muslims were determined to resist any attempt by Christians to extend their trading influence into *Dar al-islam,* or to convert Muslims to Christianity, or to bring down Islam. From 1454 to 1800, European attitudes towards Muslims grew more and more bellicose. By the nineteenth century, the new imperial powers of Europe had to seek other justifications for their desire to appropriate Muslim territories. They found them in the slave trade, especially in West and East Africa. For example, German Christian missionaries, explorers and colonial agents incited the entire German public against Islam in East Africa by their so-called eyewitness accounts of slavery in East Africa. They also advocated the forceful occupation of Muslim territory if that would facilitate the suppression of slavery. Colonel officials found satisfaction in the excuse that "there was no other way to comply with German popular demand."[18] The French and the British were exceptionally active in West Africa. The French, under Generals L. L. C. Faidherbe and Joseph Simon Gallieni, overran the entire Western Sudan, including the Great Tukulor Empire and the Niger Plains. As for the British, it was during Joseph Chamberlain's tenure in office as

British colonial secretary (1895-1903) that they conquered most of what became Nigeria, the largest colonial territory in British West Africa. Before going into action, Chamberlain delightfully boasted:

> Sooner or later we shall have to fight some of the slave dealing tribes and we cannot have a better *casus belli* ... public opinion here requires that we shall justify control of these savage countries by some serious effort to put down slave dealing.[19]

Concealing their real motives for invading Africa, reasons that were rooted in economic, political and strategic considerations, the British hastily destroyed the ancient empire of Benin (1897), the emirates of Nupe and Ilorin (1897-99) and the rest of the Sokoto caliphate (1899-1904).

To all Muslims who may have remembered the history of the Crusades, the sudden conquest of Africa by Europeans was an eye opener to the fact that European Christians had finally decided to destroy Islam. To Muslim intellectuals who had knowledge of World history, the suppression of slavery, which the invading Europeans claimed was at the heart of their project, could not have been motivated by humanitarian gestures but by the desire to undermine Islam. Muslim intellectuals knew that the Pope in Rome had blessed the enslavement of Africans and that the Roman Catholic Church was a slaveholding establishment. Muslim scholars might have known that some white Christian clergymen in the Americas owned slaves of their own while shamelessly claiming that enslavement afforded the Africans the benefits of European civilization and the opportunity to gain eternal life. If the Pope in Rome and the clergy in the Americas supported the enslavement of Africans, then how could European colonial agents justify their plunder of Africa under the pretext of suppressing the slave trade? In any case, were these not the same Europeans who, not long ago, had come to Africa in tall ships to transport millions of Africans to the Americas, where they were held down with so much barbarism? Did the Europeans not instigate wars in Africa, directly by supplying firearms, and indirectly by purchasing all available prisoners of war? And, were the British, who suddenly championed the abolition of slavery, not a few years before the foremost slave-trading nation in the world?[20]

Nevertheless, no matter what the Europeans and Muslims thought of slavery, slaves everywhere clung to the understanding that heaven only helps those who help themselves. Consequently, enslaved Africans avoided unrewarding arguments about what Holy books and Holy men thought about slavery and went on to resist the ungodly institution, even if they had to operate within the teachings of Islam and Christianity. In Brazil, for instance, Muslims rose against their masters, who happened to be Christians; in Haiti and the United States, Christian slaves rebelled against their Christian masters.

MUSLIMS AND SLAVE REVOLTS IN BRAZIL

Millions of Africans that left African shores for the Americas as captives were followers of traditional African religions. Only a small minority of them practiced Islam. There are several explanations for this. The first is that the major sources of slaves for the Atlantic slave trade were located in non-Muslim territories, and the second is that until recently, Muslims were a minority group in Western and Central Africa from where most African captives came. Furthermore, the few Muslims that were exported to the Americas were dispersed over a wide area. However, despite their small number, and the deliberate attempts by slave owners to convert them to Christianity, a sizable number of Muslims retained their faith. Some even set up their own separate communities and associations in several towns in the Americas. It would appear that the most studied of the Muslim communities in the Americas was the Muslim community of Salvador in Bahia, Brazil. Thanks to the works of João José Reis.[21]

To the Muslims of Salvador, Bahia, it was painful enough to be slaves to infidels, but more galling to their pride was the strenuous tasks they performed. Like other slaves, they undertook the unpleasant responsibility of cultivating sugar cane. The tediousness of this and other tasks, as well as the humiliation they suffered at the hands of their owners, caused discontent and resistance, which was manifested in the ancient Islamic tradition of struggle *(jihad)*. Their struggles for freedom caused great political explosions in the early nineteenth century, the most violent occurring in 1835. The unsatisfactory color and social stratification that characterized colonial Brazilian society acted as the spark that ignited the explosives.

As Joao José Reis has shown in his book, which incidentally is virtually the only one available to English speakers, the society of Bahia in the early nineteenth century was highly mixed, racially and occupationally. The urban center of Bahia was a color- and class-stratified community. This stratification generated constant conflicts, protests and rebellions.

Like the Haitian slave revolt, the slave uprisings in Bahia started from the top and filtered downwards. At the top of the social hierarchy were the principal planters. At the very bottom were slaves. In between these were merchants, state and church officials, and military officers.[22] The society of Bahia was also divided along color lines and between free and bond. The wealth of the society was controlled by a handful of very rich planters, whereas the vast population of poor whites, free people of color, and slaves remained generally deprived. Between 1823 and 1830, there were several revolts by the free people (both black and white) directed against Portuguese authorities. These revolts encouraged Muslims to organize themselves for future revolts.

Until large shipments of African Muslims began to arrive in Brazil in the 1820s, the size of the Muslim community of Bahia was small. Moreover, the realities of slavery and the social stratification of the region threatened the survival of this tiny Muslim community. More than at any other time, these Muslims wished to return to Africa. Some of them planned to capture a ship that would transport them back to Africa but their plan was exposed in 1807. The leaders of the conspiracy, most of them Hausa Muslims, were arrested and punished severely.[23] Two years later, black rebels assembled in Reconavo and then attacked the town of Navarare, ostensibly to capture ammunition and foodstuffs. The rebels were beaten back and some of them were captured. Even though the prisoners were tortured, they would not implicate their co-religionists, nor would they expose the details of their plot. During these and other uprisings that broke out in Bahia, many of the nearby *quilombos* (maroon settlements) acted as safe havens for black rebels. More importantly, it was the influx of new Muslim imports from West Africa that encouraged frequent uprisings in Bahia.

Students of West African history are familiar with the Islamic reform movements in West Africa but they may not realize how they were linked to the Muslim Slave revolts of Brazil. To fully appreciate the nature of these outbreaks, it is important for one to see the results of these West African *jihads:* first, in the Muslim population buildup in Brazil, and then, in rebellion.

The West African *jihads* broke out early in the nineteenth century as a part of an Islamic resurgence that affected the entire Grassland Belt of West Africa. They spread from Futa Toro in the west to the Adamawa Mountains to the east. These wars involved both Muslims and non-Muslims, and were fought with great ferocity and cruelty. They were wars of conversion as they were wars to reform Islam itself. For a century, these wars caused panic and instability throughout West Africa.

It is ironic yet important to note that a war that started in West Africa to reform Islam resulted in part to the export of a large number of Muslim captives to the Americas. As Mervyn Hiskett has pointed out, "The purpose of the Muslim Fulani's preaching was simply to combat mixed Islam and create an Islamic society nearer in all its aspects to the Sunni Islamic ideal."[24] But this effort became embroiled in other ideals and objectives. In particular, the societies in which these Islamic reformers lived were organized by non-Islamic institutions, even when their rulers professed Islam. Second, as the reform movement gained strength, so did many of its leaders begin to nurse the idea that they, not the traditional rulers, had been ordained by God to govern. Third, since reformers demanded full submission to Islamic law and customs from those who called themselves Muslims, the reform movement became "essentially a confrontation between Muslims at different levels of seriousness . . . not between Believers and infidels, even though the reformers sometimes pretended that it was."[25] In the Sokoto Caliphate, for instance, the Muslim leader, Nagwamatse, and his ally, Masaba, *emir* of Nupe, ransacked Gwariland and southern Zaria in endless slave-raiding wars, capturing Muslims as well as non-Muslims.[26]

The initial engagements in Yorubaland may have resulted from panic but the Yoruba fought among themselves to settle ancient quarrels. Furthermore, Oyo Yoruba, who lived in the borderlands between Yorubaland and Hausaland, suffered greatly, and since Islam had spread into northern Yorubaland, many of the Oyo-Yoruba captives were practicing Muslims. In any event, for much of the nineteenth century, the Oyo people were in constant war with the Hausa jihadists from northern Nigeria. The combatants captured both Muslims and non-Muslims and sold them into slavery. The trans-Atlantic routes facilitated the export of war prisoners to the Americas, especially to Brazil and Cuba. This explains why there were large Yoruba and Hausa populations in Brazil, sizeable numbers of them Muslims. By the time that the forced migration ended, that is, after the effective abolition of the Atlantic slave trade in the 1850s, the Yoruba as a whole had become the largest single African group in Brazil and, probably, in Cuba as well.

As already mentioned, large numbers of Muslims began to arrive in Brazil after 1820; the two most dominant groups, who also were among the largest victims of the nineteenth century wars in West Africa, were Yoruba and Hausa. These people were not all Yoruba and Hausa but might have found it convenient to claim that they were. Nonetheless, the Hausa and Yoruba Muslims might have been enemies in West Africa, but in Brazil, they could find a common identity in their religion. Islam, in this instance, played an integrating role in Bahian society and in slave resistance.

The Muslim community of Salvador was respectable and well organized. Each of its component parts brought its own peculiar trait to Brazil. For example, the Yoruba brought with them the Oyo militaristic tradition, while the Hausa brought the tradition of learning.[27] Nevertheless, neither group ever lost sight of the central message of Islam. Muslims were in the minority in Bahia, yet they formed a tightly unified group. They dressed differently and wore amulets that many Brazilians believed had magical powers. Hausa Muslims proselytized. They read the Koran and were knowledgeable in the Arabic language, which they appeared to speak fluently. They copied verses from the Koran on wooden slates, and conducted classes both for Muslims and non-Muslims. Education led to conversion, expansion, and the preservation of Islam in Bahia.[28]

Reis noted that the urban work environment allowed the slaves to retain their rich African traditions. Slaves were allowed to work away from their master's dwellings and socialize with other slaves and the free population. Petty traders gathered in the market centers; craftsmen and women practiced their skills. The Hausa dominated the local commerce in Salvador, a reflection of an ancient Hausa tradition that had earned for Kano the status of a vital entrepôt of the trans-Saharan trade. With their earnings they manumitted themselves and they formed manumission associations that encouraged members to make periodic money contributions to a fund which was used on a revolving basis to buy their freedom.[29] They also introduced an ancient African credit association known as *adashe* in Hausaland or *esusu* in Yorubaland.

The rebellion of 1835 was led predominately by Yoruba Muslims, but Hausa and other ethnic groups from West Africa also participated. That is to say that even though the rebellion has been described as Muslim, it was a slave revolt in which non-Muslims were also involved. The rebellion was unique because it demonstrated the resourcefulness and diversionary tactics of the slaves. For example, the rebels chose to strike on the holiday of Our Lady of Guidance that fell on Sunday, January 25. According to Reis, the choice of day indicated how well Africans had been integrated into the Brazilian culture. They knew that most officials would be in the countryside celebrating the Christian religious holiday. Equally important is that they planned the revolt strategically on the last day of the Islamic holy month of Ramadan. This choice of date is remarkable because it appealed to the religious sentiments of the rebels.

The Muslims' plan for a surprise attack was betrayed, however.[30] They had not prepared for a conventional fight, since they had few firearms. Despite the betrayal, and despite their relatively small number, they still found their resolve strong enough to propel them into action (only 400-500 Africans out of 20,000 blacks that lived in the vicinity actually participated). The rebels stormed through the Palace Square, banging on doors to gather rebels. They attempted to free Africans held in the city jail, and presumably, also to gather weapons. They failed, however, when they found themselves caught between two lines of fire. One came from the jail and the other came from the palace guards, who had positioned themselves on the opposite side of the square.[31] The insurgents, most of them unarmed, resorted to hand-to-hand combat, and were beaten off. The confrontation resulted in 70 deaths, mostly of blacks. Trials were held and suspects punished. Little information was gathered and most of it was distorted. Somewhat strangely, punishment fell more on freedmen than on slaves "who were overwhelmingly deemed ordinary participants in the rebellion."[32] The punishment for rebellion was particularly severe.

After quelling the rebellion, the colonial authorities tried to disperse the Muslim community of Bahia, believing that the semi-autonomous life they lived had encouraged them to indulge in endless rebellions. A crackdown was put into motion. Afro-Bahian and Islamic cultural practices came under fire. Amulets, Arabic writings, rosaries, and African clothes were confiscated and destroyed. Even African musical instruments, necklaces, and cloths were declared "harmful to law and order."[33]

Reis's work is a vital contribution to African and Diasporan studies. It is also important because it deals with a hitherto little known Muslim community in Brazil, together with their tradition of resistance against white domination. From Reis' work, one finds illustrations of linkages between nineteenth century American and continental African Muslims. Reis shows how the early Muslim communities in the Americas retained a religious practice they imported from Africa and then used it to foster black identity, unity and resistance.

ISLAMIC RESISTANCE TO FRENCH COLONIALISM IN NORTH AFRICA

The same period that marked Muslim uprisings in Brazil also witnessed the Muslims' wars of resistance to the French invasion of Algeria and Morocco. Was this a coincidence? Both conflicts were similar; they were intended to halt European domination and exploitation of Africans. The French invasion of these two North African countries began as a misunderstanding between the Turkish governor of Algiers and the French consul, a misunderstanding that brought French military personnel to Algiers. It was also a military operation abroad aimed at diverting French attention from the growing unpopularity of the regime of Charles X at home.[34] Whatever the case, from the African perspective, the wars of resistance began in 1832, when the French tried to impose themselves on the Muslim communities of North Africa. It must be stated here that this was not the first French military operation in North Africa. Napoleon Bonaparte had invaded Egypt in 1798 and looted its treasures.

Through a process of military action, scorched-earth policy, pillage and confiscation, the French government stripped the Algerian peasantry of its land and then pushed them back into the worst areas. Many Algerians, in pastoral communities for instance, were denied access to grazing lands, and were resettled in arid territories. On top of this, the French taxed the Algerians heavily and then overturned their legal system to make it administratively a part of metropolitan France. The French also introduced a policy of assimilation that was based on economic, social and political qualifications.

Deprived of land and civil rights, many Algerians immigrated to Tunisia. Some went even further east, reaching Syria, where they hoped to secure land and start life anew. This is a good example of "migration as protest," a form of maroonage or *hijra,* in opposition to colonial occupation. Rather than emigrate, however, many Algerians remained behind and resisted the French occupation.

The first Algerian insurrection began in 1832 and lasted till 1847. It was a fifteen-year-old war that was led by Abd el Kader, an avowed enemy of the French and the Turks. Abd el Kader mobilized the Algerian masses around a hierarchy of African leaders, assisted by such religious entrepreneurs as *sheiks, caids,* and *agas.* It was during Abd el Kader's resistance that a new type of relationship developed between the French and some notable Algerian rulers. These rulers were military chiefs of the Turkish government who aided the French and were used to administer Muslim populations.[35] There were also some wealthy Algerians who, for the sake of material gain, sided with the French. These notables sometimes embarked on "punitive expropriations in favor of European colonists," intended "to make the native population pay for the costs of [their] rebellion."[36] The French government in Paris supported the expropriations, which it described as a punishment for rebellion and a means of "civilizing" the Algerians. The peasants of Algeria were also subjected to bone crushing levies that were collected through the "friendly chiefs" who, according to the peasants, had taken their "skin and bones" only to return later to break the "bones to eat the marrow."[37]

It would have been impossible for the French to exploit the Algerian populations without the assistance of Algerian power holders. These Algerian collaborators supported the French in their destruction of Algerian social systems. Though the settlers had come from virtually every part of Europe, they had two things in common, namely, a collective fear and hatred for Muslims and a passionate defense of their privileges.[38]

The French finally defeated the Algerians in 1847. Abd el Kader's military forces were dispersed and, until the end of the nineteenth century, the Algerians, under a new military leader, El

Moqrani, managed to launch only one more unsuccessful major offensive against French colonialism.

Until the end of the nineteenth century, therefore, Algerians remained relatively quiet. This long period of military inactivity can be attributed to two major interrelated factors. First, the French government managed to hide behind native Algerian and Turkish power brokers as they exploited ordinary Algerians. The oppressed masses, which could not see their real oppressors, regarded the Algerian and Turkish ruling houses, rather than the French, as their real enemies. This misunderstanding instigated numerous violent clashes among the various factions in Algeria. The French, who incited the violence in the first place, stood aloof as unconcerned bystanders. The policy of using Algerians against Algerians illustrates the phenomenon often referred to as "brother set against brother," which Frantz Fanon eloquently commented on in his book, *The Wretched of the Earth*. According to Fanon, "The colonized man will first manifest this aggressiveness which has been deposited in his bones against his own people. This is the period when the niggers beat each other up, and the police and magistrates do not know which way to turn when faced with the astonishing wave of crime in North Africa."[39] Thus, rather than confront the French, who were the true enemy, the Algerians expended their energies fighting among themselves.

In the second place, many Algerians, especially those who had received a French education, and who would have led the masses against the French, failed to forge a united front against the enemy. Many vacillated. Some quarreled over tactics and strategies. A few called for closer contact and greater assimilation into French culture, while the rest asked for Algerian nationality. These debates prolonged the period of inactivity until the 1950s when some militant nationalists formed the necessary alliances with workers and peasants and began the final struggle for national liberation. This aspect of resistance constitutes the Algerian liberation movement of the 1950s and 1960s.

MAHDIST REVOLT IN THE SUDAN

Further east in the Sudan, Muslims resisted British colonialism. The most famous of these wars of resistance broke out in the last quarter of the nineteenth century and has been described simply as the Mahdist revolt. Muhammad Ahmad, who took the title of the Mahdi, led the war of resistance.

In Sunni Islam, the term, Mahdi, means "God-Guided One." It is a common belief among certain Islamic sects that before the end of time, a person from the house of the Prophet Mohammad would come to "fill the earth with justice even as it has been filled with injustice." The Mahdi, therefore, is perceived as a redeemer, a messiah whose coming is preceded by certain catastrophic signs. Because of the deep-rooted injustices that prevailed before his arrival, the Mahdi, it is further believed, must of necessity be a charismatic figure. His primary roles would include the destruction of the *al-dajjal* (the antichrist) and the return of the masses to the primitive simplicity of the old religion. The belief among Muslims that a Mahdi would come is similar to the Christian expectation of the Second Coming of Christ or the Jewish messianic movement. These ideas are rooted in the messianic and millenarian traditions of the three major universalistic religions—Judaism, Christianity, and Islam. Thus, just as Christians believe in the second coming of Christ, so do many Muslims believe in the coming of a Mahdi (God-guided One) who will bring about the victory of Islam for a millennium (thousand years) up to the Day of Judgment. Ibn Khaldun, an African historian and a fourteenth-century traveler, wrote:

> It has been accepted by all Muslims in every epoch that at the end of time a man from the family of the Prophet will make his appearance, one, who will strengthen Islam and make justice triumph; Muslims will follow him. He will gain dominance over the Muslim realm. He will be called the Mahdi. Following him the anti-Christ will appear, together with all the subsequent signs of the Day of Judgment. After the Mahdi Jesus will descend and kill the anti-Christ.

Or Jesus will descend with the Mahdi and help him
kill the anti-Christ.[40]

Ibn Khaldun stated that among those most influenced by the
Mahdist thinking were the poor and oppressed.[41] They were the
most likely to fight on the side of the Mahdi and die, if necessary, and go straight to heaven. Aziz A. Batran does not agree
entirely with Ibn Khaldun's interpretation of the conception of
the Mahdi. Nonetheless, he visualizes the Mahdist tradition as a
device to keep out the enemies of Islam, so that in the event of a
threatening intrusion by non-Muslims, it is considered a betrayal
if Muslims fail to join in a battle against them. Batran insists that
the Mahdist thinking often enabled Muslims to achieve unity
against their oppressors.[42] Throughout Muslim Africa, according
to Batran, Mahdism has inspired militant revolutionary actions
against oppressors and foreign intruders and endowed the resis-
tors with legitimacy.[43] Furthermore, it had been written that

> The more the Muslim masses have felt themselves
> oppressed and humiliated, either by their own rulers
> or by non-Muslims, the more fervent has been their
> longing for this ultimate restorer of the true Islam
> and conqueror of the whole world. And as the need
> for a Mahdi has been felt, the Mahdis have always
> appeared and Islam has risen, sword in hand, under
> their banner.[44]

Certainly, a large body of Sudanese Muslims believed that
the Mahdi had appeared in the 1880s. They also believed that
Muhammad Ahmad was the Mahdi. To them, there was no doubt
that he had fulfilled the three most important qualifications for
the Mahdi, namely, that he would be a charismatic figure, that he
would descend from the family of the Prophet Muhammad, and
that his coming would be signaled by deep-rooted injustices.

Born in Dongola province of the Sudan in 1833 or 1834 to a
boat builder, Muhammad Ahmad showed a keen interest in religious studies at a tender age, an interest he sustained throughout
his life. He belonged to the mystical Sammaniya religious broth-
erhood, and after years of intensive study, was allowed to become

a religious leader of the order, authorized to own his own flag and granted the power to admit others.[45] Ahmad then established his own residence and began to teach new disciplines. His fame as a pious mystic spread rapidly, and in 1881 he declared himself to be the expected Mahdi. Like many of his followers, he believed that he had been called out "to lead an errant, confused, and threatened people back to salvation."[46] Some of his missions were to unify the masses, ensure that their devotion to the cause of Islam transcended ethnic loyalties, wage a jihad against the infidel and purge the world of its wretchedness and corruption.[47]

Colonial authorities were enraged by these developments. They sent a small expedition to silence Ahmad, but to their surprise and disappointment, Ahmed destroyed the expedition and then withdrew to the hill of Qadir in Kordofan. From this place he sent his messengers with letters and proclamations announcing the coming of the expected Mahdi who would usher in a New World Order.[48]

Having failed to silence Muhammad Ahmad by a show of force, the Sudanese authorities tried propaganda. They publicly denounced Ahmad, calling him a pretender. They warned the Sudanese that this man was not the awaited Mahdi, nor did he possess the known attributes of the promised Mahdi. The authorities claimed that Ahmad's place of birth and his appearance were not the ones described in the popular traditions. They went on to warn the people that Ahmad was a troublemaker whose ambition was to sow the seeds of disaffection in a prosperous country. They claimed that since the Sudan was in the midst of prosperity, the conditions necessary for the coming of a Mahdi could not have been fulfilled.[49]

Ahmad refuted these claims. He described the authorities and their agents (most of who were the *ulama*) as hypocrites and mercenaries on the payroll of foreign powers. He depicted them as men who did not comprehend the plight of the Sudanese masses, men who could not distinguish truth from falsehood.[50] Of course, Ahmad knew that counter-attacking his detractors was one thing, proving that he was the expected Mahdi was another. To prove his legitimacy, he tried to reenact Prophet Muhammad's role in the creation of the Muslim community by calling on his followers to embark on a *hijra*. He then tried to evoke the life of Prophet Muhammad and the period of the first four caliphs– the "rightly guided caliphs." He went on to invoke his ancestry and the significance of the mole on his right cheek. Now, satisfied that he had satisfied these and other signs and requirements, too numerous to be listed here, Muhammad Ahmad declared war against the enemies of Islam. In November 1883 his forces attacked and captured El Obeyd and defeated an Egyptian expeditionary army led by the British commanding officer, Hicks Pasha. And while the British were making preparations for the political re-organization of the Sudan, the Mahdi attacked Khartoum (the capital city of the country), and killed General Gordon when the city fell on 26 January 1885.[51]

The colonial authorities in the Sudan were disturbed, not only by the Mahdi's fresh military successes, but also by their effects on the masses that flocked to his camp. These people had been excessively taxed and plundered by the Egyptians who had managed in the early Nineteenth century to conquer the Sudan. The main purpose of that conquest was to throw open the Sudan for exploitation for Egypt's benefit. But by the second half of the nineteenth century, Egypt's power over the Sudan had ebbed. The Sudanese might have regained their independence if the Western powers had not suddenly appeared on the scene. First, they financed a new round of Egyptian imperialism in the Sudan under Ismail (of Egypt). Then, the British occupied Egypt in 1882, and transformed the Sudan into a colony that was administered by both Britain and Egypt, hence, the term, Anglo-Egyptian Sudan. Finally, Ismail adopted a policy of appointing large numbers of Europeans and some Americans as officials in the Sudan. By the time the Mahdi proclaimed his jihad in 1882, the Sudanese masses were already waiting for someone to redeem them, not only from the British and Americans, but also from the Egyptians.

In some important respects, points out L. Carl Brown, the Mahdist revolt can be viewed as "one of several traditionalist Islamic reactions to the impact of the Western world in modern times."[52] It was a reaction against the incursion of the Western world on the Sudanese society, using Egypt as its spearhead. If so, the Mahdist revolt can be seen as an action taken to correct "what is wrong in this world" and an attempt to check Western encroachment on Muslim life. It was, therefore, a *jihad* (struggle) against the infidel, as represented by the West, and against nominal Muslims, as represented by the Muslim puppets of the West among whom was Ismail of Egypt.

The Mahdi sent panic throughout the Western World when he destroyed British military forces in the Sudan, but in the end, he failed to fulfill the purpose of his appearance. He had opposed a force that was far more sophisticated than he had expected and in the end he failed to achieve his objectives. Nonetheless, even though he failed to keep British imperialists away from his country, many in the Sudan still believed that he was the Mahdi. More important, his protest, like other protest movements of that period, aroused a chain reaction of disaffection with Westernization, which in the long run helped to advance Islamization in the region.[53] His protest also advanced anti-colonial sentiments that frequently exploded during the colonial period.

The Mahdi died unexpectedly in June 1885 and was succeeded by another militant Muslim who advanced the culture of resistance in that country. Parts of the Sudan remained a Mahdist state until 1896 when the British finally re-conquered them. "The secret of Muhammad Ahmad's achievement," wrote Trimingham, "was the strength of his personality and his power of influencing the susceptible Sudanese by suggestion. He was the 'leader,' thrown up by the times of a peculiar type of Sudanese nationalism. Behind all was his very real and unwavering belief in his divine call– a belief which exercised a compelling influence on others."[54]

OTHER MAHDIST MOVEMENTS IN THE SUDAN AND IN WEST AFRICA

R. A. Adeleye has reminded us that the Mahdist outbreak in the Sudan took place at the very beginning of European military expansion into Sub-Saharan Africa. As the European conquest of Africa south of the Sahara spread, resulting in the overthrow of the state structures of many African societies, so did new Mahdis and the wars of resistance they inspired multiply. To many Muslims, the overthrow of the indigenous African governments signified the coming of the Mahdi; consequently, new charismatic Muslim leaders emerged, determined to guarantee the independence and survival of Muslim rule. According to Adeleye, among the new charismatic leaders were many pious *mallams* (Muslim teachers and clerics) scattered throughout West Africa. "Such mallams," he added, "expressed their opposition through the Mahdist idea. They presented themselves either as the Mahdi or his precursors."[55] In the Sudan alone, there were about twenty Mahdist inspired revolts between 1885 and 1925. During the earlier colonial period, noted Trimingham, these outbreaks appeared with persistent regularity.[56] Most of them were provoked by such vexing administrative innovations as the imposition of European tax systems, or by appalling social and economic conditions. Trimingham has explained that "Mahdists have been especially frequent, have almost always been reformers and deliverers, and whenever successful have inevitably founded states."[57] In other words, Mahdis do not only fight oppression, but they also establish states. Among the Mahdis (or their precursors) who founded states in nineteenth century Africa were Muhammad Ahmad of the Sudan, Usman Dan Fodio of the Sokoto Caliphate, al-Hajj Umar Tall in Futa Toro, and Seku Ahmadu in the Western Sudan.

Some Mahdist revolts were weak or poorly organized. For instance, in 1908 in the Sudan, Abd al-Qadir preached a jihad and killed a British official, but his revolt was quickly put down.[58] On the other hand, some revolts were very strong, demanding full-scale military responses. One of them, the Satiru rebellion of

1906 in Northern Nigeria, was particularly strong. The leader of this rebellion was Dan Makafo, a resident of the town of Satiru, fourteen miles north of Sokoto.

During their first encounter with British forces, Dan Makafo's men fought mostly with bows, arrows and spears but they defeated a party of British-mounted infantry and captured their weapons. The British authorities in Northern Nigeria retaliated by sending an exceptionally large force that marched on Satiru in March 1906. Dan Makafo and his followers fought bravely but failed to repel the better-armed British soldiers. They might have minimized their losses if they had resorted to guerrilla tactics. The town of Satiru was destroyed and Dan Makafo, together with many of his followers, died in the battlefield, defending it bravely.[59]

The major colonial powers in Africa were kept in constant fear of Mahdist rebellions.[60] The endless rebellions they provoked were fueled by the popular Muslim image of Christians. This image, according to Hiskett, "was based largely on myth and fantasy, especially folkloric notions of Dajjal, Anti-Christ, the wars between him and the Mahdi, the awesome specter of Gog and Magog and their monstrous armies and, over all, the looming vision of the End of Time."[61] Call them myth or fantasy, the fact is that the sudden appearance of European troops and colonial administrators on Muslim soil was a positive sign that the hour of reckoning had come. Of necessity, Africans had to lock horns with invading Europeans. As would be expected, to most Muslims, the Mahdist revolts of the colonial period were essentially directed against Christians. Their primary aims were to drive out the Christian governments and then restore the rule of Islam.

THE RISE OF THE NATION OF ISLAM IN THE UNITED STATES

"The Black Muslim Movement," wrote C. Eric Lincoln, "had its origin in the ghetto of Detroit. The time was 1930. It was the first year of the great Depression—a time of hunger, confusion, disillusionment, despair, and discontent."[62] Lincoln should have added that the period was ripe for the coming of the Mahdi in the United States of America.

The origins of the rise of the Nation of Islam in the United States can be traced to the early twentieth century, when many blacks left their farms and plantations in the south and migrated to northern cities. A feeling of hopelessness, as well as the fear of widespread political violence like lynching had driven them north. Although some went in search of economic opportunity, a lot more were enticed by promises of jobs and better living conditions in northern industrial complexes and cities like New York, Philadelphia, Chicago, and Detroit. The white labor shortages of the First World War period actually enabled blacks to secure jobs in the northern cities but, when the war ended in 1918, the demand for black labor declined sharply. White workers and white ex-service men displaced many blacks, forcing them to congregate in the ghettos where they faced untold hardships, including police intimidation.[63] It was during this time of despair that a man appeared, like the expected Mahdi, to fill the world of the downtrodden African-Americans of Detroit with justice as it had been filled with injustice. His name was Wali B. Farad Muhammad.

Thus, the origin of the Nation of Islam can be traced, not only to the economic and political crisis facing blacks in the early twentieth century, but also to the sudden appearance of Wali B. Farad Muhammad. Farad or Fard, (as he was better known), had been employed as a salesman to market silk and other merchandise in the black ghettos of Detroit. His job enabled him to meet with blacks, to be acquainted with their plight, and to spread his message about Islam.[64] Fard took advantage of the grave economic hardships of the Depression years to attract converts. Though Christians, many of Farad's black converts were recent migrants from the south and were still groaning over a long list of unfulfilled promises and economic expectations. Between 1930 and 1933 an estimated 8,000 blacks in the Detroit area joined Fard's movement.

Even if Fard did not declare himself a Mahdi, his followers believed that "Allah (God) appeared in the person of Master W. Fard Muhammad" in July 1930, and that he was "the long awaited 'Messiah' of the Christians and the 'Mahdi' of the Muslims."[65] Fard, on the other hand, claimed that he had come from the holy city of Mecca. His light complexion and "Arab" features made his claim believable.[66] Fard told his followers that "some of his primary missions were to wake the Dead Nation in the West . . . to teach the truth about the white man, and to prepare [the people of the Nation] for the Armageddon."[67] His popularity was so high that he was able to establish the first of the Temples of Islam in Detroit. He reassured his followers that they were not "Negroes" but "Black Men." Among other things, Fard told them that Islam was the "natural religion of the Black man, and that only in Islam could the Black man find freedom, justice and equality."[68] Fard declared Christianity a white man's religion, which the white man had used for enslaving non-whites. He warned his followers that wherever Christianity had gone, men had lost their liberty and their freedom.[69]

It is not difficult to see how Fard's messages could have soothed the anxiety of a people devastated by the economic depression and social injustice of the early 1930s. Lincoln described Fard's followers as "escapists and clairvoyants," who believed that Fard was a messiah, who had come to lead them into a Golden Age that would be established "when the Black Nation in the West had thrown off the yoke of the white slave-masters."[70]

One of Fard's early converts was Elijah Poole, a Georgia-born ex-factory worker. After the sudden disappearance of Fard, apparently in 1933, Elijah Pool became the leader of the Muslim movement. He dropped the name Poole and picked up Muhammed, hence, Elijah Muhammad. He and his followers retained the name "Black Muslims," and continued with the tradition of denouncing Christianity, which they described as "an opiate designed to lull Negroes– with the promise of heaven– into passive acceptance of inferior social status."[71]

"Under Elijah Muhammed," wrote Lincoln, "the movement spread from the initial temple in Detroit to almost every major city in the country where there was a sizable black population." Elijah Muhammed became the messenger whose voice gave hope to the forgotten inner-city blacks. Among these forgotten blacks were pimps, prostitutes, con men, prisoners, ex-convicts, alcoholics, drug addicts, and the jobless. One of Elijah's strategies was to persuade his followers to recover their self-respect and aim for self-sufficiency. Moreover, Black Muslims, who had read the Bible, believed that they could not gain salvation if they continued to worship the God of their oppressors. They were also made to believe that white Christians would never accord them equality, nor could they advance themselves socially and politically under the exploitative economic system of white society. Black Muslims in America were particularly fascinated by the doctrine of separation that Elijah Muhammed preached.

THE QUESTION OF SEPARATION

The Nation of Islam's policy of separation issued from two circumstances, one sociological and the other historical. The sociological factor was born out of a feeling of isolation, compounded by a sense of minority complex. The historical factor is rooted in the age-long moral conflict between the abode of Islam and the abode of unbelief, which we have examined above.

Islamic captives in the Americas had endured their isolation, but while many reverted to traditional religions or became Christians, the rest looked forward to the moment when they could return to Africa or assert their freedom on American soil. For the time being, however, they tried as much as they could to keep themselves and their religion separate from non-Muslims. This appears to have been the attitude of most Muslims whenever they found themselves as minorities in territories dominated by non-Muslims. Certainly, this has been the attitude of the members of the Nation of Islam.

On the other hand, it has been a traditional practice for Muslims to respect non-Muslim authorities as long as these authorities do not threaten the practice of Islam. If so, why does the Nation of Islam denounce American society and seek to remain separate? The answer is not hard to find.

First, the vast majority of the members of the Nation of Islam had been Christian and had joined the Nation because of their disillusionment with white society. Second, although the members of the Nation of Islam obeyed the laws of the United States, they were certain that the authorities did not protect them against white violence and racism. Along with other African-Americans, black Muslims were treated as second class citizens, and until the 1960s, were denied the most important rights and freedoms guaranteed by the American Constitution, namely, the right to vote and the right to freedom of expression. Most of their efforts to achieve social equality with other Americans were frustrated by the racist state structure. Because of these and other reasons, the members of the Nation of Islam wanted to be separate from white Americans. Their demand for separation can, therefore, be seen as resulting from their failure to achieve integration and equality within the socio-economic order of the country. It is, therefore, accurate to regard black separatism as an aspect of Black Nationalism.

How separate the members of the Nation of Islam want to be is hard to determine, but it must be borne in mind that black separatists advocate either territorial separation (nation within a nation) or repatriation to Africa. Like Harriet Tubman, the leaders of the Nation of Islam did not believe in the back-to-Africa movement. Instead, they favor territorial separation, which would entail the creation of an African or Muslim territory within the boundaries of the United States, where they could practice their religion and run their own political and economic institutions unmolested. Malcolm X summarized this aspiration when he said:

> There is something that the white man can do to avert [disaster]. He must atone – and this can only be done by allowing black men, those who choose, to leave this land of bondage and go to a land of our

own. . . . He should give us separate states here on American soil, where those of us who wish can go and set up our own government, our own economic system, our own civilization.[72]

It must be stated, however, that the idea of separation is not new. As we have seen, it was rooted in Muslims' ideas about the contradictions between the abode of Islam *(dar al-islam)* and the abode of war *(dar el-harb)*. When, therefore, Fard, Elijah Muhammad, and Malcolm X advocated the creation of a separate state for black Muslims on American soil, they were, in fact, asserting one of the principles of Islam. As was mentioned earlier, Mahdis do not only fight oppression, they also build nations. Like many Mahdis, Fard and Elijah Muhammad were convinced that they were engaged in the act of building a nation, the Nation of Islam. As one can gather from the teachings of Elijah Muhammad, this seems to be a central preoccupation of the Nation of Islam.

Malcolm X sometimes spoke for blacks as a whole, sometimes specifically for black Muslims.[73] When he advocated the creation of a black state on American soil, he might have spoken for African-Americans as a whole, but it is also conceivable that, as a spokesperson of the Nation of Islam, he spoke specifically for black Muslims.

The members of the Nation of Islam decried all blacks that supported integration. They believed that "the offer of integration is hypocritical and is made by those who are trying to deceive the black people into believing that 400-year-old open enemies of freedom, justice, and equality are, all of a sudden, their 'friends.'"[74] As is well known, neither Martin Luther King Jr. nor the leaders of the National Association for the Advancement of Colored People (NAACP) advocated the separation of blacks from whites. Instead, they struggled for integration. If Malcolm X preached separation, then he could not have spoken for all African-Americans.

Today, while the leaders of the Nation of Islam remotely pursue their dream of separation, they concentrate their efforts on the more practicable mission of salvaging their followers from moral and economic decadence. They discipline their members and try to replace their sense of despair with a feeling of hope. Among other things, they rehabilitate some ex-convicts, improve family life, and provide financial assistance for members who wish to open small businesses. Many of its followers give up the more observable anti-social habits like stealing, drug dealing, smoking, and the consumption of alcoholic beverages. Until his death, Malcolm X remained grateful to the reforming program of the Nation of Islam. According to Malcolm,

> I am a good example of why Islam is spreading so rapidly across the land. I was nothing but another convict, a semi-illiterate criminal. Mr. Muhammad's teachings were able to reach into prison, which is the level where people are considered to have fallen as low as they can go. His teachings brought me from behind prison walls and placed me on the podiums of some of the leading colleges and universities in the country. . . . This is the best example of Mr. Muhammad's ability to take nothing and make something, to take nobody and make somebody.[75]

As a religious movement, the Nation of Islam remained relatively unknown nationally until the 1950s when the civil rights movement gathered momentum. The outspokenness of leaders like Malcolm X enabled the organization to attract media attention. The humanitarian program of the Nation of Islam also continued to attract inner city dwellers. Even when they resisted conversion to Islam, large sections of the downtrodden population of the black ghettoes of the United States agreed with the Nation's message of racial solidarity and self-help. In other words, an African-American does not have to be a Muslim to perceive the benefits of racial solidarity and self-help. Moreover, although some well-educated African Americans have joined the Nation, the bulk of its recruits are still drawn from low-income, inner city dwellers.

Rather than praise the Nation of Islam for its good works, however, Americans denounce it. Some black political leaders claim that the Nation of Islam's activity is harmful to integration and racial harmony. The lukewarm acceptance of the Nation of Islam by the more successful blacks can be attributed to the Nation's strategy for advancing black liberation. For example, even though most blacks share the same concerns about white racism, they are frightened by the Nation's central political ideology, which is anchored to the principle of separation of the black man's world from the white man's world. Black businessmen and women, entertainers and sports men and women, who amass wealth from the wider American society, cannot objectively practice separation.

Moreover, many Americans still believe that Muslims, including members of the Nation of Islam, threaten the political stability of the country. Perhaps, this fear stems from America's loss of popularity in the Arab World and from the fact that some leaders of the Nation of Islam sometimes indulge in violent rhetoric of violence. The truth, however, is that the members of the Nation of Islam are harmless, and cannot in any way be compared to the members of the Ku Klux Klan, the Neo-Nazis, the skinheads, and other white supremacist hate groups that are staffed by Christians, fascists and atheists.

The Nation of Islam participated actively in the struggle for civil liberties in the United States. Like Muslims in Africa and Brazil, they fought against the degradation of black people, thereby contributing to the spread of the black culture of resistance. Much of what we know about Black Muslims and their preferred methods of achieving freedom and justice for African-Americans comes from Malcolm X. It was largely through his efforts that black Muslims became transformed into Muslims, a process that began, not in the 1930s, but in the 1960s.[76] One must read his speeches and his autobiography to understand the central message of the Nation of Islam, bearing in mind, however, that he revised his views on certain aspects of the Nation's political and religious ideologies. Although Malcolm X later left the Nation of Islam, he professed Islam until the last days of his life. It is also important to point out that Malcolm X followed the path paved by Marcus Garvey. Like Garvey, Malcolm recommended self-help and self-reliance as avenues to black redemption. He urged blacks to be enterprising, resourceful, self-sufficient and self-reliant, and to cultivate a sense of pride and accomplishment. Working through and with the assistance of the Nation of Islam, Malcolm encouraged the establishment of schools, mosques, unions, small-scale businesses, and banks in black communities. He also encouraged blacks to own their own businesses, to provide employment for blacks, and to prevent capital flight from the black community.

I cannot end this discussion without stating that in this chapter I have tried to look at the role of Muslims in the development and spread of the black culture of resistance in Africa and the Diaspora. I have tried, however, to stay away from Islamic doctrines, devotional duties, internal conflict and power struggles. Regarding Islam in the United States, I recognize that there are many Muslim sects in the country, some conservative, some moderate and some militant. Nonetheless, I consider the Nation of Islam to be the most relevant organization to examine in this chapter. This is not only because of its militancy and concern for the poor, but also because of its unique contributions to the struggle for civil rights in the United States and proven commitment to the principle of black liberation everywhere.

Notes

1. Michael Crowder, *A Short History of Nigeria* (New York: Frederick A. Praeger, 1962), 199.
2. Asghar Ali Engineer, "On Developing Liberation Theology in Islam," In Asghar Ali Engineer (ed.), *Islam and Revolution* (Delhi: Janta, 1984), 29.
3. *Ibid.,* 33.
4. *Ibid.,* 35.
5. Eric Wolf, *Peasant Wars of the Twentieth Century* (New York: Harper & Row, 1969), 218.
6. See Mervyn Hiskett, *The Development of Islam in West Africa* (New York: Longman, 1984), 265-301.
7. Engineer, *"On Developing Liberation Theology in Islam,"* 25-7.
8. *Ibid.,* 27.

9. R. A. Adeleye, *Power and Diplomacy in Northern Nigeria, 1804-1906: Sokoto Caliphate and its Enemies* (New York: Humanities Press, 1971), 121.

10. William Montgomery Watt, *Islamic Fundamentalism and Modernity* (London: Routledge, 1988), 6-16.

11. *Al-Qur'an,* Chapter II, Verse 139, taken from *A Contemporary Translation* by Ahmed Ali (Princeton: Princeton University Press, 1988), 28.

12. *Ibid.,* Chapter II, Verse 136.

13. *Ibid.,* Chapter II, Verse 139.

14. Mervyn Hiskett, *The Development of Islam in West Africa* (London: Longman, 1984), 223.

15. *Ibid.,* 202.

16. Alan Isaacman, *The Tradition of Resistance in Mozambique: The Zambesi Valley 1850-1921* (Berkley: University of California Press, 1976), 1-2.

17. Hiskett, *The Development of Islam in West Africa,* 204-5.

18. *Ibid.,* 216.

19. Suzanne Miers, *Britain and the Ending of the Slave Trade* (New York: Africana, 1974), 24.

20. See Philip D. Curtin, *The Atlantic Slave Trade: A Census* (Madison: University of Wisconsin Press, 1969).

21. João José Reis, *Slave Rebellion in Brazil, The Muslim Uprising of 1835 in Bahia,* (Baltimore: John Hopkins University Press, 1993),

22. *Ibid.,* 8.

23. *Ibid.,* 43.

24. Hiskett, *The Development of Islam in West Africa,* 159.

25. *Ibid.,* 159.

26. *Ibid.,* 186.

27. Reis, *Slave Rebellion in Brazil,* 141.

28. *Ibid.,* 106

29. *Ibid.,* 165.

30. *Ibid.,* 74.

31. *Ibid.,* 81.

32. *Ibid.,* 206.

33. *Ibid.,* 203.

34. Wolf, *Peasant Wars*, 211.

35. *Ibid.*, 218.

36. *Ibid.*, 220.

37. As quoted in *ibid.*, 220.

38. *Ibid.*, 224.

38. Frantz Fanon, *The Wretched of the Earth* (New York: Grove Press, 1977), 52.

39. Quoted in Peter B. Clarke and Ian Linden, *Islam in Modern Nigeria: A Study of a Muslim Community in a Post-Independence State, 1960-1983* (Mainz: Gruneald, 1983), 109.

41. *Ibid.*, 109.

41. Aziz A. Batran, *Two Essays on Islam and Revolution in Africa* (Brattleboro, VT: Center for Arab-Islamic Studies, 1983), 27.

43. *Ibid.*, 29.

44. Quoted in *ibid.*, 28-9.

45. J. Spencer, Trimingham, *Islam in the Sudan* (London: Frank Cass, 1965), 93.

46. L. Carl Brown, "The Sudanese Mahdiya" in Robert Rotberg and Ali A. Mazrui, (eds.). *Protest and Power in Black Africa* (New York, Oxford University Press, 1970), 150.

47. Trimingham, *Islam in the Sudan*, 94.

48. *Ibid.*, 94-5.

49. Batran, *Two Essays on Islam and Revolution*, 30.

50. *Ibid.*, 30.

51. Trimingham, *Islam in the Sudan*, 95.

52. Brown, "The Sudanese Mayday," 160.

53. *Ibid.*, 166-7.

54. Trimingham, *Islam in the Sudan*, 151.

55. Adeleye, *Power and Diplomacy in Northern Nigeria*, 321.

56. Trimingham, *Islam in the Sudan*, 158.

57. *Ibid.*, 149-50.

58. *Ibid.*, 159.

59. Adeleye, *Power and Diplomacy in Northern Nigeria*, 323-4.

60. *Ibid.*, 326.

61. Hiskett, *The Development of Islam in West Africa*, 225.

61. C. Eric Lincoln, *Black Muslims in America* (Boston: Beacon Press, 1973), xxii.

63. *Ibid.,* xxiv.
64. Clifton E. Marsh, *From Black Muslims to Muslims: The Transition from Separatism to Islam, 1930-1980* (Metuchen: The Scarecrow Press, 1984), 4, 51-2.
65. As quoted in *ibid., 64.*
66. *Ibid.,* 51.
67. Lincoln, *Black Muslims in America,* xxiv.
68. *Ibid.,* xxvi
69. *Ibid.,* xxv.
70. *Ibid.,* xxvi
71. David Gallen, *Malcolm X as they knew Him* (New York: Carroll & Graft, 1992), 110.
72. *Ibid.,* 129.
73. See, for instance Bruce Perry, (Ed.) *Malcolm: The Last Speeches* (New York: Pathfinder, 1989). See also George Breitman (ed.), *Malcolm X Speaks: Selected Speeches and Statements* (New York: Pathfinder, 1992).
73. Quoted in Marsh, *From Black Muslims to Muslims,* 64.
75. *Ibid.,* 124.
76. *Ibid.,* 62.

Chapter 6

BLACK LIBERATION THEOLOGY AND RESISTANCE IN AFRICA AND THE UNITED STATES

Christianity's role in resistance in Africa and the diaspora is somewhat bizarre. Although many African communities initially resisted the teaching and spread of Christianity, a large number accepted the Bible and then used it in their struggle against European domination. Some of the most articulate Pan-Africanists and civil rights advocates were baptized Christians. These were the men and women who organized the most prominent political associations that eventually overthrew colonialism and segregation in Sub-Saharan Africa, the West Indies and the United States. European missionary and colonial agents, who had hoped to make the blacks docile by converting them to Christianity, were disappointed.

Black Christians' success can be explained by invoking five interrelated factors. First, they manipulated the Bible to suit their own purposes. Second, many Africans compared their own pain to Christ's suffering on earth, and then added him to the great council of African ancestors. Even the saints and angels found nichés in some African-based religions. For example, Voodoo devotees equated their serpent god, *Damballah,* to Saint Patrick who, according to myth, banished snakes from Ireland. Also, the Voodoo goddess, *Ozoli,* became the Virgin Mary, mother of Christ. Third, Africans did not completely give up their ancestors and their worldviews even when they converted to Christianity. This process involved both the Christianization of different aspects of African traditional religions and the Africanization of Christianity. That is to say that, just as the Europeans Europeanized Christianity and used it to establish relations of domination in their dealings with non-European nations, so did the Africans Africanize Christianity and then used it as an instrument of resistance against European domination. Fourth, Africans believed that Christianity, Islam and Judaism enhance (not weaken) traditional African religions. Fifth, the black culture of resistance, whose origins and sustenance came from European violence and racism, was too strong to be neutralized by the ephemeral appeal to Christian brotherly love.

To start with, we must call attention to certain aspects of Afro-European relations that are often misunderstood. One of them is the fact that since Roman and Byzantine times, Europeans have tried to use Christianity to establish a pattern of domination over the people of Africa and to exert a deep impact on African cultures and institutions. This was the case during the first seven centuries of the Christian era, when parts of North and East Africa, including Egypt, Ethiopia and Nubia, were converted to Coptic Christianity. Again, after the re-entry of Christianity into Africa in the fifteenth century, following the Portuguese adventures in Africa, all African Christian converts were subject to the authority of the Pope in Rome. Following the introduction of the Atlantic slave trade in the same period, European slave owners used Christianity to reinforce the doctrine of race superiority among African exiles in the Americas. The tendency was further advanced in the nineteenth and twentieth centuries, when European imperialists recruited Christian missionaries to serve as a cultural wing of European colonial expansion into Africa. Acting in concert with European anthropologists and colonial officers, missionaries peddled the ideology of white supremacy and ensured that Africans were treated as second-class citizens even in their own countries. In Algeria, for instance, the French adopted a policy that made the lowest European settler the superior of any African.[1] In the Congo, the Roman Catholic priests placed themselves above the laws of the country, claiming that as representatives of the Pope in Rome, they were not the subjects of the King of Congo.

In their dealings with black people, Europeans ingeniously fused religious with secular ideas and then turned the Bible into a potent tool for enforcing obedience to their oppressive order. They lifted verses from the book and used them to demand unquestioned obedience from their slaves and colonized converts. Europeans, armed to the teeth as they plundered and colonized the world, could not see the contradiction in their actions when they told the oppressed to love those that misused and abused them. "Love your enemies," they readily quoted from the Bible, "[and] do good to those who hate you, bless those who curse you, pray for those who abuse you. To him who strikes you on the cheek, offer the other also . . . ."[2] Black converts were asked to be meek for the meek shall inherit the earth, yet blacks must seek first God's Kingdom and lay their treasures in heaven (for all treasures that were stored on earth, such as the gold and diamond deposits of South Africa, belonged to the white people). The logic of these religious injunctions is hard to find; the meek that would inherit the earth must first lay their treasures in heaven.

Furthermore, Africans were told to be obedient to God and to God's representatives on earth. Of course, these representatives were no other than European invaders of Africa--men like King Leopold in the Congo, Cecil Rhodes in Zimbabwe, Frederick Lugard in Nigeria, and General Gallieni in the Western Sudan. These were the aggressors whose hands were drenched in African blood. Their conscience soiled with stolen minerals and art treasures.

Frantz Fanon was right when he placed DDT, a type of pesticide, on the same level as Christianity. According to Fanon, as pesticides kill germs, so does Christianity destroy the traditions of the colonized peoples.[3] Fanon might not have had any quarrels with Christianity except with the way European imperialists used it to enslave and colonize black people. Even if he had, he had every right to be, for the painful truth is that Christianity does not guarantee Africans equality with Europeans. Considering the way the religion was paraded in the colonies, it could not have called the Africans to the infinite ways of the Lord.

It is not difficult to see why many Africans in Africa and the diaspora resisted Euro-centric Christianity. They agreed with the central message of Christianity, which was based on the ideas of love and eternal life. What the Africans did not agree with was the brand of Christianity that degraded their humanity and undermined their cultures.

FROM A THEOLOGY OF SOLACE TO A THEOLOGY OF LIBERATION

While the Christian missionaries and colonial agents tried to use Christianity to promote white supremacy, many blacks in Africa and the diaspora perceived the liberating qualities of Christianity. During the course of their struggles against European domination they developed a theology of liberation, an African or Black Christian liberation theology.

Liberation theology refers to an attempt to use religion to achieve freedom, equality and justice. One can therefore speak of an African Christian liberation theology, or an Islamic liberation theology, and so on, provided that each addresses the questions of freedom, equality and justice. As Asghar Ali Engineer has cautioned, liberation theology is not theology of solace but that of struggle.[4] Such a theology does not consider established institutions as sacred and unalterable. Instead, it treats values, not institutions, as sacred.[5] The primary function of liberation theology, therefore, is to emancipate the masses from the grips of their oppressors and exploiters. It seeks to instill in the oppressed the need to act with revolutionary zeal with which to overturn tyranny, exploitation, and persecution. Engineer has cautioned that liberation theology transforms religion into a powerful instrument of political struggle and change.[6] The South African radical, Steve Biko, believed that African Christian (liberation) theology endeavors "to relate God and Christ once more to the black man and his daily problems. It wants to describe Christ as a fighting god, not as a passive god who allows a lie to rest unchallenged . . . .It seeks to bring back God to the black man and to the truth and reality of his situation."[7] Thus, while the Christian theologian of solace admonishes a convert to surrender all his problems to the will of God, the liberation theologian invokes the co-operation of God in his or her struggle against tyranny.

African Christian liberation theology evolved simultaneously in Africa and the Americas in response to European aggression. The first African Christian theologians to emerge in Africa during the last five hundred years lived in the Congo-Angola region. As will be explained shortly, the Congo-Angola region has continued to produce the more articulate continental African Christian liberation theologians. Other centers of strong African liberation theology were South Africa, West Africa, the West Indies and the United States. Wherever it might have been located, African liberation theology evolved in response to European violence, racism and economic exploitation of the black man. Sometimes also referred to as Black or Ethiopian Churches, these centers of liberation theology were born out of protest. Most of their leaders were Christian liberation theologians who functioned within the tradition. The new religious houses did not appear overnight, but evolved over a long period of time. Born in extremely hostile times, their development called for great sacrifice and ingenuity. To appreciate the difficulties that Africans encountered when developing their own brand of Christian liberation theology, it is necessary to trace the experiments to their historical roots.

In the beginning, slaveholders in the Americas tried to use Christianity to reinforce the ideology of slavery. They hated everything that was of value to the Africans. Even meaningful African names were offensive and had to be replaced with some meaningless European names. The continued practice of African traditional religions enraged the Catholic Church. Wherever the white missionaries went in Africa and the diaspora, they arrogated to themselves the responsibility of smashing what they regarded as heathen practices and witchcraft. In the Congo, noted John

Thornton, "since their arrival in 1645, the Capuchins had made the suppression of what they considered witchcraft their special duty, and they pursued it with a zeal that other religious groups did not." Even the Jesuits, who had been working in the Congo since 1619, shared the views of the Capuchins on the matter of witchcraft and therefore could not tolerate its practice. The priests of both orders were ready, whenever they wished to seize and destroy any sacred objects they considered fetish, idolatry or witchcraft.[8] When slaveholders encouraged slaves to convert, they did so: not necessarily to save their souls, but to strip them of their African cultures and make them docile. Africans in the Americas were falsely promised eternal life through conversion, humility and good behavior. In Brazil, as Stuart B. Schwartz has shown, Christianity was imposed on slaves and owners allowed them access to such European kinds of institutions as marriage and religious brotherhoods. In 1633, Father Antonio Vieira preached to slaves in Bahia the virtues of "patience and martyrdom." His sermon must have offended blacks that knew that "no African or Indian slave was justly captured."[9]

In Haiti, slave owners tried to use Christianity as an opiate for slaves and to discourage flight and disobedience. Sermons were carefully fabricated to urge slaves to forget their servile status or to bring back runaway slaves. Father Fauque was found warning a group of runaways:

> Remember my dear children that though you be slaves you are nevertheless Christians like your masters; that from the day of your baptism you profess the same religion as they which teach you that those who do not live the Christian life shall be cast into Hell after death. How unfortunate for you if, after having been slaves to men of this world and time you should become slaves of the devil for all eternity. This misfortune will certainly fall upon you if you do not return to your duty since you are in a condition of habitual damnation for in addition to the wrong you do your masters by depriving them of your labor, you do not come to Mass on holy days;

> you do not approach the sacraments. . . . Come to me
> then my dear friends.[10]

A similar admonition, directed to a runaway, stated:

> Unfaithful and wicked servant, since you have strayed
> from the service of your master and the obedience
> you owed to God and the Holy Church in order to
> give way to the sinfulness of your heart and to expose
> yourself to the certain loss of your salvation and
> your life, we, by the authority of our holy ministry,
> condemn you to serve penance for the period of . . .
> warning you that should you fail in this and show no
> clear proof of repentance and making amends you will
> be rejected among Christians, forbidden entry to the
> church and abandoned to a death without sacrament,
> without mourners, and without a burial place.[11]

Since the teachings of the Christian priests were at variance with
the African worldview, the latter ignored the priests and preoc-
cupied themselves with a counter ideology of struggle. They
stuck to their African traditional religions, which emphasized
self-help and personal achievement, not to subservience and
docility. However, in due course, and as these African captives
became increasingly familiar with Jesus and the Old Testament
stories, they began to blend their African worldviews with Christian worldviews. They also began to identify their ancestors
with Christian saints and biblical heroes. In 1891 a Trinidadian
newspaper described how the black communities of the island
paraded themselves as Christians, yet continued to give the
priests of their traditional African religious cults great respect and
engaged in what were described as *obeah* and *Chango* worship.
The census records of that period described most of these people
as Catholics, because publicly they were practicing Catholics, but
in private they engaged in *African* religions and identified their
African gods with the saints of the Roman Catholic Church.[12]

Meanwhile, noted Mechal Sobel, as the walls that separated
black and white societies slowly crumbled, so did the black
national culture merge with non-African cultural elements to

create a unique form of black behavior. Despite the inconsistencies that one may find in this behavior, "blacks never gave up the basic African understandings and usage regarding spirit and soul-travels which [in North America], under the pressure of slavery, fused with Christian understandings of Jesus and individual salvation, to create a coherent Afro-Christian faith, whose reality was reflected in a vibrant and known institution, a black Baptist church, the history of which goes back to the 1750s."[13]

Certainly, blacks in the Americas owed the fundamentals of their thought, worldviews, and cultures to Africa even though these were later blended with Euro-American cultures, resulting in a style which, nevertheless, was uniquely African.[14] What this means is that even though most slaves retained their African worldview, and even if their owners did not always permit them to learn to read and write, still they were strongly exposed to the Bible message. Many slaves became practicing Christians; some trained as preachers.

Mechal Sobel has warned against the notion of the so-called hidden institution. According to him, the black church of the slave period was not hidden at all. Instead it was a known and well-established institution.[15] These facts are born out in correspondents from white churches, which described certain aspects of the lives of the members of these churches and their patterns of social organization. They established independent churches that were formerly organized, with written covenants and membership rolls.[16]

Sobel further explained that even though many Afro-Americans eventually lost touch with the source of their images and their understandings, lack of consciousness did not alter the black Christians' ties to the African sacred cosmos.[17] The fusion of traditional African thought with the Christian religion continued to produce a peculiar African identity and pattern of behavior that conditioned the nature of slave revolts. For example, the blending of the African worldview with the Christian worldview made it possible for blacks to appropriate the story of the Hebrew slaves and their redemption. Black slaves often compared themselves to the Hebrews and sometimes claimed direct descent from Abraham himself. They insisted that as the children of Israel freed themselves from the chains of bondage by leaving the land of Egypt, so would they free themselves from New World slavery and go to heaven, which was the same as returning to Africa, where "they would find mother, father, and kin-folk there, waiting."[18]

As most continental Africans would have turned to the leaders of their religious sects or cults in moments of crisis, so did many enslaved Africans in the United States turn to Jesus in their search for redemption. To them, Jesus was not only the head of their religious organization, but also a personal redeemer. "Nobody knows de trouble I see. . . . Nobody knows but Jesus," they would sing, for they believed that "a little talk with Jesus makes it all right." They would also turn to him with high expectations because they hoped that he would fulfill every promise he had made. Did he not say "Come unto me, all ye that labors, and are heavy laden, and I would give you rest?" Altogether, many Africans in slavery drew much inspiration from the suffering of Jesus. To them, it was not for nothing that

> They crucified my Lord; An' he never said a mum-
> balin' word;
> They crucified my Lord; An' he never said a mum-
> balin' word,
> Not a word, not a word, not a word.
> They nailed him to the tree . . . . They pierced him in
> the side,
> The blood came twinklin' down . . . . He bowed His
> head an' died, An' He never said a mumbalin'
> word. . . ."[19]

Sobel insisted that this existential contact with Jesus, as with Noah, Gabriel, Joshua, Daniel, Moses, and other biblical personalities, was made possible by the nature of the vision experience.[20] In other words, many slaves did not find any contradictions between the Christian worldview and African cosmology, nor did they lose ties with the African sacred cosmos. But while many may overlook the revolutionary potential of this mixture, the slaves recognized it and used it effectively. For, even though the Christian worldview expected African converts to be docile and passive, not to say "a mumbalin' word" when European mobs lynched them in the streets of the United States, the African component of the mixture constrained them to resist every form of intimidation. Ultimately, Africans in slavery operated from two seemingly diametrically opposing, yet complementary positions, namely, the African culture of resistance, in which magical folk beliefs readily provided the necessary inspiration and courage to violently resist oppression, and the Christian promise that the meek shall inherit the earth. Eugene Genovese, Mechal Sobel, Lawrence Levine, Stephen B. Oates, together with a host of other scholars are certain that it was the blending of the Christian world view with the African spirit and soul-travels that inspired Denmark Vesey's conspiracy and Nat Turner's insurrection. These freedom fighters and their followers saw Jesus, Abraham, Daniel, Moses, together with the endless saints of the Catholic Church and the pantheon of the Holy Bible, including the Cherubim and Seraphim, as members of the great family of African ancestors.

Enslaved Africans in the Americas did not find many contradictions between certain vital elements of Judaism, Christianity, Islam and African traditional religions. For example, Hebrew and Islamic circumcision rituals and the practice of polygamy were consistent with African customs. Beliefs in possession by the Holy Spirit and the idea of God as the maker of the universe were as central to all African religions as they were to Judaism and Christianity. These assertions are illustrated in a dialogue between Mr. Brown, a Christian missionary, and Akunna, an Igbo chief in Chinua Achebe's novel, *Things Fall Apart*. "You said that there is one supreme God who made heaven and earth," said the chief to the missionary. "We also believe in Him and call Him Chukwu. He made all the world and the other gods." Mr. Brown acknowledged that Chukwu was the same as God who made the world but disputed that Chukwu made the other gods.[21] It was not the Igbo chief's fault, however, that the missionary could not see that the gods were emanations of Chukwu.

Meanwhile in the United States, black Christians worshipped in integrated churches until 1758, when the first African American Baptist Church was founded and was led by two white preachers. The Church did not survive; it folded up within a year. Fifteen years later, a new congregation was founded, and it was led by four black preachers. This attempt was successful. In July 1794, under their leader, Richard Allen, blacks in the city of Philadelphia started the Bethel African Methodist Episcopal Church.[22] The first purpose was to be able to worship God in an environment that was free from discrimination, and the other was to be able to re-establish ties with the African continent. Others emulated these examples and, during the next few decades, black churches sprang up in several American cities.

AFRICAN LIBERATION THEOLOGY AND SLAVE REVOLTS IN THE UNITED STATES

Whites were nervous about the mushrooming of separate black churches; whites did not want blacks to worship with them, nor did they want blacks to worship alone. The fears of the whites were not altogether unfounded, for, as time went on, blacks turned some of their churches into centers of underground plotting. Left alone in their religious establishments, blacks searched the Bible and found in it the necessary inspiration to plot against the institution of slavery. Gabriel Prosser's rebellion of 1800 in Richmond, Virginia, was one of the first recorded revolts in which the church was directly implicated. Although some scholars have rejected this assertion, the overwhelming evidence suggests that the Old Testament message played a role in it.[23] Gabriel Prosser was a local preacher who emphasized the relevance of the story about Moses and the Israelites to the conditions of African captives in the Americas. He assured his congregation that their time was coming too and, like Moses, he would lead them out of bondage.

Then came Denmark Vessey! Working from Charleston, South Carolina, he used his sermons to spread information about an imminent rebellion. He quoted extensively from Bible scriptures, showing similarities between Hebrew salvation and African redemption. He told his congregation that in the beginning God created the world and then all men with equal rights, whites and blacks.[24] He then went on to conspire with 9,000 men who would enter Charleston and begin a "general massacre" of whites. They would also attack any blacks who would not join them, as well as any other person who dared to resist their anti-slavery efforts. But before the plot could be hatched, some slaves alerted their masters about the conspiracy. Vessey and some of his co-conspirators were captured, tried and then hanged on July 2, 1822. Thirty-five more were hanged in subsequent weeks. A sizable number was forced into exile. The story of what would have happened frightened white society. It was, according to Mary Frances Berry, the only time in the United States that an organized effort was made to implement a large-scale city revolt.[25] One interesting revelation that came out of the trials and investigations was that some whites supported the plot. These whites were motivated by different reasons—anti-slavery, anti-racism—but four were convicted on the allegation that they had hoped to use the occasion to loot property.

There was yet Nat Turner, whose insurrection was religiously inspired. Born in Virginia in 1800, Turner grew up believing that he was destined for some divine purpose because of a few birthmarks on his head. He later became a preacher, but the harsh conditions of slavery and the Bible message of redemption combined to turn him into a freedom fighter. Turner identified with the prophets of the Old Testament and was encouraged by the Biblical admonition, "seek yea the kingdom of heaven and all things shall be added onto you."[26] He claimed to have seen a number of signs that he believed were sent by God telling him to lead a rebellion against the slave owners. He also believed that just as the Lord had anointed Ezekiel in the Old Testament, so had he been anointed in the United States. There is every reason to conclude that the emerging Black liberation theology nurtured Nat Turner's longing for freedom, justice and equality. He recalled that he heard a loud voice in the heavens. At the same time, the Spirit appeared to him saying, the Serpent is loosened and Christ has laid down the yoke he bore for the sins of men. Take it on and fight against the Serpent for the time is fast approaching when the first should be the last, the last should be the first.[27]

In August of 1831, in Southampton, Virginia, Nat Turner placed himself at the head of a band of 70 rebels and ransacked the town, killing more than fifty white slave owners and their family members.[28] But the insurrection was quickly put down and Turner was arrested. At his trial, he stated that the time and place for attacks on slave owners had been divinely revealed to him. He went on to explain that on the day of the rebellion an eclipse of the sun, together with what appeared to be dried blood on tree leaves and strange atmospheric conditions that produced a colorful haze in the air in the early morning, were signs from God that the time had come to overthrow the slave system.

The cases narrated above clearly illustrate how the Bible message, or more specifically, the emerging African liberation theology, instigated slave revolts. The leaders of these acts of resistance were preachers who had a vast knowledge of the Bible. Their relatively comfortable stations in life did not undermine their determination to seek freedom for their people. The age of African or Black Christian Liberation Theology had dawned.

Although blacks in bondage in the Americas used religion to fight white brutality, it must be stated that Black churches developed under very different circumstances. Also, it must not be forgotten that early Black churches were not equally committed to the principle of liberation. Some were militant and others moderate even though they all had their eyes on the goal of achieving equal rights for all worshippers. These were some of the Black churches that steered the course of the Independence Movement in Africa and the Civil Rights Movement in the United States. The separate or breakaway churches acted as centers for the development of Black Nationalism, where black nationalists sought refuge from white racism. Breakaway churches were similar to slave churches which, according to Stephen Oates, were not only the centers of underground plotting against the master class, but also "the focal point of an entire subterranean culture the blacks sought to construct beyond the white man's control."[29]

MANIFESTATIONS OF AFRICAN CHRISTIAN LIBERATION THEOLOGY ON THE AFRICAN CONTINENT

Before Ethiopian churches began to spring up on the African continent, many blacks on both sides of the Atlantic Ocean had established contacts among themselves, even during the peak period of the slave trade. As far back as 1774, before the American war of independence, many Africans had traveled to the United States, some of them registering at American Negro colleges.[30] At the same time, some Africans in the Americas visited the African continent periodically. These contacts increased, especially after the Emancipation proclamations of the first half of the nineteenth century, when thousands of blacks returned to Africa from Brazil, the West Indies, and the United States. This influx of returnees resulted in the strengthening of religio-political ties between continental Africans and the Africans of the diaspora.

The Ethiopian churches they established on arrival in Africa provided the African returnees with the necessary forum to assert their identity in the face of an emerging European colonial presence in the last quarter of the nineteenth century. As African-Americans used the Black churches to protest slavery and racism, so did continental Africans of the early colonial period use the African churches as training grounds for African nationalism. The more repressive the colonial regime, the greater was the appeal of African churches. This was particularly so in Angola, the Congo, South Africa, Nigeria, and Ghana, where political protests were expressed through the Ethiopian churches.

Meanwhile, partly because of the activities of Africans returning from the Americas, and partly because of the evangelical drive of European Christian missionaries, a sizable number of continental Africans converted to Christianity in the nineteenth century. Most of these converts were confined to the coastal towns of western and southern Africa such as Free Town,

Accra, Lagos, Cape Town and Natal. Some of them teamed up with European missionaries to push the Christian faith into the interior, preaching the Gospel and building schools at the same time. By the early 1900s, hundreds of thousands of Africans had been partially assimilated into European cultures through these endeavors. These half-assimilated Africans are sometimes described as Western-educated elite or westernized Africans. Some of their common traits included a dislike for agricultural life and a strong tendency to work as teachers, clergymen, lawyers, civil servants, journalists, doctors and engineers. They dressed like Europeans and, because of their Christian upbringing, they shunned African institutions like polygamy.

The Western-educated Africans suffered from a severe psychological problem, however. They admired European culture, but were everlastingly disappointed that no matter how much they mimicked the ways of the white man, the Europeans never treated them as equals. Commenting on this phenomenon, Lawrence Levine stated that "the reward of imitating whites were never very certain.... The world of the whites, attractive [to slaves and colonial subjects alike] as it might appear at times, offered little but the certainty of arbitrary and perpetual enslavement and inequality."[31] Though assimilated to the white man's world, these educated Africans soon realized that assimilation contained strong elements of subordination. Neither the French, nor the English, nor the Portuguese were ready to treat them as equals.

Thus, to correct the wrongs, many Western-educated Africans agreed to resist European racism and economic exploitation. Rather than resort to armed rebellion, as the peasant masses were doing, they adopted a strategy involving intellectual and religious revolutions. These modes of resistance were non-violent; they were consistent with the principles on which the Ethiopian churches were formed.

Ethiopianism and the new intellectual revolution developed, therefore, in reaction to pseudo-scientific racist theories, which stated, among other things, that Africans were inferior to Europeans because of their skin color. This theory was reinforced by the Hermitic Hypothesis, which stated that the Hermitic people, an alleged branch of the Caucasian race, had brought everything useful in Africa there. The Ethiopian churches stood up against such bodies of misinformation.

Some Africans justified the founding of Ethiopian churches on the grounds that European Christian missionaries confused race with religion and were quick "to identify technical superiority with spiritual superiority." Believing that the European Christian theology was irrelevant and harmful to Africa, African theologians insisted that "African Christianity, in order to play its part in emergent Africa must work out its own theology from its own experience."[32]

Some believed that the new African Christian theology would benefit not only Africa but world Christianity as well. Those who propagated this idea explained that in most African separatist sects, there was a return to ancient rituals that were fundamentally closer to the ancient Christian rituals that were practiced by the early Christian fathers. They argued that European Christianity had failed to solve the racial problem that slavery created. European colonial conquest and exploitation of Africa, they insisted, compounded this problem.[33]

Ethiopianism inspired the birth of many African churches. Controlled by Africans themselves, the leaders of these churches introduced into them certain rituals and doctrines that conformed to African cultures. The Ethiopian churches uplifted the Africans, rather than degrade them. The leaders of these religious movements emphasized "self-improvement, self-rule, and political rights," insisting at the same time on "the self-government of the African Church under African leaders."[34] By the beginning of the twentieth century, Ethiopianism had become a powerful and revolutionary instrument of resistance against European racism and cultural imperialism, even though it stuck to the principle of non-violence.

Since Ethiopianism and the new intellectual revolution were carried out by peaceful means, the armed rebellion of Rev. Chilembwe of Malawi was both an exception and a sign of things to come. Chilembwe had accompanied the radical European evangelist, Reverend Booth, to the United States in 1897 and was ordained a priest soon after. When he returned to Malawi, he established a mission post, a school and a farm for youths but he was appalled by the hypocrisy of the colonial administration that exploited helpless African peasants rather than "uplift them." Chilembwe described colonialism as "a mockery of Christianity," and when the First World War broke out, he criticized the Europeans for forcing poor Africans to participate in a conflict that did not concern them. He also called upon the citizens of the world to witness this shameful practice of sending poor Africans to die for a cause that was not theirs.[35] In January 1915, when he could no longer stomach the endless exploitation and oppression of the Africans, he declared war on the British rulers of Malawi. His rebellion was quickly crushed, however. He also lost his life in the conflict.

Chilembwe's rebellion seems to have attracted much attention even though similar eruptions occurred in the Congo, Uganda, Nigeria and elsewhere. In parts of Nigeria, for instance, some communities thought that the outbreak of the First World War signaled the time to drive the British out of Nigeria. At the same time, and throughout the colonial period, the leaders of African churches never tired of using their congregations as platforms for expressing political discontent, even though they rejected the principle of armed rebellion. Closely linked to the Ethiopian church movement was the rise of millenarian churches. Three examples come from the Congo and Angola where African Christian liberation theologians used their knowledge of the Bible to battle European domination. Three excellent examples come from the Congo and Angola regions.

DONA BEATRIZ

As already mentioned, the Congo and Angola regions were among the first African regions to develop a brand of African Christian liberation theology during the last five hundred years. While some African women like Nanny of Jamaica used their knowledge of African traditional religions to resist European domination in the diaspora, others like Dona Beatriz of the Congo used Black Christian liberation theology for similar purposes. It is interesting to note that Nanny's resistance against British slave owners of Jamaica began at about the same time that Dona Beatriz mounted her resistance against the Portuguese who enslaved the Congolese. It is also important to remark that a century before Richard Allen and his black followers started the Bethel African Methodist Episcopal Church in the city of Philadelphia (July 1794), Dona Beatriz had launched in the Congo a Christian religious movement known as "The Antonians." This name derived from her claim that she had had visions of St. Anthony "who gave her his spirit and a new understanding of the Christian religion."[36]

John K. Thornton, who has made a detailed study of the life of Dona Beatriz, has stated that the Antonian movement she started was aimed not only at "ending a long-lasting civil war and reestablishing a broken monarchy," but was also a popular movement directed against the slave trade from the region.[37] The endless wars, intrigues and betrayal among the ruling elite helped to shape Dona's political and religious thought and action. She had hardly turned into an adult when she began to see visions, which some Congolese interpreted as spiritual gift.

Dona Beatriz stood up against the false teaching of European missionaries as well as the Portuguese slave dealing in the Congo-Angola region. She suspected that the actions of the Catholic priests in the political and personal realms might have been motivated by selfish ends. For in the Congo, Roman Catholic priests exercised a wide range of unprecedented powers. For instance, the Capuchins had the effrontery to insist that because they were the servants of God, they had to be "strictly respected by every Congolese, even by the King and the nobility." Consequently, the priests tried to place themselves above the laws of the Congo.

The Catholic fathers did not protest enslavement. They all knew that chiefs who made war knew that wars always resulted in the capture of people as slaves. In fact, Catholic fathers often claimed that enslavement was "a just punishment, which the Church itself had specified as appropriate for hardened *ndokis* (witches)."[38]

On the other hand, for the chiefs and the aristocratic families, the trade in captives was driven by consideration of profit. With the profits they derived from the trade, the nobility bought hats and other disposable fancy materials, and made "no distinction between the innocent and the guilty." In the event of a war, anyone, combatants and non-combatants became objects of enslavement. The countryside was depopulated because of the fear of enslavement by advancing armies that foraged for food and supplies. In the battlefield, the opposing armies enslaved each other. The most affected were the numerous porters who were inadequately armed and whose numbers included many women and children. Victory in war meant the capture and enslavement of thousands of people.[39] "Slaves were valuable throughout the Kongo," noted Thornton, "for they provided additional workers on the lands of their owners and potentially allow the fielding of large armies or the population of large areas."[40] It is only with the knowledge of these events that we can begin to understand the political and religious mission, that is, the liberation theology of Dona Beatriz.

Dona Beatriz believed that blacks had no business mixing with whites because the latter's only mission in the Congo was to enslave people. Blacks must, therefore, form their own separate churches and institutions. Along with the Antonians, Dona Beatriz endeavored to restore the old capital of the nation, Sao Salvador that had gone into decay as a result of Portuguese slaving activities. She also resisted the Portuguese misrepresentation of Christianity among the Bakongo and the false teachings of Portuguese missionaries.

Dona Beatriz (or Kimpa Vita) was born to a noble family and was converted to Christianity as a result of the work of early Portuguese missionaries, who, at that time, concentrated their energies in converting the members of the royal families. Like

many African communities that embraced Christianity at that
time (and even to this day), the new religion conferred on them a
false sense of superiority over their non-Christian neighbors. For
in much of Africa, Christianity exposed its adherents to Western
education, European languages, a feeling of belonging to an
assumed superior foreign culture and an exploitative mode of
production that was capitalist driven. The more Beatriz studied
the scriptures, the more she uncovered what she perceived to be
the false teaching of the white missionaries. She became convinced that Christianity was rooted in African traditions, but
rather than acknowledge this fact, the Portuguese distorted it to
suit their own purposes. For example, she charged that the Capuchins were not telling the Nativity story correctly. The correct
story, she said, was that Jesus was a black man, born in the Congo.
His birthplace was the royal city of Sao Salvador, and when the
catechism mentioned Bethlehem, it was this city that was meant.
Also, the claim that Jesus was baptized in Nazareth was not the
true story; the real place of his baptism was the northern province of Nsundi. Dona Beatriz insisted that Jesus and Mary were
actually Congolese.[41]

Dona Beatriz also preached that Saint Anthony was the most
important saint. She warned that Jesus was angry and was about
to unleash his punishment. But the Congolese who followed
Saint Anthony needed not be afraid of the impending disaster.
She claimed that Saint Anthony had taken over her body, adding
that her arrival meant that the Congo could have saints of their
own just as Europeans did.[42] She found justification for her
thought, as she testified, when Saint Anthony appeared to her,
not in the form of a white man, but a black man.

Her utterances not only meant that she was revising the
history of the Church, they also meant that she was reforming it.
For instance, she urged the introduction of a new, truer version
of prayers. Furthermore, in her teachings, she denied the power
of the sacraments. What mattered, she claimed, was the intention of the believer rather than the performance of sacraments.

Like many Congolese of her time, Dona Beatriz could not understand why the missionaries should have portrayed Jesus, the Virgin Mary and the saints as Europeans when in fact they were not. Furthermore, she was unhappy because the Catholic priests who performed mass at congregations in the Congo were Europeans. Beatriz therefore decided to preach the re-Africanization of the scriptures and the abrogation of all the falsehoods that the Portuguese had added onto them.

Dona Beatriz was not a mere visionary who tried to manipulate the Bible story for her own selfish ends. Instead, she was a realist, a liberation theologian, who was disturbed by Portuguese adventurers who used the teachings of Christ to conceal their imperial designs on the continent of Africa. The erosion of Congolese culture, which the agents of Portuguese imperialism had set in motion, also perturbed her.

Dona Beatriz stood in opposition, not only to the Portuguese, but also to the king of the Congo who could not protect his people against the Portuguese slave raiders and traders. Like many aristocrats of his day, the king behaved like the Portuguese with whom he collaborated to trade in slaves and to provoke inter-group conflicts whose sole purpose was to harvest captives.

But trouble was brewing fast. Sao Salvador was a great city, reputed to have been inhabited by nearly 100,000 people. However, the city had been sacked in 1678 and almost all its inhabitants had fled. The fear of further attacks prevented many people from settling there. In its hay day, the city had public squares, cathedrals and stone buildings. However, since its abandonment, it had been overtaken by dense bush and large herds of wild animals. Everyone wished that the city should be restored but felt that a restoration could not take place while evil and selfish people retained the power to make the decisions.[43] Dona decided to bypass these "evil and selfish people" and go on with the restoration effort, not by force, but by moral persuasion.

She was destined to run into a grave problem, however. For apart from annoying the Catholic Church by her religious zeal, she was now stepping on the toes of the nobility when she decided to lead the restoration movement. For example, King Pedro IV was also anxious to undertake the restoration of the city. He was sure that God and Saint Francis had selected him (not Dona Beatriz) as the means by which the cathedrals of Sao Salvador would be restored.[44]

Responding to Dona Beatriz's call for reconciliation and reconstruction of Sao Salvador, people flocked into the city that had been avoided like a plague. They now were ready to either worship with the Antonians or to participate in the rebuilding effort that was going on there. And as her popularity soared, so did the capital city grow in size. Euphoria and excitement were so high that a European observer described Dona Beatriz as "the restorer, ruler, and lord of the Congo."[45]

Some community leaders allied themselves with Dona Beatriz but many more remained loyal to the Portuguese and the Pope in Rome. Although King Pedro IV opposed her teachings, he showed some reluctance to arrest her, despite mounting pressure from the Portuguese and the Roman Catholic Church. The king's uneasiness increased day by day as Dona Beatriz's power and popularity waxed. The Portuguese continued to pressure King Pedro to arrest her. Eventually he did but not before he had became fully aware of the political implications of the movement that Dona Beatriz had launched. Arrested and then charged with heresy, Dona Beatriz was sentenced to death on July 2, 1706.[46] She was burned alive on a stake, with her infant baby clenching mortally to her chest.

If the purpose of true revolutions is to overthrow existing corrupt systems, then Dona Beatriz was one of Africa's true revolutionaries. Again, if liberation theology is an attempt to transform religion into a powerful instrument for political struggle or to use religion to emancipate the masses from the grips of their oppressors and exploiters, then Dona Beatrice was a true liberation theologian. We must, therefore, remember Dona Beatrice as a revolutionary and a liberation theologian who attempted to re-Africanize Christianity in the Congo as well as provide the

Africans with the psychological tools to withstand European cultural, political and economic violence.

The death of Dona Beatriz did not put an end to the development of African liberation theology in Africa, which continued to develop, even during the peak period of the slave trade. As we have seen, the violent trade did not prevent blacks who lived on both sides of the Atlantic Ocean from establishing contacts among themselves and exchanging ideas about African liberation.

KIMBANGUISM: A CONGOLESE RELIGIOUS PROTEST MOVEMENT

Early Portuguese Christian missionary activity had produced a sizeable number of native African converts and a tradition of Christianity in the Congo despite the failure of the mission, which, as we have seen, was caused largely by Portuguese involvement in the Atlantic slave trade. Despite the failure and strained relations between the Congolese and the Portuguese, the former retained some amounts of Christian faith well into the last quarter of the nineteenth century. The Congolese retained their independence until the decisions reached by the Europeans at the Berlin Conference of 1884-85 gave the Portuguese an opportunity to resume their aggressive moves into the interior of Africa. But the new Portuguese aggression had to face a new form of African religious nationalism that began in the 1880s to sweep through Africa south of the Sahara. This religious nationalism was manifested in Ethiopian and millenarian church movements. It was within this religious nationalism that the Kimbanguist movement operated.

The founder of this Congolese-based movement was Simon Kimbangu. Born in 1889, Simon became a Christian in 1915 and then spent three years as an evangelist and teacher in a mission school where he advanced his knowledge of the Bible.[47] Kimbangu became a Baptist missionary and in 1918 he heard in his dream a voice proclaiming, "I am Christ. My servants are unfaithful. I have chosen you to bear witness before your brethren and to convert them. Tend My flock." Believing himself unworthy of the responsibility, Kimbangu avoided it for three years. His indecision and doubts finally melted away on April 6, 1921, when, passing through a neighboring village, he chanced upon a woman who was critically ill. Kimbangu entered the woman's home, "laid his hands on her and healed her in the name of Jesus Christ."[48] Kimbangu is believed to have performed numerous other miraculous acts in which he made the blind to see, the deaf to hear, the crippled to walk, and the dead to resurrect. The story of these deeds spread far and wide and marked the beginning of the Kimbanguist movement. "As far as the followers of Kimbangu were concerned," noted Marie-Louise Martin, "nothing less than a new Pentecost had come. The Holy Spirit had evidently descended on Simon Kimbangu and had given him authority to heal and to preach."[49]

The political and racial implications of these healing miracles are evident; they were spectacular in the sense that they were performed within the Christian tradition. Some Africans interpreted this to mean that God had now revealed his power in the very heart of Africa, and therefore, Christianity was not a religion of any particular race. Neither Kimbangu nor his apostles claimed that Kimbangu was Christ; instead, they said that Christ appeared through Kimbangu in the Congo. He preached obedience to God, and he admonished his followers to have faith in Christ and to seek the kingdom of God.

Simon Kimbangu became famous almost overnight. Large numbers of people embarked on pilgrimages to N'Kamba, his residence. European capitalists, missionaries and colonial officials were infuriated when workers abandoned their tasks to join the pilgrims. Fearing that a revolt was brewing, and that the religious movement would turn into a political movement, Europeans decided to take action. On the first day of June 1921, less than two months after Kimbangu performed his first healing miracle, the Belgian administration assembled the leaders of the Catholic and Protestant missions in Mbanza-Ngungu and requested them to repudiate Kimbangu and other prophetic movements.[50] The next day (June 2, 1921) an order for the arrest of Kimbangu and his associates was issued. The attempt to arrest Kimbangu sparked the very trouble that the government wanted to avert. The country was on the brink of a major uprising. A skirmish occurred between soldiers and civilians in N'Kamba when railway workers and civil servants threatened to go on strike. Some prominent Protestants schemed to take over the Kimbanguist movement as Kimbangu went into hiding and was shielded by the peasants. Many arrests were made and the supporters of other prophetic movements came out in the open.

However, after evading the Belgian officials for three months, Kimbangu turned himself in. He claimed to have heard the voice of God saying, "Return to N'Kamba to be arrested." His followers had tried to persuade him to the contrary but Kimbangu insisted on going to see the authorities. He even exhorted his followers to face suffering courageously, not to use violence and not to repay evil with evil. [51]

Simon Kimbangu was arrested, tried, and then sentenced to 120 lashes and death. King Albert of Belgium reduced the sentence to 120 lashes and life imprisonment. Kimbangu began to serve his imprisonment in November of 1921 in Elisabethville where he remained for thirty years until his death in 1951.

Kimbangu's decision to turn himself in has some remarkable parallels with the life of Jesus Christ, especially in regard to re-enacting the arrest, torture, sentencing, and condemnation to death of Jesus Christ. To many Congolese, there were other parallels. Simon Kimbangu, like Jesus Christ, was a man of peace. Moreover, as the Europeans condemned Jesus Christ to death, as represented by Pontius Pilate, so did Kimbangu suffer death at the hands of Europeans, as represented by the Belgians. These feelings reinforced Congolese resentment for European colonialism. It is evident that the martyrdom of Kimbangu reinforced the Congolese appeal for the Black Church and advanced the development of the black culture of resistance.

In keeping with the teachings of Jesus Christ, Kimbanguists accepted the principles of love, non-violence and obedience to authority. Kimbanguists agreed to obey those in authority, to love their enemies, and to repay evil with kindness. They obeyed these rules so rigidly that in 1925 the solicitor general of the colony noted that "[Kimbanguists] pay their taxes promptly and [are] exemplary subjects."[52] Though impressed by the Kimbanguists' peaceful and law-abiding posture, the colonial authorities still refused to grant them religious freedom. To the Portuguese imperialists, religious freedom, like all forms of freedom, was inimical to the successful implementation of colonial policies.

The "Church of Christ on Earth through the Prophet Simon Kimbangu," under the leadership of Simon Kimbangu's youngest son, Joseph Diangienda, created many splinter organizations and suffered persecution in the Congo for forty years before being accorded official recognition. During this time, many Kimbanguists became members of Protestant or Catholic churches while either meeting secretly with their fellow Kimbanguists or waiting patiently for the call to return to their faith. When the time came, the Kimbanguist church emerged as one of the largest organized churches in post-colonial Congo.

Until then, the Kimbangu church allowed its members to join political parties, and to express their political views without fear. This was a different policy from that of the Tokoist church, which we will discuss presently. Furthermore, the Kimbanguists opened their doors to people of all races.[53] This was a shrewd move, intended to reassure European racists that the movement was not anti-white. Although the church portrayed itself as a purely religious organization, colonial government officials still suspected that the Kimbanguists were subversives who ought to be silenced. The authorities had other reasons to be disturbed by the growth of this Pentecostal movement whose members were willing to suffer persecution for the sake of religious freedom. The authorities knew that a people who today are ready to endure persecution for the sake of religious freedom will tomorrow endure persecution for the sake of political freedom. It was only in 1959, after a long struggle, that the Kimbanguists were finally granted religious immunity and placed at the same level as Catholics and Protestants.[54] Until then, the Kimbanguists stuck to their belief that God had sent them an African prophet to deliver them from the evils of colonialism. The advent of Kimbanguism and its puritan program, wrote Alfredo Margarido, "was set up to oppose white enterprise through a new rationalization of the Congolese societies. In addition, even if Simon Kimbangu never preached Congolese nationalism, members soon identified the new church with the ancient Kongo kingdom, the greatest myth in the history of the Bakongo population."[55]

THE TOKOIST MOVEMENT: RELIGION AND RESISTANCE IN ANGOLA

One of the offshoots of Angolan resistance to Portuguese colonialism was the Tokoist Messianic and syncretic movement. It was born within the Bakongo community at the time when the "Church of Christ on Earth through the Prophet Simon Kimbangu" was suffering from its forty years of persecution.

Simao Toko was the founder of the Tokoist movement. Like Simon Kimbangu, Toko was a Bakongo, a baptized Christian, and a product of Christian mission schools. After his education, Toko worked as a teacher among his people before embarking on his missionary work, which rapidly resulted in a religious movement.

The Tokoist movement provided the Angolans with the opportunity to criticize both traditional institutions and imported colonial systems. The peasants had waged anti-European wars in Angola but their loyalties were to the ethnic groups, as the modern Angolan nationality had not yet been formed. For three centuries, as we have seen, the Portuguese exploited Angolan ethnic disunity to secure slaves who were shipped off in chains to Brazil and other Portuguese colonies.

By the 1870s, wrote Alfredo Margarido, a new breed of Angolan intellectuals and city dwellers had begun to construct an Angolan nationalism and to discover what it meant to be black in a racially divided society like Angola. They discovered that what was valuable to the "Angolan nation" was inconsistent with Portuguese interests. Trapped between traditional values and the realities of life in a colonized society, Angolans began to seek an explanation for the unequal distribution of wealth, which characterized colonial society. They did not find the answers in the real world, so they sought it elsewhere, in religion and myth.[56]

One of the more vivid and painful grievances had to do with the impact of the slave trade on Angola. The Portuguese enterprise, especially their manipulation of the slave trade, had overturned everything that was of value to the Angolans. The sheer loss in numbers to family-based social structures had undermined Angolan stability and independence and created deep tensions in its social and political fabrics.

The Tokoists believed that white rule was the root of all suffering in African societies. They believed that Africans were capable of doing good but could not demonstrate this virtue because of white domination. The Tokoists then concluded that if an African society functioned badly, it was not because it was fundamentally bad, but because the whites had imposed foreign regulations upon it. Therefore they (the blacks) had become accomplices in the destruction of African society.[57]

Despite their hatred for white domination, however, the Tokoists preached obedience to colonial authority because it was "in their best interest to be obedient to all authority." Though critical of white rule, the Tokoists recognized that white society had organizational qualities that enabled it to rule. The Tokoists insisted that their church would have a dual function. "It must not only find its Angolan identity, but also seek to appropriate the logic and organizational ability of the whites."[58]

The Tokoists avoided direct political opposition to colonial authority, not only because of their awareness of its strength, but also because of "the weakness of their own position." To the Tokoist, pacifism did not mean inaction or docility. They argued that Africans should be aware of the political situation and use it to seek solutions to problems. Africans must recognize that white men crush people even though their contributions to human development may be beneficial. White men may run efficient political, technical and economic institutions, yet they are an established evil, which must be destroyed. Above all, the beneficial institutions of the whites must be appropriated, not blindly imitated.[59]

The Tokoists therefore advocated a total separation of the black person from the white person's world because, while the white world was a world of politics, of the profane, the black world was a world of the sacred. The Tokoists then argued that to avoid the white man was to escape from evil and to return to the basic goodness of the Africans. Whites must, of necessity, be kept out of the Tokoist church, because the world of the whites was a world of regulations. "The whites set up revenue regulations, police regulations, work systems, and laws for everything."[60]

Margarido states that by exposing their followers to a thorough comprehension of colonial order, and by fostering passive yet dangerous resistance, the Tokoists made an invaluable contribution to Angolan resistance to Portuguese rule. By rejecting all political activity, they summoned the faithful not to concern themselves with the particular political situation in Angola. And by separating themselves from the world of the white man, the Tokoist created a dualism in society which was inimical to the functioning of a biracial society, capable of breeding mistrust between the rulers, who were white, and the ruled, who were black. Furthermore, by obeying colonial regulations, the Tokoist found the justification to insist that Portuguese administrators adhered strictly to the rules established by colonialism itself. Because of their knowledge of the working of colonialism and their refusal to resort to armed violence, their criticism of the colonial system was taken seriously by the Portuguese authorities.[61] The Tokoists adopted a legal strategy of protest and were able to exert some amount of control over the activities of colonial administrators. Yet, the Tokoist movement produced another unexpected benefit. The Tokoists, who became disillusioned or frustrated by the pacific stance of Tokoist philosophy, became the militants who spearheaded the war of liberation in Angola. Though the Tokoists continued to detach themselves from politics, insisting on the separation of the sacred from the profane, the Tokoist church succeeded in exposing its followers to "the reality of colonialism," and in spreading the spirit of protest.[62]

Like the Kimbanguists, the Tokoists studied the Bible and led pious lives. They also studied colonial society, which enabled them to work out their relationships with it. Like the Kimbanguists, the Tokoists promoted Bakongo unity and provided the masses an alternative platform upon which nationalist agitation could be carried out. Furthermore, both movements tried to reconstitute Bakongo family structure and clan organizations that had been shattered by centuries of slavery and colonialism. Although they endeavored to live peacefully within the colonial structure, they ensured that they were not part of it. The Tokoists, in particular, advocated a total separation of the black person from the white person's world. However, while the Kimbanguists insisted that the tie that bound the new extended African family should be Christianity, the Tokoists insisted that the tie was Angolan nationalism. Finally, both the Tokoists and Kimbanguists were black separatists but, while some black separatists like the Nation of Islam advocated the creation of a separate territory for blacks on American soil, the Kimbanguists and Tokoists wanted to avoid the world of the white man on African soil.

Until this day, black Christians all over Africa and the Americas have continued to fight European racism, usually by non-violent means. As they combat white racism, however, they remain conscious of the fact that Christianity did not create racism. They know that slavery created racism. Black Christians are angry, not with Christianity, but with European Christians who have failed to solve the problems created by slavery, racism and colonialism. Black churches are against the hypocrisy of European Christians who preach love and unity in Christ but practice racial discrimination. The historical roles that the Black Church, especially African Christian liberation theology, has carved out for itself are to right these age-long wrongs and to make Christianity play the historical role that Jesus Christ wanted it to play. It was also to re-Africanize all African Christian converts who had strayed from the rightful path when they placed their faith on the very

Europeans who degraded and oppressed them. The problem with the early white missionaries was that they went to Africa with preconceived negative ideas. One of them was that everything about the continent was evil, hence the expression, "the Dark Continent."[63] As we have seen, the early missionaries claimed the right to smash whatever they considered as heathen practices or witchcraft among the Africans. The Europeans also believed that every African was ignorant and backward and therefore in dire need of the paternalistic guidance of the Europeans. Nor must we forget the pervasive notion of white superiority over blacks. Such unfounded notions were capable of breeding mistrust and conflict. This certainly explains why black-white relations were never altogether cordial.

Notes

1. Eric R. Wolf, *Peasant wars of the twentieth century* (New York, Harper & Row, 1969), 224.
2. Luke 6: 27-30.
3. Frantz Fanon, *The Wretched of the Earth* (New York: Penguin, 1967), 42.
4. Asghar Ali Engineer, "On Developing Liberation Theology in Islam," in Asghar Ali Engineer, (ed.), *Islam and Revolution* (Delhi: Janta Publications, 1984), 23.
5. *Ibid.,* 23.
6. *Ibid.,* 24.
7. Steve Biko, "Black Consciousness and the Quest for a True Humanity," in *Black Theology: The South African Voice,* edited by Basil Moore (Atlanta: John Knox Press, 1973), 43. See also J. N. K. Mugambi, *African Christian Theology* (Nairobi: Heinemann, 1989).
8. John K. Thornton, *The Kongolese Saint Anthony: Dona Beatriz Kimpa Vita and the Antonian Movement, 1684-1706* (Cambridge: Cambridge University Press, 1998), 71, 85-6.
9. Stuart B. Schwartz, "The Mocambo: Slave Resistance in Colonial Bahia," in Richard Price (ed.) *Maroon Societies: Rebel Slave Communities in the Americas* (Baltimore: Johns Hopkins University Press, 1979): 207n.

10. Quoted in Jean Fouchard, *The Haitian Maroons: Liberty or Death* (New York: Edward W. Blyden Press, 1981), 325.

11. *Ibid.* 325.

12. Owen Charles Mathurin, *Henry Sylvester Williams and the Origins of the Pan -African Movement, 1869-1911.* (Westport: Greenwood Press, 1976), 5.

13. Mechal Sobel, *Trabelin On: The Slave Journey to an Afro-Baptist Faith* (Westport: Greenwood Press, 1979), xvii.

14. *Ibid.,* xvii.

15. *Ibid.* xvii.

16. *Ibid.,* xvii-xviii.

17. *Ibid., xxiv.*

18. *Ibid.,* 125.

19. *Ibid.,* 124-25.

20. *Ibid.,* 124.

21. Chinua Achebe, *Things Fall Apart* (Portsmouth: Heinemann, 1996), 126-7.

22. Vincent Bakpetu Thompson, *Africa and Unity: the Evolution of Pan-Africanism* (London: Longman, 1969), 11.

23. Lawrence W. Levine, *Black Culture and Black Consciousness: Afro-American Folk thought from Slavery to Freedom* (New York: Oxford University Press, 1977), 75.

24. *Ibid.,* 75-6.

25. Mary Frances Berry, *Black Resistance/White Law: A History of Constitutional Racism in America* (New York: A Lane, 1994), 18-19.

26. Stephen B. Oates, *The Fires of Jubilee: Nat Turner's Fierce Rebellion* (New York: Harper and Row, 1975), 26.

27. *Ibid.,* 41.

28. Levine, *Black Culture and Black Consciousness,* 76-7.

29. Oates, *The Fires of Jubilee,* 25.

30. Thompson, *Africa and Unity.*

31. Levine, *Black Culture,* 139.

32. Quoted in Thompson, *Africa and Unity,* 11.

33. *Ibid.,* 11.

34. A. Adu Boahen, *African Perspectives on Colonialism* (Baltimore: The Johns Hopkins University Press, 1987), 72-3.

35. As quoted in *Ibid., 74-5.*

36. Marjorie W. Bingham and Susan H. Gross, *Women in Africa of the Sub-Sahara, Vol. I, From Ancient Times to the 20th Century* (St. Louis Park, MN: Glenhurst, 1982), 130.

37. Thornton, *The Kongolese Saint Anthony*, 1.

38. *Ibid.,* 90.

39. *Ibid.,* 98.

40. *Ibid.,* 99.

41. *Ibid.,* 113-14.

42. *Ibid.,* 112.

43. *Ibid.,* 53.

44. *Ibid.,* 71.

45. *Ibid.,* 130.

46. *Ibid.,* 130.

47. Marie-Louise Martin, *Kimbangu: An African Prophet and His Church* (Oxford: Basil Blackwell, 1975), 42-3.

48. *Ibid.,* 44-5.

49. *Ibid.,* 47.

50. *Ibid.,* 58.

51. *Ibid.,* 60.

52. *Ibid.,* 80.

53. *Ibid.,* 112.

54. *Ibid.,* 108.

55. Alfredo Margarido, "The Tokoist Church and Portuguese Colonialism in Angola" in Ronald H. Chilcote (ed.), *Protest and Resistance in Angola and Brazil: Comparative Studies* (Berkley: Univ. of California Press, 1972), 37.

56. *Ibid.,* 33.

57. *Ibid.,* 47.

58. *Ibid.,* 47.

59. *Ibid.,* 47.

60. *Ibid.,* 48.

61. *Ibid.,* 49.

62. *Ibid.,* 52.

63. See Philip Curtin, *The Image of Africa.*

Chapter 7

BLACK POPULAR MUSIC OF RESISTANCE IN THE USA: FROM BLUES TO RAP

BLUES

What makes one form of performance more culturally meaningful than the other depends on its cultural context, the peculiar circumstances surrounding its evolution, its historical value and the socio-political message it strives to convey. These facts are indispensable to an understanding of the art form known as Blues. The origins of Blues have been traced to West Africa. It was from there that Africans first transplanted this art into the semi-barren musical arena of the United States.

Africans in captivity led a sad life and had to accept music as one strategy for coping with their anguish. The available range of musical instruments was limited and, until they fashioned new ones for themselves, or adopted existing ones, they chanted their native songs. Sometimes referred to as work songs, these chants were rendered as call-and-response, or shouts and hollers. "The work song," wrote Tilford Brooks,

> was a part of African culture long before Blacks came to America, and it remained an integral part of Black culture long after their arrival in the New World. Thus the work song was present in the culture of the slaves earlier than any other form of music. Because it retained the greatest number of Africanisms, the

> work song forms a strong link between pure West
> African music and the music of the slaves.[1]

The work song eventually lost some of its African elements, partly because slave owners pressured slaves to give up their native cultures, and partly because of differences in language and ritual, as we saw in chapter three. Scholars are certain that Blues developed out of the slaves' work songs, spirituals and field hollers, and that all these musical forms were rooted in African traditions.[2] However, what scholars are not too certain about is the exact time that blues detached itself from its antecedents. Some believe that it occurred during the mid-nineteenth century; others place it in the last quarter of the nineteenth century. What scholars do agree on is that emancipation played an important role in the emergence of Blues as a distinct musical form.

The end of slavery, noted Brooks, brought with it many opportunities but not without some complications. First, it de-centralized the black community, which had been southern based. Second, it inserted blacks into a New World that was more complex and uncertain than the world of slavery. It was out of these social and cultural complexities and change that Blues was born. "With emancipation," wrote Brooks, "Blacks were promised freedom of the kind enjoyed by other Americans. The failure of Blacks to gain true freedom created the psychological milieu in which the blues was developed."[3] Emancipated blacks were confronted with the experience of being alone, for the first time. The work gangs had died with slavery; ex-slaves had to deal with the realities of the reconstruction era.

On the other hand, emancipation enabled most southern blacks to gain access to mobility, for the first time. The traveling musician now sang songs that reflected his or her new mood. The dominant themes of their songs were concerned with loneliness and hardship. It was at this time that "primitive" or "traditional" Blues was born. For the rest of the nineteenth century, however, the field hollers and "primitive" Blues remained intertwined in terms of structure.

John Rublowsky stated that once outside the plantation-based economy, many ex-slaves turned to music as a means of earning their livelihood, and bands of newly emancipated street musicians appeared throughout the south. No other American city, he stated, attracted these Black musicians more than New Orleans where bands proliferated.[4] They played "primitive" or "traditional" Blues, which was "almost a conscious expression of the Negro's individuality and equally important, his separateness," but as time went on, and as they traveled to distant cities, the "primitive" Blues singers had to adjust to changes in speech patterns to make themselves understood by other Americans. By the turn of the century, they could no longer detach themselves from the diverse sociological and musical influences of the new American society. They appropriated some of the elements of popular American music and, in the process, transformed "primitive" or "traditional" Blues into what, in the 1920s, became known as "classical" or "city" Blues.[5] Unlike traditional Blues, which had been an expression of the black person's loneliness and isolation, classical Blues was a statement about the new changes that were taking place in the wider American society. Thus, while primitive Blues belonged to the private domain, classical Blues belonged to the public sphere. The latter was an acknowledgment of the black person's new sense of time and place within the American society that had changed substantially since the days of the field holler.

Classical Blues was destined to change its form and become commercialized. The opportunities that came with the First World War persuaded many southern blacks to move northward in search of better economic well being. There was an expansion of industries in the North and many blacks moved into such cities as Chicago, Detroit, and New York, where they soon realized that Blues could be used to entertain people. Recording companies began to produce Blues music for the black market. The golden age of classical blues had come.

These happy moments would soon come to a sudden end, however. The Great Depression arrived in 1929, spreading unem-

ployment and hardships. Some disillusioned blacks returned to
the South.

The Second World War and its aftermath brought new
opportunities but could not resurrect the golden age of Classical Blues. Instead, it witnessed the emergence of Contemporary
Blues and Rhythm and Blues. These changes never altered the
fundamental role that Blues had been cut out to play. Blues never
lost its emphasis on the social and cultural messages that it always
tried to convey through its unique lyrical patterns. It remained
one of the ties that bound contemporary black society to the
work gangs and then to Africa.

Blues is a musical form that enabled blacks in America to
endure the crises of emancipation, reconstruction, and integration into the wider contemporary society of America. Both black
and white musicians today play or sing the Blues but, unfortunately, black musicians have profited little from their recordings.
Instead, white-owned recording companies favor white imitators
of Blues. Among these white imitators are the Rolling Stones,
the Beatles, Eric Clapton, and the Animals. Some of their songs
are taken from the original compositions of Black Blues singers
who receive little or no recognition or financial reward for their
efforts and creativity.[6]

CONTEMPORARY BLUES AND RHYTHM AND BLUES

Born after the Second World War, Contemporary Blues and
Rhythm and Blues (R&B) exhibited low level resistance qualities.
For one thing, the economic prosperity of the Post-World War Era
stifled most forms of protests until the second half of the 1950s,
when the Civil Rights Movement began. Moreover, blacks had
become sufficiently integrated into the main stream of American
society and had no real compelling reasons to protest their situation as blacks of the Reconstruction period did. Moreover, as the
American society became more and more mixed, blacks could no
longer monopolize Contemporary Blues and R&B as they had
done during the era of "Classical Blues." The names of the leading
Contemporary Blues and R&B artists of the 1950s through the

1970s clearly illustrate these assertions. It was only after the birth of Rap and Hip Hop in the late 1970s and early 1980s that black artists once again began to dominate R&B and to use both Rap and Hip Hop as instruments of protest.

RAP AND RESISTANCE IN CONTEMPORARY AMERICAN SOCIETY

Blues has played its historical role well, but many American youths may not be fully aware of its significance. Instead, many want to identify with a newer kind of music that is more relevant to today's society than the slave society in which their great-grand parents might have lived. Like most contemporary events, the true purpose of Rap (and Hip-Hop) is still being debated. My objective here is to explain Rap from the point of view of Rap artists, or from the point of view of those who research them, not from the eyes of those who have constructed a negative image of Hip-Hop culture.

It is important for students to see the connections among the five most universally popular musical forms--Jazz, Blues, Rhythm and Blues (R&B), Rock, and Rap. All of these musical forms have their roots in Africa. Rap, Rhythm and Blues, Rock, and Jazz are derived from Blues. As explained above, Blues is derived from the work songs and field hollers of enslaved Africans. It then went though certain transformations, from "primitive" blues to classical Blues, then to contemporary Blues and Rhythm and Blues. It was in New Orleans and several other cities of the southern states that classical Blues interfaced with certain Voodoo and Black spiritual music to produce Rock. Rap is a modified version of Rhythm and Blues but it makes a greater use of percussion sound. Jazz, the most sophisticated of all, is derived from an admixture of Blues, Spirituals and Voodoo sacred drums. It must be understood that the youngest of these popular American musical forms, Rock and Rap, came of age only in 1954 and 1974, respectively. Jazz, according to some observers, matured before 1913, while Blues, the oldest of them all, dates back to the Emancipation and Reconstruction periods (1861-1877). It is difficult for any modern popular music to escape the influence of Blues. For example, both American Country music and *Reggae* are derived from Blues and Rhythm and Blues.

Although Rap is related to Rhythm and Blues, its origins go even further back in time and space. Rapping is an ancient African tradition, an aspect of chanting that African captives took to the Americas. In West Africa, where the roots of Rap have been traced, Rap was part of praise singing and social commentary of griots. In South Carolina, the Gullahs still sing "rap" songs, which they inherited from their great-grand parents, who had brought the tradition from Africa. "Rap is not new at all, of course," insists Christopher Small, "but stems from the perennial admiration given in black culture to the possessor of highly developed speech skills."[7] This is understandable because African culture is an oral culture. In West Africa, those who possessed these skills, like the griots, were universally admired. Contemporary American rappers can be pictured as the descendents of these griots. Like the griots, rappers do not always praise; they also admonish and ridicule. Also like the griots, they keep records of historical events. Rap is used for record keeping; it can function as a historical text. Yet, it is a resistant music, a child of protest.

Like all musical forms, its primary function is to entertain, but beneath this purpose is an attempt to expose the ills of contemporary society. As Brian Cross has testified, "As a term that describes a colloquial way of speaking, rapping has been part of the social fabric of black America since English became a language of the slaves. This form, usually in rhyming couplets, is a powerful tool of resistance, a way of delineating community and of communicating history."[8]

Contemporary American Rap emerged from the black ghetto music of the 1970s. Some believe that it started in 1974 in the South Bronx, when Joseph Saddler (also known as Grandmaster Flash), began playing his DJ turntables in a nearby park. He was quickly copied by other youths in the New York area. However, it was not until 1979 that Sugar Hill Records of New Jersey, a company that had been floated by Sylvia Robinson, released a disc called "Rappers Delight." The disc went up the Pop charts to become a hit.[9]

The New York originators of contemporary Rap, it is further contended, were reacting to the tendency of the white middle-class to appropriate disco. They also were reacting to the decay that afflicted the Bronx when the middle-class white neighborhoods disappeared in the 1960, leaving behind a trail of decadence, crime and drug problems.[10] In due course, rappers rapped about the crisis of the inner-cities and their deteriorating class and race relations, along with junkies, hustlers, derelicts, bag ladies, and suicide.[11]

It is wrong to claim that Rap is all about resistance. Much of it deals with private matters. There is also a genre of rap that is capitalist driven. The perpetrators of this type of music are motivated by the quest for money and, so, care very little about the political and cultural value of what they rap about. These are the artists who promote sex, promote the drug habit, and glorify violence and ostentatious life-styles. They have no qualms calling every woman a hoe.

However, I have decided in this work to concern myself only with those aspects of rap music that contribute to political consciousness and the development of the black culture of resistance. I will be looking specifically at those aspects of the music that comment on such burning social and political issues as public education, police brutality, racial profiling, the crisis of the drug culture, the media, and public space. These aspects also dwell on the frustrations of black people in this unfair world, as well as the impediments that are placed on their way to socio-economic advancement. Among these artists are Dead Prez, Talib Kweli, Lauryn Hill, Tupac Shakur and many others. For example, Tupac Shakur, in a MTV talk interview stated: "My skin is my sin," by which he meant that it is a sin to be black in the United States. But what Tupac expressed in the 1990s had been common knowledge to African-Americans for a very long time. For instance, during the Second World War, African American soldiers serving in the European theaters of war were discriminated against and then treated worse than the German prisoners of war (PWOS) they might be guarding.[12] Moreover, although Tupac described having a black skin as a sin, others might consider it a heinous crime against humanity. Another case in point in 1945, when Walter Winchell asked a young black woman in Harlem how Adolph Hitler should be punished for his crimes against humanity, she replied, "Paint him black and send him over here."[13]

Rap artists are also quick to see the connections that link the systems of exploitation and dehumanization of the black people to the school and prison systems. As dead Prez puts it,

> Man that school shit is a joke
> The same people who control the school system
> Control the prison system, and the whole social
>   system
> Ever since slavery, know what I'm saying?

Because many pioneer Rap artists are raised in inner cities, they understand the plight of the poor very well. They know how dangerous and frustrating it can be to live in poverty in a wealthy country. The psychological impact of feelings of destitution and helplessness is well articulated by Tupac Shakur in his song, "I Got Nothing To Lose," in which he declared: "Do or die, walk a mile in my shoes and you would be crazy too with nothing to lose."[14] Martin Luther King Jr. attributed this sense of destitution to the evils of segregation to which Africans in America were subjected. "The segregation of the Negroes," said King, "with its inevitable discrimination, has thrived on elements of inferiority present in the masses of both white and Negro people. Through forced separation from our African culture, through slavery, poverty, and deprivation, many black men lost self-respect."[15] Rappers did not need Martin Luther King Jr. to teach them this aspect of Pan-African history. The evidence is everywhere in their neighborhoods.

Female rappers use their music to expose and ridicule sexism as well as other social ills. As Tricia Rose has pointed out, songs and music videos contain specific references to localized and current oppression.[16] In this regard, rappers can be seen as the voice of neglected inner-city communities. As B. Adler has explained, the language that rappers use acts as both poetry and journalism. Some rappers regard rap as "black America's CNN."[17]

Like many *Reggae* artists, some rap artists rap about Pan-African consciousness and solidarity, Dead Prez, for example, reminds his African- American audiences that they were Africans and not necessarily African-Americans. He therefore admonished them to anchor their identity on their original motherland, not in the artificially created community that exploited them. In his piece, I'm A African, Dead Prez proclaims:

> I'm a African, never a African-American
> Blacker than Black, I take it back to the origin.[18]

Dead Prez expounds his Pan-African idea by urging solidarity not only among all black people in Africa and the United states, but with every one in Puerto Rico, Haiti, Jamaica, New York, and California.

> No, it ain't about where you stay
> It's about the Motherland

Furthermore, like many *Reggae* artists, Rap artists believe that the economic and political systems of the West are repressive and exploitative to the extreme. They visualize a world that is divided into two: one occupied by the oppressors and the other by the oppressed, a world in which the oppressors are determined to exterminate the oppressed through brutality and scare tactics. However, unlike some *Reggae* artists who urge blacks to return to Africa, rappers admonish the oppressed to get organized wherever they might be and fight back. For example, Chuck D warns against white people's genocidal intentions and urges blacks to fight back. He sings:

> The Ku Klux Klan is on the loose
> Training their kids on machine gun use

Hot rod policemen
Zipping through the ghetto streets in jet mobiles
Trampling niggers
Killing babies/Beating sisters/ into miscarriages
Killing us whenever they want to
Scared/Scared/Scared/Scared all the time.
Surrounded by guns in worse shape than South Africa
Brothers we better get hip and come off this trip--
Warriors come forth and lead our people to freedom
. . .[19]

Some rappers visualize two worlds: one privileged and exploitative, the other, underprivileged and exploited. In the song,
"White Heaven/Black Hell," Public Enemy explains this division
and the relationship between the two:

Black History - white lie
Black athletes - white agents
Black preacher - white Jesus
Black drug dealer - white government
Black entertainers - white lawyers
Black police - white judge
Black business - white accountants
Black record company - white distribution
Black politicians - white president
Black genocide - white world

This characterization of a world divided into White Heaven
and Black Hell is reminiscent of Frantz Fanon's depiction of the
colonial world that is cut into two—one white, the other non-
white—one privileged, the other deprived. As Fanon put it,

The zone where the natives [non-whites] live is not
complementary to the zone inhabited by the settlers
[whites]. The two zones are opposed, but not in the
service of a higher unity. Obedient to the rules of pure
Aristotelian logic, they both follow the principle of
reciprocal exclusivity. No conciliation is possible, for
of the two terms, one is superfluous. The settlers' town

is a strongly built town; all made of stone and steel. It is a brightly lit town; the streets are covered with asphalt, and the garbage cans swallow all the leavings, unseen, unknown and hardly thought about. . . . The settler's town is a well-fed town, an easygoing town; its belly is always full of good things. The settlers' town is a town of white people, of foreigners.

The town belonging to the colonized people, or at least the native town, the Negro village, the medina, the reservation, is a place of ill fame, peopled by men of evil repute. . . . It is a world without spaciousness; men live there on top of each other, and their huts are built one on top of the other. The native town is a hungry town, starved of bread, of meat, of shoes, of coal, of light. The native town is a crouching village, a town on its knees, a town wallowing in the mire. It is a town of niggers and dirty Arabs.[20]

Rap artists do not need to read Frantz Fanon to either visualize the world as one big mass in which one group wants to exterminate the other, or to see it as a place that is divided between exploiters and the exploited. What is important is that Rap artists are able to reassert black identity and to publicize the frustrations of the black masses through music. They show a strong misgiving for the constant distortion of the black image by whites who happen to control the television network, the press, radio, public libraries, and the school system. The media, they charge, is the supreme organ of deceit and manipulation. It manipulates the self-consciousness of the masses and renders them easy to control. The victims of the media do not believe any thing unless it is carried by the television network, the radio or the newspaper. Some Rap artists, therefore, warn against an uncritical acceptance of the information that the media spreads.

Rap artists not only denounce the media's misrepresentation of black people, but they also call attention to the poor public services that state and public officials provide black communi-

ties. In its song, "911 is a Joke," Public Enemy exposes a painful
daily experience.

> Hit me, going, going, gone
> Now I Dialed 911 a long time ago
> Don't you see how late they're reactin'
> They only come and they come when they wanna
>
> 911 is a joke we don't want 'em
> I call a cab 'cause a cab will come quicker
> [The technicians] flick you off like fleas
> They be laughin' at ya while you're crawlin' on your
>   knees.

This song ridicules the familiar lateness of 911 ambulances and
the deplorable attitudes of some medical professionals towards
poor blacks. It might be a true account of certain personal experiences, but because blacks are not always able to change official
attitudes, rappers let out the collective frustration through music.
However, realizing that officials can reprimand them and censure
their works, Rap artists often disguise their resistant messages in
coded speech. They have no difficulty in doing so because the
black community as a whole is skilled in the use of mainstream
and non-mainstream languages.[21]

Although Rap artists speak up against certain ills of society,
many Americans, including some blacks, find their brand of
music extremely distasteful. Rappers have been called promoters
of sexism and violence against women, children, and law enforcement agents. The term "gangsta rap" is revolting to some who
insist that nothing good can come out of gangs, forgetting that
rappers live in a hostile world and cannot easily detach themselves
from what goes on around them. As we have seen, contemporary
Rap was born in an age of urban decay in addition to worsen-
ing class, race and gender relations in American society. Nelson
George has, in this regard, warned that it is futile to blame the
ever-widening circles of violence on rappers or on black youths.
Commenting on the violence that broke out at a Rap concert in

Long Island on September 10, 1987, George charged that no one tried to understand that deadly conflict was a symptom rather than the cause of violence. "They wanted to blame the kids. They wanted to blame rap."[22] In any case, the most outrageous cases of shooting in the United States, including those that occurred in 1999 at a high school, at several work places, in a church, and at a Jewish center were not instigated or perpetrated by Rap artists.

Some sections of society find rappers' language offensive to an extreme. The most criticized Rap groups are those that deliver their messages in a less-disguised language. For example, the mere title of the song, "Fuck the Police," by NWA of Los Angeles, is enough to turn many Americans against the group, even when it sings about the familiar allegation of police brutality and harassment. Part of the song states:

> Fuck the police commin' straight from the under-
> ground
> A young nigger got it bad 'cause I'm brown
> And not the other color
> Some police think
> They have the authority to kill a minority
> Fuck that shit 'cause I ain't the one
> For a punk motherfucker with a badge and a gun.

Some critics may charge that the language used in this song is indecent. Others may point out that it is not different from the language that certain groups in American society use and understand. That this type of language is also used on TV comedies and even in Hollywood movies is an indication that it may be a language that is commonly used and understood by many Americans. After all, commented one observer, Rap takes ordinary street language, uses it in a poetic way and brings it back to the street. Nor can we lose sight of the fact that the main consumers of Rap music are young white males from the suburbs. Certainly, these white consumers of Rap understand and appreciate the language in which the music is rendered. Moreover, many white Rap groups have recently made Pop charts. In any case, what is important is that inner city youths (white, black and brown) fully relate to the message that rappers convey.

At any event, we are not as much concerned with "rap talk" as we are with its cultural value, especially in the context of black resistance and survival. Our interest here is that the black culture of resistance finds an outlet through Rap. Rap is an authentic, indigenous black art. Its birthplace is the South Bronx. From there Rap spread westward to Los Angeles and then to the rest of the country and beyond. Contemporary Rap music is now popular in Africa, Europe and Asia. In Japan, for instance, hundreds of Rap groups perform in clubs and public drinking places every night. Little did the originators of modern Rap, who spun out tunes from their turntables in the parks of South Bronx, realize that they were leaving an indelible mark on popular culture globally.

Be that as it may, some Rap lyrics provide American youths (black, white and brown) not only with entertainment, but also with a safe outlet for their frustrations. Some of these youths live in huge "concentration camps" or projects, ghettoes and slums. They witness all sorts of vice, especially drug dealing, alcoholism, and unnecessary death. They understand the problems of their community. They see drug pushers and the police take over their space. They are often the victims of what they perceive as police brutality. They also see themselves as the neglected majority. The government, they say, is doing too little to protect them. Menaced by the continual presence of the police, who encroach upon their freedom and privacy, these youths may as well rap than lose their minds. Other youths that live in affluent neighborhoods and are not in any way disturbed in the manner just described, also listen to Rap music—purely for entertainment and recreational purposes.

On the whole, however, Rap has enabled some black youths to reassert their separate identities, identities that are being threatened by the dominating white middle-class culture. Rap artists are also able to publicize what goes on in the inner cities, where the majority of blacks live and die. In this regard, Rap stands on the same artistic, cultural, and political levels *as Reggae,*

Samba, Capoeira, Rumba, Blues, and other black-resistant music and dances.

Notes

1. Tilford Brooks, *America's Black Musical Heritage* (Englewood Cliffs, NJ, 1984), 42-3.
2. *Ibid.,* 52.
3. *Ibid.,* 52.
4. John Rublowsky, *Black Music in America* (New York: Basic Books, 1971), 122.
5. Brooks, *America's Black Musical Heritage*, 56-8.
6. *Ibid.,* 185.
7. Christopher Small, *Music of the Common Tongue: Survival and Celebration in Afro-American Music* (London: John Calder, 1987), 391.
8. Brian Cross, *It's Not About A Salary: Rap, Race, and Resistance in Los Angeles* (New York: Verso, 1993), 3.
9. Arnold Shaw, *Black Popular Music in America: From the Spirituals, Minstrels, and Ragtime to Soul, Disco, and Hip-Hop* (New York: Schirmer Books, 1966), 292.
10. Cheryl L. Keyes, "At the Cross Roads: Rap Music and the African Nexus." *Ethnomusicology,* Vol. 40. No. 2, 1996, 226-9.
11. Shaw, *Black Popular Music in America*, 293.
12. Douglas T. Miller and Marion Nowak, *The Fifties: The Way We really Were* (Garden City, New York: Doubleday, 1977), 183.
13. *Ibid.,* 183.
14. See Alan Light (ed.) *The Vibe History of Hip Hop* (New York: Three River Press, 1999).
15. Martin Luther King, Jr., *I have a Dream: Writings and Speeches That Changed the World,* edited by James M. Washington. San Francisco: Harper, 1992, 4.
16. Tricia Rose, *Black Noise: Rap Music and Black Culture in Contemporary America* (Hanover: Wesleyan University Press, 1994), 123.
17. Janette Beckman, *Rap: Portraits and Lyrics of a Generation of Black Rockers* (New York: St. Martin's Press, 1991), xviii.
18. Dead Prez, I'm A African, in Let's Get Free album.

19. Anthony Hamilton (Father Amdee), "Kill," Black Voices on the Streets of Watts, 1971. (Reproduced in Cross, *It's Not About A Salary*), 9.

20. Frantz Fanon, *The Wretched of the Earth* (New York: Grove Press, 1977), 38-9.

21. Rose, *Black Noise,* 123.

22. Nelson George (ed.), *Stop the Violence: Overcoming Self Destruction* (New York: Pantheon Books, 1990), 11.

Chapter 8

BLACK MUSIC OF RESISTANCE IN SOUTH AFRICA, 1818-1994

INTRODUCTION: MUSIC, DANCE AND ANTI-COLONIAL PROTESTS IN AFRICA

Continental Africans have danced and sung songs for thousands of years, but the European colonial presence in the nineteenth and twentieth centuries ushered in new sets of songs and dances. Among the anti-colonial songs and dances were those that ridiculed colonial tax and labor systems. Colonized Africans sang about the useless and unrewarding white man's work, about the cruelty of recruiting officers who beat workers, and about the unnecessary death that often occurred in labor camps. Many hated the colonial armed forces and ridiculed Africans who served as soldiers. For instance, the Igbo people sang:

> *Nne muru soja amuro nnwa.*
> The mother of a soldier is a childless person.

Although formal colonialism ended in Africa decades ago, the older generations of workers still recall some anti-colonial songs that helped them cope with their ordeals. For example, the Igala people of Central Nigeria sang:

> *Ikpa ka ce ki ma nu'gwa,*

The road work that has no reward
Itali ce ugwa
The whip is the reward[1]

The Igbo of southeastern Nigeria sang:
Anyi jeko ibu okwute,
We are going to carry stones
Onye nwuru ozulike
One finds rest only after death
Obuzikwa olu oyibo?
Is that not what the white man's work is all about?

Because of the bizarre nature of the colonial labor system, many Nigerians have remained disenchanted with all forms of wage labor. They therefore describe all wage labor as "the white man's work," even when they work for other Nigerians or for their own governments. Wage labor is therefore dubbed *aikin bature* (Hausa), *olu oyibo* (Igbo) or *ise ijoba* (Yoruba).

In Kenya, Africans mocked not only the colonial labor system, but also Christian missionaries who interfered with local customs. For example, the anti-colonial association, *Karing'a,* developed dance-songs, known collectively as *muthiriga,* purposely to ridicule the missionaries and to reaffirm indigenous African traditions. Furthermore, during the Mau Mau uprising, freedom fighters sang: "You Europeans, you are robbers even though you pretend to lead us. Go away. Go away . . . ."[2]

BLACK MUSIC OF RESISTANCE IN SOUTH AFRICA

Ngoma: A Dance against the Enemy

Songs and dances to ridicule or protest the white man's work abound, but it was in South Africa that such dances and songs were best developed. Following the discovery of gold and diamond deposits in South Africa in 1867 and in 1884, Europeans used different forms of violence and intimidation to force blacks into the capitalist labor system. The emerging conditions of labor exploitation produced in South Africa a peculiar form of dependency. Whites kept most of the land and forced the Africans onto reserves or Bantustans. The land allotted the Africans (13.7% of the entire country) was too small and too unproductive to support a decent living. Conditions in the Bantustans were so appalling that Africans had to migrate to distant places to seek wage labor.

Until the collapse of apartheid in 1994, black wages remained profoundly low. Blacks who left the Bantustans had to scramble for the lowest paying jobs in the white economy, where black unemployment rate exceeded 50%. Holding onto a job was as difficult as finding one, for the recruiting officers used all forms of tactics to maintain a steady flow of poorly paid, oscillating labor force. White supervisors took advantage of the superfluity of black labor to abuse African workers who then were forced to conceal their rage in resistant songs:

> The white man be damned
> They call us Jim.[3]

Large numbers of migrant workers lived in hostels or dormitories in the major townships. Some hostels housed up to 1500 men apiece, and it was not uncommon to find sixteen men sharing a single room. Fearing spontaneous protest against the deplorable conditions that workers lived under, city authorities policed the hostels. For six days a week, black workers did the most arduous jobs, but on weekends, they reclaim their pride. They come together to dance *ngoma*, a dance against the enemy. This act of defiance is replayed every week deep inside of the black townships.[4]

The major instrument of *Ngoma* was the base drum, which might have fascinated the Zulu people when they clashed with the British in the second half of the nineteenth century. Those who performed *Ngoma* also copied the regimental march but turned it into *Ngoma*. Perhaps they chose the base drum and the regimental march because these were part of the European traditions of war, or simply to mock the enemy. It must be borne in mind that in pre-colonial days, one of the many ways to fight the enemy was to copy or capture his instruments and symbols of power such as masks, wooden gongs, and war-drums. This custom was carried into the colonial period and was employed by such African nationalists as Nnamdi Azikiwe, Kwame Nkrumah and Jomo Kenyatta, when they journeyed to the white man's country to learn the secrets of his organizational skills. Also in South Africa, Nelson Mandela studied Afrikaans, the language of his tormentors, to understand their thought processes. In chapter six above we saw how the Tokoists of Angola urged the Africans to appropriate the beneficial institutions of the white man, not blindly imitate them. When, therefore, South African black workers gathered each weekend in the middle of the black townships to dance *Ngoma,* it was to do battle with the enemy, using his (the enemy's) own symbols of war—a musical instrument and a military drill. It is also to redeem their pride, and to re-enact the history of the battles that their forebears waged against the enemy—the white man. *Ngoma* was a dance of resistance, a symbolic dance against the enemy. The migrant workers were angry but could no longer engage in real wars against the Europeans. And since their aggression had nowhere to go, they danced in competitive display against one another.[5]

Music lovers all over the world know Miriam Makeba as "Mama Africa" because she epitomizes true African womanhood. Says Makeba, "There are three things I was born with in this world and there are three things I will have until the day I die: hope; determination; and song"(Makeba &. Hall; p.l). These three words have come to characterize the life history of Miriam Makeba. From her early struggles with South African apartheid to the apex of her singing career as a world-renowned entertainer and a symbol of resistance to racial struggle, Makeba has retained these gifts and empowered many as she empowered herself. Her depth of soul, expressed through song, has moved millions and informed them of the evils of apartheid. Although she never obtained a college degree, she has gracefully and competently performed the job of national diplomats in her fight against apartheid. Despite her many accomplishments, she retains a humility matched by few others of her stature.

Miriam Makeba was born on March 4, 1932 in South Africa to Caswell and Christina Makeba. She was the only child born to Caswell and Christina. Her mother had three older children from a first marriage: Hilda, Mizpah, and Joseph. Many black South Africans have both an English and an African name, and it is a custom for someone's African name to comment on the circumstances surrounding his or her birth. Makeba's African name is *Uzenzile,* "You have no one to blame but yourself." This was Makeba's grandmother's somewhat serious, yet playful comment to Christina after a difficult childbirth and in light of previous warnings that another child could endanger her life. In 1932 the Depression was felt in South Africa and Makeba's family was going through great financial hardship and could scarcely afford a child, so the family doubted their little girl would make it. Caswell, who was from the Xhosa tribe and whose African name was Mpambane, spent most of his time away in Johannesburg trying to find work in order to support the family. Christina, who was from the Swazi tribe and whose African name was Nomkomndelo, was a trained nurse. The deep spirit that was later manifested in Makeba's songs may be traced back to her close relationship with her mother and grandmother, both of whom became *isangomas* later in their lives. An *insangoma* is a diviner and tribal doctor respected in the community and sometimes possessed by ancestral spirits. The community depends on the *isangoma* as a medium between the living and their dead ancestors.

Eighteen days after Makeba's birth, police raided her house and discovered *umqombothl,* an African beer her mother made. The authorities claimed that Africans are not "civilized" enough to drink so drinking was illegal for blacks. Some households secretly brewed cornmeal and malt to make *umqombothi,* a good source of income and an alternative to other beer. Since the family could not pay the eighteen-pound fine for possessing an alcoholic beverage, Christina and Miriam Makeba spent six months in jail. Hence, racial injustice affected Miriam Makeba very early in her life. The political climate in South Africa would become worse as the hateful Dutch gained full control of the government.

Fortunately, music was a big part of Makeba's childhood and she used it to cope with the harshness of racial injustice. Her mother was a talented singer who also played several traditional instruments. On Sundays all the children and adults in the neighborhood would get together in a common courtyard to sing and dance. Makeba embraced Christianity because she enjoyed singing in the Sunday school choir. She recalls singing hymns like "Nearer My God to Thee" and "Rock of Ages" both in Afrikaans and English; she also sang Xhosa and Zulu hymns. Makeba's exposure to the Bapedi as a child opened her eyes to the power of music as a therapeutic agent and as a means of coping with hardship. The Bapedi were tribesmen from the northern Transvaal who worked the worst jobs in Johannesburg. They were very musical people whose happy outward appearance, especially while playing their drums, belied their awful existence. Commenting on her observation of the Bapedi, Makeba said, "Is it the music that makes them act like they don't have a care in the world, I wonder? It must be. Already I have discovered that music is a type of magic." She then concluded, "Who can keep us down as long as we have our music?" (Makeba & Hall, p. 15)

Under the direction of choir director Joseph Mutuba at the Kilnerton Training Institution, a senior high school, Makeba learned how to communicate the message of music on stage. Mntuba recognized Makeba's talent and encouraged her to continue singing. He formed a trio with Makeba and two other girls—this was Makeba's very first singing group. The trio performed at fund raisings, community centers, churches, and other schools. The girls learned how to move on stage and since not everyone in their audience understood Zulu or Sotho, they had to use gestures and facial expressions to convey the message of their songs. Under Mutuba's direction, Makeba sang for King George as he drove through the township with his daughter, Princess Elizabeth. As she matured as a young singer and performer, Makeba was also exposed to American jazz.

Makeba recalls listening to Ella Fitzgerald and Billie Holliday for hours with friends. Her brother, Joseph, taught her American lyrics even before she understood the words and had her perform for friends. This would later prove very useful for Makeba, as she would become the first to combine black American culture with that of South Africa to create a unique mix that won the love of millions all over the world.

A few months after King George's visit, the candidate of the Afrikaner's Nationalist party, Doctor Milan, won the national election. This was a major change that would greatly affect blacks all over South Africa. Until that time, the English always held political power in South Africa due to Britain's victory in the Boer War many years before. "Boer" is the Dutch word for peasant; the Boers, descendants of the Dutch, called themselves Afrikaners. Their language, Afrikaans, is a mixture of Dutch and German. There was great animosity between the English and the Afrikaners; the English were the administrators, while the Afrikaners were the farmers, policemen, and more or less a buffer between the blacks and the English. Milan charged up the Afrikaners in order to win the election: "We are oppressed, yet we are the majority. We were the first to get here and this is our land" (Makeba & Hall, p. 25). After they gained power, the Afrikaners began to create the South Africa they had always wanted. During that year, 1947, apartheid was institutionalized. "Apartheid" is Afrikaans for "Aparthood" (*heid*="hood"). The new government declared that when Dutch settlers arrived at the Cape of Good Hope, there was no one on the land; they said that the black South Africans that lived among them migrated down from the north. Black South Africans were no longer called natives but Bantu. The Immorality Act made interracial relations illegal and the Group Areas Act segregated housing for the blacks. Thousands were relocated to wastelands called "homelands-" The Bantu Education Act redesigned the school curriculum for blacks so that all were prepared to enter servant jobs and menial work. The South African government essentially made blacks foreigners and prisoners in their own land. Although the government tried to create a kind of Utopia for the white minority, they built a fictitious glass world that would surely shatter.

Things continued to get worse for Makeba as she left home to get her first job. She was first a nanny for a Greek family near Pretoria. Since the family could scarcely afford her service, the wife accused her of stealing a watch and called the police. Fortunately, the husband was kind to Makeba and told the police that his wife hid the watch. Another nanny job near Pretoria proved equally unsuccessful because of the family's harshness. Shortly after going home she dated a young man named Gooli and became pregnant with his child at seventeen. She named her child Bongi, which means "we thank thee" (Makeba & Hall, p. 37). Although Gooli married Makeba and took her into his family's home, he became physically and verbally abusive. The marriage ended when Makeba caught her husband cheating with her sister, Mizpah. She brought Bongi to her mother and stayed with some extended family in Johannesburg.

Life began to improve greatly for Makeba after she moved to Johannesburg. She joined her first band, the Cuban Brothers, which was headed by her cousin Zweli Ngwenya. The group had a piano player, a drummer, and some brass players; Makeba was the lead singer. Together they entered amateur contests, and sang at fund raising, community centers, and churches. One day after one of their gigs at the Donaldson Community Center in Orlando East, the leader of the Manhattan Brothers, Nathan Mdlhedlhe, told Makeba that they were looking for a female vocalist and invited her to audition for the part. The Manhattan Brothers was the most popular group in South Africa at the time and Makeba could not believe what had happened. Miriam Makeba became the female vocalist for the Manhattan Brothers and toured in Swaziland, Lesotho, and Lourenco Marques, a Portuguese colony. It was against the law for black performers to record in English, so the group only recorded tribal songs. Although the Manhattan Brothers was successful, life was not easy. Said Makeba: "Just because we are performers does not mean that life is easier for the Manhattan Brothers or myself.

Nothing can change the fact that we are still black. The apartheid laws bind us just as tightly. In fact, life is even more difficult for us because we have to travel, eat at restaurants, and stay at hotels all the time. Nathan makes sure that all our papers are in order. Still, this does not guarantee that we will not be harassed" (Makeba & Hall, p. 53).

At Gallotone Records, where the Manhattan Brothers recorded, Makeba was asked to make her own record. A songwriter in the United States liked one of the songs on the record and wrote lyrics to it; "Lakutshuna Ilangu," a Xhosa tune, became "You Tell Such Lovely Lies." Gallotone Records insisted that Makeba sing the new lyrics. The song became a hit and, at a risk to Makeba, was played on the radio—in South Africa and abroad. After one other performance with the Manhattan Brothers, Makeba met Nelson Mandela when, as a young lawyer, he and others were drafting the Freedom Charter in which they proclaimed, "South Africa belongs to all who live in it, black and white" (Makeba fc Hall, p. 55).

Three years after her debut with the Manhattan Brothers, in 1956, Gallotone Records created a new group with Makeba, the Skylarks (¹Makeba, sound recording). She was the leader with three other young women as backup singers: Mamie and Mary Rabotapi, and Abigail Kubeka. The Skylarks created a unique blend of Western pop music with traditional tunes. The songs commented on the social and political conditions of the time. The group performed live before audiences in the Pretoria area.

In 1959 Miriam Makeba had a landmark year as she appeared in two very successful productions: the musical *King Kong* and the documentary *Come Back Africa*. King Kong was the nickname of a famous African boxer, Ezekiel Dihmini, whose talent was forced to rust because his predecessor, another African boxer named Jake Tule, killed a white man in a boxing match in London. This was unacceptable and could not happen again, so the authorities did not allow Dihimini to travel abroad to box. He began drinking and killed his girlfriend (her role was played by Makeba) and went to jail.

Shortly after being jailed, authorities said that he drowned in a pond of water. In depicting Dihimini's life, the jazz opera alluded to the terrible racial injustice that was rampant in South Africa. *Come Back Africa* also dealt with the plight of blacks in South Africa, but it was more explicit in its message and very controversial. The documentary was made by an American filmmaker, Lionel Rogosin, and appeared in the Venice Film Festival. After an invitation by Rogosin, Makeba quietly left the country to join him and his wife at the prestigious film festival in Italy. *Come Back Africa* was a huge success and it won Makeba accolades from the United States and Europe. Makeba's trip to Italy, however, would mark a thirty-year period in which she would be unable to return to her home land.

Miriam Makeba: A Vital Link Between the Struggle against Apartheid in South Africa and the Civil Rights Movement in the United States

The active involvement of Miriam Makeba in the struggle against apartheid and white racism in the United States actually began in 1959, when she met Harry Belafonte in London. Belafonte was a big fan of hers and wanted to help her get started in the American music industry where she would both grow and be in a better position to help her people in South Africa. In November 1959 Makeba made her US debut in the Steve Allen Show, where she sang for an audience of sixty million people. Shortly afterwards, she appeared on the Village Vanguard, a small jazz club in New York where she had a four-week contract. For the next ten years, Makeba worked very closely with entertainment giant Harry Belafonte. Through her association with Belafonte, she met other entertainers like Nina Simone, Duke Ellington, Miles Davis, and Sidney Poitier. Belafonte held press conferences before Makeba's shows and they talked about South Africa and increased the United States' awareness of apartheid. Although she is very shy and has never considered herself a politician, Makeba inevitably talked about political situations in South Africa because of endless journalist inquiries: "Journalists come and ask me questions. I try to talk about my music, and they politely write down what I say. But they ask me questions about South Africa and apartheid. They want to know if I am associated with the African Nationalist Movement. 'Please' I say, 'Let's not talk about polities'" (Makeba & Hall, p. 87).

Makeba's initial reluctance to talk about conditions in South Africa soon faded. After her mother's death in 1960, she went with her daughter Bongi to the South African consulate in order to get the necessary paperwork to attend her mother's funeral. South Africa, however, still perceived Makeba as they perceive all other black South Africans, and she became a threat. Said Makeba about her experience at the consulate:

> I am nervous when I go into the South African con-sulate. Here I am once again nothing but a native black without rights. The darling of the American newsmagazines and music industry the girl who charmed New York sophisticates... here she is just a *kaffir* [derogatory term for black South Africans] who doesn't know her place. The man at the desk takes my passport. He does not speak to me, but to himself when he says, 'Miriam Makeba,' as if he was expecting this moment. He takes a rubber stamp and slams it down on my passport. Then he walks away, I pick up my passport. It is stamped 'INVALID" (Makeba & Hall, p. 98).

Makeba was exiled. Although this imposed separation from her family and roots was very painful, she soon realized she had the kind of freedom that most black South Africans could only dream of and this came with a measure of responsibility. Soon after her exile she said, "All the newspapermen and the radio and TV people give me a valuable chance to speak up about the crimes that are being committed against my people at home. I must no longer be shy. I ask myself how many black South Africans enjoy the attention of the press all the time, and I can only answer: one" (Makeba & Hall, p. 103).

In 1963 Miriam Makeba addressed the United Nations Special Committee on Apartheid. This unique opportunity came

through her association with many African delegates at United
Nations functions. Makeba eloquently spoke about the plight of
her people and the harshness of apartheid in South Africa. She
urged the United Nations to impose a complete boycott of South
Africa, especially with respect to arms. When South African
authorities heard of her address, they banned her records in the
country; it became illegal to sell even the old records she did
with Gallotone Records back in South Africa. The ban, however,
only increased Makeba's importance and black South Africans
became more committed to her records, which were sold under
the counter. Makeba became a spokesperson for her people: "My
appearance before the UN Special Committee changes my life, or
at least the way people think of me. The person Miriam Makeba
is no longer just an African singer to them. I am a symbol of my
repressed people. To be in such a position is to live with a great
responsibility. It is as if I am more than myself (Makeba & Hall, p.
113). As Makeba fought in the United States, the South African
government became more stringent and oppressive. Authorities
arrested Nelson Mandela while he was returning from a meeting
with some African heads of state from the African National Congress. He was put on trial and then sentenced to life in prison.
In 1964 Makeba went before the UN Special Committee on
Apartheid a second time. This time she appealed for the release
of South Africa's political prisoners.

Makeba's transformation from singer to singer and symbolic
figure occurred as her popularity continued to skyrocket both
in America and abroad. She performed at major entertainment
centers all over the world and sang for President John F. Kennedy
at his birthday party; the same time Marilyn Monroe sang happy
birthday to the president. The album *An Evening with Harry
Belafonte & Miriam Makeba* won the Grammy and Makeba
became the first South African to win that award. She later
released Pata Pata, which became a worldwide hit. When independent African nations met in Addis Ababa, Ethiopia, to form
the Organization of African Unity all the heads of state asked
for only one performer: Miriam Makeba. Some of the African

leaders at the meeting were Emperor Haile Selassie, the host
Léopold Senghor of Senegal, Kwame Nkrumah of Ghana, and
Sekou Toure of Guinea, who later became very close to Makeba.
After her performance at the Pan-African Festival in Algiers,
the Algerian president gave her a diplomatic passport from his
country. Algeria was the first of several African countries that
made Makeba an honorary citizen.

During the Sixties, Makeba certainly was not alone in her
fight for civil liberty. Black American leaders like Dr. Martin
Luther King, who was acquainted with Makeba, and Malcolm
X made their voices heard and were helping to pave the way
for a better America. All this inspired Makeba. While she was
hospitalized for cancer of the cervix at Hollywood Community
Hospital in California, Makeba watched Dr. King's march to
Washington and listened to his famous "I have a Dream" speech.
At the conclusion of the speech she said; "I have a dream too- I
would like to see my people free. I would like to see the black and
white children of South Africa walk hand in hand. I would like
to go home again... This is something for me to live for" (Makeba
& Hall, p. 124).

The year that Dr. Martin Luther King was assassinated, 1968,
was the year that Miriam Makeba fell in love with Stokely Carmichael Carmichael, then president of the Student Nonviolent
Coordination Committee (SNCC), who had strong views and
was seen as a threat, so the American government watched him
very closely. When he and Makeba decided to get married, the
public wasted no time to show their disapproval. Entertainment
centers all over the country began canceling Makeba's scheduled
shows. Many were afraid that her shows would finance radical
activities. The FBI began to keep a close eye on her. The riots that
spread throughout the country shortly after Dr. King's death did
not ameliorate Makeba's situation. This is when she decided to
leave the United States and accept an old offer from Sekou Toure
to live in Guinea. Carmichael moved with his wife to Guinea,
where he continued to network with African leaders and engage

in the activist movement in the US through groups like SNCC. He and Makeba were married for ten years.

While in Guinea, Makeba began performing more in Europe and Africa, and she fought apartheid in an expanded capacity. President Toure asked Makeba to be one of the Guinean delegates to the United Nations and in 1975, he asked her to deliver the annual Guinean speech to the General Assembly. Makeba talked about the accomplishments of the nationalist movement, the role that superpowers should play in Africa's development and apartheid. In case her speeches at the UN were not enough, Makeba was sure to speak against apartheid at her concerts:

> I sang songs that are written by South Africans... Some of these songs protest the treatment of our people... Sometimes I think I must sound like a revolutionary when I say we must rise up against the criminal regime of [South Africa]. Afterward, I get scared of the things I say on stage. I say to myself, 'My goodness, next time maybe I shouldn't say that.' But the next time comes and I don't care. If I die on stage I guess I'll be the happiest person, because I will be dying like a soldier on the battlefield (Makeba & Hall, p. 224).

Miriam Makeba's remarkable musical career spans four decades and she continues to use her success to help her people in South Africa and the world. Her endless efforts to awaken the world to the plight of her people was recognized in Brussels in 1986 when she received the Dag Hammarskjold Peace Prize. After Nelson Mandela's release from prison in 1990, Makeba returned to South Africa. Her recent album, *Homeland* (2000), expresses her love for her people and the country. The first track in the album, Masakhane (see Songs below), calls for post-apartheid unity and hope. While she recognizes the troubles that pervade the continent, Makeba remains hopeful. "I think our people should be commended," she says. "After inheriting all the problems our government inherited from the apartheid era, they tried their best. Change is slow because there's no money. But the very fact that even after all that suffering

people are trying to live together and move forward is impressive"
(www.ritrnoartists.com/Makeba/raves_mm.htm). Makeba is also
impressive. Through her music, she captured her culture and the
traditions of her people and shared it with the world. Her determination and positive outlook continues to shine to this day. Like
she has said more than once, she was born with and will always
have hope, determination, and song.

SONGS

Masakhane "Let us Build Up One Another"

This song urges the people of South Africa to come together
and build the nation for a better future for all.

> Lyrics:
> Ngiwu ambe umhlaba wonk ba
> Ngaze ngaba tshela ngo sizi ebesinalo
> Silubonile nosizo Iwabe zizwe
> Sithi enkosi siyabonga
> Siyabonga, rea leboha
> Enkosi bantnbomntanami
> Ibonakel, imi sebenze yenu
> Sibabonile be didizela
> Ngo June sixteenth 1976
> Sengi buyele mna sengibuyile khaya
> Kwasi kwamnand, ekhaya we vumanibo
> He mn He mn He mn
> Chorus
> Mina ku mele ngakhiwe nguwe
> Wena wakhiwe yimi
> Thina sonke masakhane
> Enkosi bo mama bomthandaze
> Izwakel, imi thandazo yenu
> Ngoba thina sinjenje sinjenjenje
> Ngmithandazo
> Enkosi zinkokheli, enkosi bafundis
> Bethu sithi ngo Babu Sisulu;
> Enkosi Babu Thambo, Enkosi
> Enkosi Madiba

Who siyabonga John Dube,
Siyabonga Babulu Tuli,
Siyabonga Bhutaleze

Pata Pata (²**Makeba; sound recording**)

Saguguka sathi beka
Saguguka sathi beka
Saguguka sathi beka
Saguguka sathi beka
Yi yo mama yiyo mama
(Nantsi, pata pata)
Yi yo mama yiyo mama
(Nantsi, pata pata)

'Cause We Live For Love

The morning sun shines full of laughter
Waking up, all walks of life
Shining on love he says
It's a brand new day
Give all the warmth you can away
And!!
Open your hearts
For our children and the universe
To love and hold
Embracing the good
In those who feel they must give of themselves
'Cause we live for love
And love lives through all
The evening star (shines on) each person
With a sparkle of light and a smile
Touching the hearts for all to feel
The presence of love, for it's real!
So!!
Open your hearts
For our children and the universe
To love and hold

Embracing the good
In those who feel they must give of themselves
'Cause we live for love
And love lives through all
Let the rainbow rain showers on you
Raining down, all colours for all
Sowing seeds and dreams of the future
A though of love and peace forever more
Open your hearts
For our children and the universe
To love and hold
Embracing the good
In those who feel they must give of themselves
'Cause we live for love
And love lives through all
'Cause we live for love through love

Homeland

Now that those days are gone
I will spend each day with only
joy in my heart
Through many times I've cried
I'll always find the strength
to wipe the tears
From my eyes
I remember those days
I prayed to come home
And I know that someday I'd be here
Memories of days gone by
When I felt so alone
In the end all that matters is I'm home
Homeland
Ngai nazongiI
Mboka na ngai
Po na seko
Homeland
Ngai nazongiI
Mboka na ngai

Kino liwa
If you ever feel this way

Think about my story how
it came to play
My heart is beating fast
Finally today
Now at last I'm home

Zenizenabo "Bring Them with You or Be Victorious" (³**Makeba, p. 31**)

This is a Xhosa war chant about old tribal feuds.

Lyrics:

Bring them with you,
You idealistic cowards.
Bring them with you,
You idealistic cowards.
You cherish high ideals.
[These five lines are sung seven times.]
Hit, man, hit,
Son of my father hmm, hmm, hmm, ho—o
Ho-hmm, son of my father;
Hit hard.
As for your idealism,
Hey, ho, hey, ho, hey, ho,
Son of my father.

Jikele' Maweni "Go Round to the Rocks" (³**Makeba, p. 45**)

This is also a Xhosa battle song. It is a warrior's cry of defeat in battle.

Lyrics:
The boys' sticks will come to life at the river
Yo Homm!
When sticks knock against one another

I yo Homm!
Men are afraid of going to the river
Yo Homm!
Because sticks are knocking one against another.
I yo Homm!

Go round to the rocks,
We are going soon.
[These two lines are sung four times.]

The boys are dancing.
They dance beautifully.
The boys are dancing,
They dance to celebrate
Their departure for the mines.
[These five lines are sung twice.]
Go round to the rocks,
We are going soon;
[These two lines are sung four times.]

The men met,
It was beautiful.
The men met,
They met for the trip to the mines.
They met and it was beautiful.

Mayibuve "Restore Africa to its Owners" ([3]Makeba, p. 91)

This Xhosa song speaks of black South Africa's resentment to white rule. It is one of several patriotic African folk songs.

Lyrics:
We true South Africans have suffered for a long time
As a result of white people laws.
Awake, my people.
The time for our liberation has come.
This land is ours.
Remember Kings Umshoeshoe, Dingaan,
Umzilikazi, and Ngqika.
They fought for this land.

Awake, ye Africans;
Remember the words of King Shaka
Which he spoke on the arrival of white people.
"Do no trust the white man,
Because he has come to take your land."
Oh, my Father! Unite my people
I beg you, let's fight for our land.
We have long been ruled by the Dutch;
We have long suffered under their rule.
The time for your liberation has come.
The whole of Africa is ready to fight for our
        freedom.
You Zulu, Xhosa, Shangane, Basuto, Venda unite.
There is no more time for crying.
Restore Africa right now.
Follow the road of our forefathers
And fight for our land
Which was taken by white people.
We want our liberation now.
Beware, my people.
Awake Mandela and Sisule,
Sobukwe and you Luthuli, Tambo, Nokwe, and
        Resha.
Awake, ye Africans.
Remember the words of Ngqika,
"Do no trust the white man,
Because he has come to take your land."
Oh my Father! Unite my people
I beg you, let's fight for our land.
We have long been ruled by the Dutch.
We have long suffered under their rule.
The time for your liberation has come.
The whole of Africa is ready to fight for our
        freedom.
You Zulu, Xhosa; Shangane; Basuto^ Venda unite.
There is no more time for crying.

References

Makeba, Miriam and Hall; James, *Makeba: My Story*, New York, NY: NAL Penguin Inc., 1987.

Makeba; Miriam, *The best of Miriam Makeba & the Skylarks* [sound recording], USA: Kaz Records, 1992.

Makeba, Miriam, *Welela* [sound recording]. New York, NY: Reprise Records, 1968.

Makeba, Miriam, *The World of African Song*, Chicago, IL, 1971, pp. 35, 41, 91.

www.ritmoartists.com/Makeba/raves mm.htm

www.putumavo.com/cd/makeba/inakeba.htm

Notes

1. P. O. Okwoli, *A Short History of Igala*, (Ilorin, 1973), 99.
2. L. S. B. Leaky, *Defeating the Mau Mau* (London: Methuen, 1954), 63.
3. Reproduced from "The Black Music of Resistance: South Africa" (Visual)
4. *Ibid.*
5. *Ibid.*

Conclusion

Black people in Africa and the diaspora are no longer satisfied occupying the lowest rungs of the social ladder because of slavery, colonialism and racism, but rather need to pull themselves to the top. After all, slavery and colonialism have been toppled, and racism is no longer as virulent as it was a hundred years ago. Nevertheless, to prepare for the future, black people must fully acquaint themselves with what happened to their forebears over the last five hundred years.

I have attempted to explain what happened to black people during the last five perilous centuries. Restated, Africa's predicament began in the fifteenth century when Europeans arrived on African shores with ships and guns, supposedly to trade, but how could any commercial intercourse carried out at gunpoint be described as trading? Their major items of commerce were human beings, secured by systematically wrenching them from their homelands. Europeans then went on to objectify Africans in order to justify their enslavement. The result was racism.

Africans fought back. They challenged these systems of violence and racism, and, in the process, developed a black culture of resistance. The black culture of resistance matured over time and was passed down from one generation to the next. Expressed through political mobilization, religious nationalism, popular culture, and economic determinism, the black culture of resistance satisfies the definition of "culture."

Over the course of the past five centuries, Europeans used different tactics to retain their stranglehold on the Africans. They conspired to dispossess the Africans of their land, their mineral deposits, and everything else that was of value. Europeans even used Christianity, Western education and assimilation strategies to subordinate the people of African descent to the whims of Europe. They eventually partitioned the African continent, divided its people, and planted the seeds of discord among them. However, what the Europeans did not seem to take into account was that the more repressive their actions, the more determined were the black people to halt their aggression.

Africans everywhere recognized the monstrous nature of white domination and railed against it. The peculiar circumstances and resources available to them conditioned the methods that they used. For example, maroons, as rebel slaves, could think of only one way out of white domination--that of counter-violence. And since they were outnumbered and outgunned, they accepted guerrilla tactics as their preferred military strategy.

On the other hand, plantation slaves chose strategies that helped to ameliorate the harsh conditions of slavery. Until they were satisfied that the time for an armed insurrection had come, they occupied themselves with flight and other forms of non-violent resistance.

On the African continent, most peasant communities responded to the initial European invasion violently and sometimes invoked assistance from religious beliefs. The organizers of the Mahdist movements evoked certain Islamic traditions, just as the organizers of the Maji Maji, Nyabingi and Mau Mau uprisings turned to African traditional belief systems. In Jamaica, Africans in captivity massed behind the *Kumina* cults, while in Brazil, Cuba and Trinidad, slaves turned to such Yoruba-derived religious affiliations as *Candomblé, Santeria* and *Shango.*

The attitudes of black peoples towards Christianity were mixed. Most blacks were appalled by the way Europeans used Christianity to expand their power, but they were often unsure about how best to fight it. In northern Nigeria, the initial instinct of Muslim leaders was to keep the Christians out of Muslim territory. Elsewhere, as in Zanzibar, Muslim leaders preferred to act as a buffer group and to use their association with the colonial powers to entrench themselves as leaders of non-Muslim African communities. Whatever methods they may have chosen, it is evident that Muslim opposition to the Europeans derived, not necessarily from religious differences, but from what the Muslims perceived as the disruption of Muslim society by non-Muslims.

Unlike the Igbo people who first opposed the presence of the Christian missionaries before following Christ *en masse,* the Gikuyu people of Kenya first embraced Christianity and then used it as an instrument of protest against the missionaries and colonial administrators. When the Mau Mau movement was launched, many Kenyan Christians joined it and participated in traditional oath-taking ceremonies. However, while the Gikuyu fought European cultural imposition, the Igbo ultimately found out that Christianity and Western education were useful tools with which to negotiate the exploitative colonial system.

It should be stated that, generally, Africans did not always oppose the Christians on religious grounds. What they opposed was the way foreign missionaries used Christianity to divide indigenous communities. African elders were worried about the impact of the new religion on traditional educational systems and morality. They feared that what the Christians taught was at variance with traditional ideas of community life, and that the colonial educational system was designed evidently to infuse European values, European superiority, and submission to European authority. Elders recalled that when the European missionaries first arrived, they had promised to teach skills in the three Rs--Reading, (w)Riting and (a)Rithmetic. Missionaries introduced the three Rs all right, but padded them with a new set of Rs--Racism, Reverence for the white man and (dis)Respect for African cultures.

Moreover, European-trained missionaries were the first to distort African history. They were also the first to turn some African youths against the customs of their fathers. It was through the European mission schools and churches that European cultures filtered down to African societies. The primary aims of the mission schools and churches, noted Leonard Barrett, were to "de-Africanize the Africans," a process, which in Jamaica, for example, meant the total "rejection of all things African: speech, lore, food, dress, religion, and, if necessary, even your ancestors, especially if they were Black."[1] The missionaries and European schoolteachers paraded themselves around with an air of superiority because, in their view, they were the conveyers of civilization and the providers of the good life. Some of the first native graduates of the mission schools also behaved like the European missionaries; they saw themselves as superior to the other members of their own communities and acted as the conduit through which European cultures could be transmitted.

In the United States, separate black churches mushroomed partly because whites did not want blacks to worship with them, and partly because blacks wanted to be able to serve God in an environment that was free from discrimination. In due course, however, black Christians quickly turned their new churches into centers to develop Black nationalism. These centers of worship also sheltered the emerging "black" culture, and acted as sanctuaries for anyone wishing to escape from white racism. In the early nineteenth century, removed from the watchful eyes of white society, black church-leaders like Gabriel Prosser, Denmark Vessey and Nat Turner used their churches as centers for underground plotting against slave owners. In the twentieth century, church-leaders like Martin Luther King Jr. and Ralph Abernathy used similar establishments to launch the Civil Rights movement.

Elsewhere in Africa and the diaspora, some Christian liberation theologians, like the Black Zionists in Jamaica, the Spiritual Baptists in Trinidad, and the Tokoists in Angola, used their organizations to reconstitute the African family structures that had been battered by centuries of slavery and colonialism. The Tokoists were black separatists but, while the Nation of Islam, a separatist Muslim sect, advocated the creation of a separate territory for blacks on American soil, the Tokoists wanted to avoid the world of the white man on African soil. Unlike the Tokoists and the Nation of Islam, however, the members of the black churches of the United States wanted to be integrated into the white man's world, even though they preferred to be left alone in their sacred devotional spaces.

Mention must also be made of the contributions of African captives in the Americas to their own liberation. African slaves did not just sit by waiting for the abolitionists to set them free. Continual rebellions fed into the politics of abolition and hastened the drawing up of emancipation programs.

Resistance to European domination and exploitation took several other forms. For example, South African women's refusal to observe the obnoxious pass laws, together with the decision of some Africans to make a living from the informal sector of the colonial economy, were forms of resistance. The Rastafarians' habits of smoking marijuana in public and wearing dreadlocks were acts of resistance--a refusal to conform to the behavior patterns of the ruling classes. Even flight was a form of resistance. In West Africa, for example, many blacks who lived in the territories occupied by the French, protested with their feet; their mass exodus to neighboring British colonies caused major labor problems for the French colonial administration. Also in North Africa, Muslims who left Algeria and emigrated eastward re-enacted the religious duty that required Muslims to withdraw from a land dominated by infidels. This act of protest, subtle as it might seem, increased disaffection against European rule.

Some blacks sought to solve the crisis of European domination by economic self-sufficiency. Among the advocates of economic self-sufficiency were Marcus Garvey and the members of the Nation of Islam. These nationalists believed that blacks must prevent capital flight from the black communities; they must get involved in business ventures that benefit blacks.

There was one thing that black people never disagreed about, namely, that culture, including music and dance, were indispensable instruments of survival and resistance. Africans danced and sang songs to conceal their rage, or to expose and ridicule the evils of enslavement and colonialism. In some instances, blacks sang to prepare themselves for battle. It was significant that blacks in

Brazil played *Capoeira*, just as African-Americans rapped about the oppressive racist system in which they found themselves. In South Africa, black migrant workers danced *Ngoma* against the enemy, and in Jamaica, *Reggae* artists sang redemption songs. In chapter six, we saw how music and dance advanced the black culture of resistance.

BLACK INTELLECTUALS AND THE BLACK CULTURE OF RESISTANCE

At this point, I must devote some space to the attitudes and contributions of black intellectuals to the struggle for freedom. This is important because it was through their efforts that Africans at home and abroad finally regained their independence. But when the struggle for independence raged, these black intellectuals vacillated between non-violence and counter-violence on one hand, and on the other hand, between integration and separation. They were very much unlike the maroons in the Americas and peasant communities on the continent of Africa, who saw no other way out of slavery and colonialism other than counter-violence and separation. Some black intellectuals supported counter-violence; others opposed it for various reasons. For example, Nnamdi Azikiwe of Nigeria thought that it was unprofitable for unarmed Africans to stage revolutions.[2] Even some European historians expressed similar sentiments. They claimed that Africans who rose in arms against European colonizers of Africa had nothing to gain from their actions since they had only limited access to modern war instruments. African leaders, they added, were not even united. So if one group decided to resist, there was always another group that was ready to collaborate with the invaders.[3] "If [African leaders] were far-sighted and well-informed," wrote Roland Oliver and John D. Fage, "and more particularly if they had access to foreign advisers such as missionaries or traders, they might well understand that nothing was to be gained by resistance, and much by negotiation."[4]

Black intellectuals shunned violent political protests largely because they expected to be heirs to the colonial structures. Many of them opposed the colonial regimes, yet they wanted to be part of the European World and to be treated with respect. Some of them began to preach counter-violence only when they became convinced that assimilation did not really confer on them the privileges that their European masters enjoyed.

While some black intellectuals vacillated, others remained committed to the philosophy of counter-violence. Fanon, Cabral, Malcolm X and a host of other black revolutionaries placed much faith in the potency of counter-violence. Although these militants were criticized by the advocates of non-violence, events in Algeria, Guinea (Bissau), Mozambique, Namibia, South Africa and Zimbabwe proved them right. The stubborn posture of the colonial powers in these places warranted the transition to armed struggle.

Although disunity and low-levels of arms supplies created many problems for African freedom fighters, those problems were surmountable. By the early 1950s, blacks had forged bonds of unity among the various sections of the Black World, thanks to the Pan-African movement. Moreover, encouraged by the changing world political climate, black freedom fighters and intellectuals had begun to secure guns from the Soviets and the Chinese. When Ghana became independent in 1957, self-rule for other African countries was only a question of time. For example, after their expulsion from Southeast Asia, the French became so anxious to get out of Africa that they worked forcibly to liberate some French African countries.

It was in the United States of America that indecision over ways to combat European domination was most pronounced. As we have seen, some African-Americans supported integration with white society, while others advocated separation. Some wanted to achieve justice by non-violent means; others wanted to include counter-violence. Moreover, while some preached self–sufficiency through black enterprise, others opposed capitalism. The divergences in ideology created many conflicts, not only between the various associations that claimed to speak for the black community, but also among the members of the same associations. Mostly, this was because some African-Americans failed to listen when Malcolm X admonished them to keep their eyes on the objectives of the struggle and not to quarrel over methods or be mystified by the fetish of organization.

One of the greatest achievements of black intellectuals in the freedom struggle was the formation of the Pan-African movement. Black intellectuals were quick to perceive that counter-violence, religion and divine inspiration, together with dance and music may have sustained the black culture of resistance, but they lacked the necessary force to unify all black people against their oppressors. It was partly to remedy this shortfall that black intellectuals launched the Pan-African movement in 1900. The Pan-African movement was not only a political association; it was also a cultural movement that aimed to rehabilitate the African past. Thus, the historical roles that the Pan-African movement eventually played went far beyond fulfilling the ideals of its founders. Among other things, it promoted the idea of African Unity, Black Nationalism, African Redemption, African Personality, Negritude, Black Consciousness, and Black Power.

We must also remember that black intellectuals have continued to contribute to the spread and preservation of the black culture of resistance through their public speeches, writings, and works of art. They challenge the assumed inferiority of the black race. They also refute the unfounded claim that Africans made no contributions to world development. Their opposition to the dominant Euro-centric viewpoint is based on the understanding that false testimonies have political and economic implications; they often justify the subjugation and exploitation of people. Determined to right what is wrong, black intellectuals use their skills to explain African genius, initiative and creativity.

Some black scholars, especially in the United States, go even further. They retreat to the land of the pharaohs and the pyramids--to ancient Egypt, Axum and Kush--to re-arm themselves for a new war against European cultural imperialism. They devise new systems of knowledge as alternatives to the narrow Euro-centric perspective of the world. Their prime objective is to recover for black people a stolen legacy. In the vanguard is a host

of Afro-centrists. Like Amilcar Cabral, these intellectual nationalists believe that culture is an indispensable tool for resistance.

Some militant black intellectuals like Frantz Fanon explain
the inter-connections between colonial violence and counter-
violence. They show that any political system that thrives on
violence will be destroyed by its own contradictions. They demonstrate that oppressiveness and racism are essential elements of
Western culture, which are directly responsible for the spread
of violence and protests around the world. They then admonish
all oppressed peoples to shake off foreign domination by force
because colonialism and its dependency relationships are established by violence and are maintained by the same means. Unlike
some moderate Pan-Africanists, the militants have no faith in
settling the colonial question by non-violent methods because
colonialism is an unbridled monster that will yield only when
confronted by an equal and opposing force. Frantz Fanon, one
of the most articulate advocates of counter-violence, insists that
colonialism "is violence in its natural state, and will only yield
when confronted with greater violence."[5] To Fanon, therefore,
counter-violence does not only guarantee the native his freedom;
it makes him fearless and restores his self-respect.

Fanon is not original in his advocacy of colonial counter-violence. One hundred years earlier, Frederick Douglass had warned
that blacks must liberate themselves from the shackles of white
domination by turning to violence. Douglass insisted that black
people "had no hope of justice from whites, no possible hope
except in their own right arms. It must come to blood; they must
fight for themselves, and redeem themselves, or it would never be
done."[6] Thus, long before the advent of the Bolshevik and Chinese
revolutions, Frederick Douglass, like Toussaint L'Ouverture, had
recognized that revolutions involved bloodshed and that repressive political systems could be overthrown only by violence.
Malcolm X was correct then when he told African-Americans
that those people who sang "We Shall Overcome" and indulged
in public exhibition of piety, believing that they were engaged in
a revolution, knew not what revolutions entailed.

As already explained in chapter nine, Malcolm spoke frequently about meeting violence with violence. His intention
was not to promote armed conflicts but to warn his audiences
not to confuse methods with objectives. He stated that methods
may change but objectives should not change. He explained that
the objective of the African-Americans was to secure freedom,
equality and justice. The methods by which this objective could
be achieved might change, but the objective must remain constant. How the objective could be achieved would be determined
by the means available—the ballot box, the bullet, separation, or
integration.

Malcolm X's eloquence, notwithstanding, it is remarkable
that in the United States, Latin America, the West Indies and
Africa, the launching of a black counter-violence movement was
a clear demonstration that blacks could also withhold peace from
their oppressors, just as their oppressors had denied them peace.

Not all black scholars and political activists advocate counter-
violence, though. Some believe that since cultural penetration is
an aspect of European strategy for controlling non-Europeans,
resistance should also be carried out by non-violent, cultural
means. One of the advocates of non-violence was Rex Nettleford
who argued that dance and music were important elements of
black culture for resistance and survival.[7] There were also men
like Martin Luther King Jr., Ralph Abernathy, James Lawson and
many other black nationalists who admonished their followers to
embrace the philosophy of non-violence. Like Gandhi of India,
however, they warned that non-violence should not be mistaken
for inaction.

Believing that resistance was useless without unity, black intellectual nationalists advocated African unity. Kwame Nkrumah,
the apostle of African Unity, insisted that blacks all over the world
must unite because, "All peoples of African descent, whether they
live in North or South America, the Caribbean, or in any other
part of the world are Africans and belong to one African nation."[8]
As we have seen, W.E.B. DuBois cautioned that until Africa was
free, black people everywhere could not escape chains.[9] And

long after achieving independence, African leaders still kept their eyes fixed on the virtues of African unity. Nkrumah reassured all black people that independence for Ghana was meaningless if the other segments of the Black World remained disunited.[10] Also, Julius Nyerere, the "father of Tanzanian nationalism," declared that only political union among African nations could save the continent from neo-colonial attacks and economic exploitation. "As long as there remain separate African nations," Nyerere explained, "there will remain too a danger that other states will exploit our differences for their own purposes. Only with unity can we ensure that Africa really governs Africa. Only with unity can we be sure that African resources will be used for the benefit of Africa.[11] Certainly, all black intellectuals and statesmen subscribe to the sentiment of black unity.

SOME ACHIEVEMENTS OF THE BLACK CULTURE OF RESISTANCE

At this stage, I will only outline a few of the achievements of the black culture of resistance since they have already been explained in the preceding chapters. First, the black culture of resistance has enabled black people to survive five hundred years of white domination. Second, it has united the disunited peoples of African origin for a common struggle against European violence. Finally, the black culture of resistance has enabled black people to wrest political independence and civil rights from the white ruling classes.

At the sociological and psychological levels, the black culture of resistance transformed blacks when it gave them a new political consciousness and self pride. Blacks no longer have to bow their heads in shame because of the color of their skin, the texture of their hair, their individuality, and their heritage. In the United States, the Civil Rights movement paved the way for integration; it also created a legacy of political activism, mass education, economic opportunity and access to the ballot box and political offices. It even expanded Black Studies programs and ushered in a renewed interest in African studies.

Today black people may boast that they have overturned colonial rule and racial segregation. However, as they celebrate their "flag" independence, or the collapse of legal segregation, they must remain conscious of the fact that the struggle for black liberation is not yet over. They must be reminded that white domination has changed its tactics but not its basic nature, and that black people everywhere are still being exploited, no longer by the old slave and colonial masters, but by the new multinational corporations, the World Bank and the International Monetary Fund. Hiding behind the pale veil of globalization, white capitalists wrecked havoc on unsuspecting black communities. Burdened with high interest payments on IMF loans and currency devaluation, black people in Africa and the Caribbean are deprived of the fruits of their labor. They are also left out of the current worldwide economic prosperity.

Worse still, black people suffer from the consequences of environmental degradation--air pollution, deforestation, poisoned rivers and lakes--but while the industrialized nations grow fat because of their reckless abuse of the environment, black people are left in abject poverty. It is, therefore, necessary for blacks to join the struggle against the wanton destruction of the environment. They must resist the continued neo-colonial exploitation of the Third World and, above all, remain conscious of the fact that real freedom and justice can be secured only through economic self-sufficiency.

Furthermore, the available evidence confirms that white people have not given up their tendency to divide the world into superior and inferior races. Legal segregation may have ended, but certain vestiges of discrimination may still prevent many blacks from achieving meaningful social and economic well being. In the United States, cases of police brutality, racial profiling and hate crimes abound. Incomes, housing and educational facilities for blacks are still deplorable. Inferior education gives rise to low incomes and poor access to justice. Poor education promotes low self-esteem. Perhaps, it is not by coincidence that millions of blacks in the United States are first confined to the projects before they are locked up in prisons.

On the other hand, a close look at the achievements of the black culture of resistance reveals some of its shortcomings. As we saw in chapter seven, the Pan-African movement has failed to solve many problems confronting Africa and the diaspora. The unity that it achieved for Africa is extremely fragile; Africa has never been able to insulate itself from Western machinations, nor has the OAU been able to deal with the conflicts that constantly erupt in Africa. Many African leaders have succumbed to neo-colonial pressure, and have aided the multinational corporations in plundering African resources.

On the whole, both black and white people must be reminded that the black culture of resistance owes its entire existence to the white culture of domination. Like all cultural elements, the black culture of resistance bears its inner meaning; it does not matter whether or not non-blacks understand it. What matters is that as long as black people retain the collective memory of white violence, and as long as white people refuse to make reparations for past transgressions, the black culture of resistance will continue to advance.

Notes

1. Leonard E. Barrett, *The Sun and the Drum: African Roots in Jamaican Folk Tradition* (Kingston, Jamaica: Sangster's Book Stores, 1976), 13.

2. Nnamdi Azikiwe, *My Odyssey* (New York: Praeger, 1970), 162.

3. Roland Robinson, "Non-European Foundations of European Imperialism: Sketch for a Theory of Collaboration," in *Imperialism: The Robinson and Gallagher Controversy*, ed. William Roger Louis (New York: New Viewpoint, 1976), 132-33.

4. Roland Oliver and John D. Fage, *A Short History of Africa* (Baltimore: Penguin Books, 1962), 203. See also Norman Leys, *Kenya* (London: Frank Cass, 1973), 342.

5. Frantz Fanon, *The Wretched of the Earth* (New York: Penguin, 1967), 61.

6. Carleton Mabee, *Sojourner Truth: Slave, Prophet, Legend* (New York: New York University Press, 1993), 84.

7. Rex M. Nettleford, *Dace Jamaica: Cultural Definition and Artistic Discovery: the National Dance Theater Company of Jamaica, 1962-1983,* (New York: Grove Press, 1985), 20.

8. Kwame Nkrumah, *Class Struggle in Africa* (New York: International Publishers), 87.

9. See chapter 7.

10. Kwame Nkrumah, *Africa Must Unite* (London: Panaf Books, 1963).

11. As quoted in Frederick A. O. Schwarz, Jr., *Nigeria: The Tribes, the Nation, or the Race--The Politics of Independence* (Cambridge: The M. I. T. Press, 1965), 223.

Bibliography

Achebe, Chinua. *Things Fall Apart*. Portsmouth: Heinemann, 1996.

Adeleye, R. A. *Power and Diplomacy in Northern Nigeria, 1804-1906: Sokoto Caliphate and its Enemies*. New York: Humanities Press, 1971.

Ajayi, J. F. Ade, and Michael Crowder (eds.). *History of West Africa, Vol. 2*. New York: Columbia University Press, 1976.

Alethra, Lindstrom J. *Sojourner Truth: Slave, Abolitionist, Fighter for Women's Rights*. New York: J. Messner, 1980.

Alkalimat, Abdul, (ed.). *Paradigms in Black Studies: Intellectual History, Cultural Meaning and Political Ideology*. Chicago: Twenty-first Century Books and Publications, 1990.

Anderson, Terry H.. *The Movement and the Sixties*. New York: Oxford University Press, 1995.

Al-Qur'an, A Contemporary Translation by Ahmed Ali (Princeton: Princeton University Press, 1988).

Aptheker, Herbert. "Resistance and Afro-American History: Some Notes on Contemporary Historiography and Suggestions for Further Research," in Gary Y. Okihiro, (ed.) *In Resistance: Studies in African, Caribbean, and Afro-American History*. Amherst: The University of Massachusetts Press, 1986: 10-20.

Arhin, Kwame (ed.). *The Life and Work of Kwame Nkrumah*. Accra, Ghana: Sedco Publishing Limited, 1991.

Aseka, Eric. *Jomo Kenyatta: A Biography*. Nairobi: East African Educational Publishers, 1992.

Azikiwe, Nnamdi. *My Odyssey*. Westport: Negro University Press, 1970.

_____. *Renascent Africa*. London: Frank Cass, 1968.

Barrett, Leonard E. *The Rastafarians: A Study in Messianic Cultism in Jamaica*. Rio Piedras, Puerto Rico: Institute of Caribbean Studies. 1968.

_____. *The Sun and the Drum: African Roots in Jamaican Folk Tradition*. Kingston, Jamaica: Sangster's Book Stores, 1976.

Bastide, Roger. *African Civilisations in the New World*. New York: Harper & Row, 1971.

_____. "The Other Quilombos," in Richard Price, (ed.), *Maroon Societies: Rebel Slave Communities in the Americas*. Baltimore: The John Hopkins UniversityPress 1979.

Beckman, Janette. *Rap: Portraits and Lyrics of a Generation of Black Rockers*. New York: St. Martin's Press, 1991.

Berry, Mary Frances. *Black Resistance, White Law: A History of Constitutional Racism in America*. New York: A Lane, 1994.

Batran, Aziz A. *Two Essays on Islam and Revolution in Africa*. Brattleboro, VT: Center for Arab-Islamic Studies, 1983.

Bhardwaj, K. K. *Namibia: Struggle for Independence*. New Delhi: ABC Publishing House, 1989.

Biko, Steve. "Black Consciousness and the Quest for a True Humanity," in *Black Theology: The South African Voice*, Edited by Basil Moore. Atlanta: John Knox Press, 1973.

_____. *I Write What I Like*. New York: Harper & Row, 1978, 49.

Bingham, Marjorie W. and Susan H. Gross. *Women in Africa of the Sub-Sahara,Vol. I, From Ancient Times to the 20th Century*. St. Louis Park, MN: Glenhurst, 1982.

Birmingham, David. "The African Response to Early Portuguese Activities in Angola, in Chilcote, Ronald H.. (ed.) *Protest and Resistance in Angola and Brazil: Comparative Studies*. Berkeley: University of California Press, 1972: 11-28.

_____. *The Portuguese Conquest of Angola*. London: Oxford University Press, 1965.

"Black Music of Resistance: South Africa" (Visual).

Blum, John Morton. *Years of Discord: American Politics and Society, 1961-1974*. New York: Norton, 1991.

Boahen, A. Adu. *African Perspectives on Colonialism*. Baltimore: Johns Hopkins Univ. Press, 1994.

Bradford, Sarah. *Harriet Tubman: The Moses of Her People*. Secaucus, NJ: The Citadel Press, 1974.

Bernstein, Hilda. *For Their Triumphs and For Their Tears: Conditions and Resistance of Women in Apartheid South Africa*. London: International Defence Aid Fund for South Africa, in Co-operation with the United Nations Center Against Apartheid, 1978.

Brathwaite, Edward Kamau. *Wars of Respect: Nanny, Sam Sharpe and the Struggle for People's Liberation*. Kingston, Jamaica: Published by API for National Heritage Week Committee, 1977.

Breitman, George. *Malcolm X Speaks: Selected Speeches and Statements*. New York: Pathfinder, 1992.

Brodber, Erna and Edward J. Greene. *Reggae and Cultural Identity in Jamaica*, Working Papers on Caribbean Society. Institute of Social and Economic Research, Mona Campus, Kingston, Jamaica. University of the West Indies, 1981.

Brooks, Tilford. *America's Black Musical Heritage*. Englewood Cliffs, NJ, 1984.

Brown, L. Carl. "The Sudanese Mahdiya" in Robert Rotberg and Ali A.   Mazrui, (eds.). *Protest and Power in Black Africa*. New York, Oxford University Press, 1970: 145-168.

Browning, Barbara. *Samba: Resistance in Motion*. Bloomington: Indiana University Press, 1995.

Burns, Stewart. *Social Movements of the 1960s: Searching for Democracy*. Boston: Twayne Publishers, 1990.

Bush, Barbara. *Slave Women in Caribbean Society, 1650-1833* (Kingston: Heinemann, 1990.

Cabral, Amilcar. *Return to the Source: Selected Speeches by Amilcar Cabral*. African Information Service, 1973).

___. *Unity and Struggle: Speeches and Writings*. New York. Monthly Review Press, 1979.

Campbell, Horace. Pan-Africanism: *The Struggle Against Imperialism and Neo-Colonialism. Documents of the Sixth Pan-African Congress with an assessment by Horace Campbell*. Toronto: Afro-Carib Publications, 1975.

_____. *Rasta and Resistance: From Marcus Garvey to Walter Rodney*. Trenton, NJ: Africa World Press, 1987.

Cantarow, Ellen *et. al. Moving the Mountain: Women Working for Social Change*. New York: Feminist Press, 1980.

Carothers, John Colin. *The Psychology of Mau Mau*. Nairobi: printed by the Government Printer, 1954.

Carson, Clayborne. *In Struggle: SNCC and the Black Awakening of the 1960s*. Cambridge: Harvard University Press, 1981.

Césaire, Aimé. *Discours sur le Colonialisme*. Paris: Presence Africaine, 1976.

Chaliand, Gerard. *Armed Struggle in Africa: With the Guerrillas in Portuguese Guinea*. New York: Monthly Review Press, 1969.

Chevannes, Barry. *Rastafarai: Roots and Ideology*. Syracuse: Syracuse University Press, 1994.

Chevannes, Barry. *Rastafari and other African Caribbean Worldviews*. Houndmills, Macmillan, 1995.

Chilcote Ronald H. (ed.). *Protest and Resistance in Angola and Brazil: Comparative Studies*. Berkley: University of California Press, 1972.

Clarke, Peter B. and Ian Linden. *Islam in Modern Nigeria: A Study of a Muslim Community in a Post-Independence State, 1960-1983*. Mainz: Gruneald, 1983.

Cliffe, Lionel et. al. *The Transition to Independence in Namibia*. Boulder: Lynne Rienner, 1994.

Clough, Marshall S. *Mau Mau Memoirs: History, Memory, and Politics*. Boulder Colo.: Lynne Rienner, 1998.

Conrad, Earl. *Harriet Tubman: Negro Soldier and Abolitionist*. New York: International Publishers, 1942.

Crahan, Margaret and Franklin W. Knight. *Africa and the Caribbean: the Legacies of a Link*. (Baltimore: Johns Hopkins Univ. Press, 1979).

Cross, Brian. *It's Not About A Salary: Rap, Race, and Resistance in Los Angeles*. New York: Verso, 1993.

Crowder, Michael. *A Short History of Nigeria*. New York: Praeger, 1962.

_____ (ed.) *West African Resistance: the Military Response to Colonial Occupation*. New York: Africana Publishing Corp. 1971.

Curtin, Philip D. *The Atlantic Slave Trade: A Census*. Madison: University of Wisconsin Press, 1969.

_____. *The Image of Africa, British Ideas and Action, 1780-1850*. Madison: Univ. of Wisconsin Press, 1964.

Daniel, Yvonne. *Rumba: Dance and Social Change in Contemporary Cuba*. Bloomington: Indiana University Press, 1995.

Davidson, Basil. *No Fist Is Big Enough to Hide the Sky*. London: Zed Press, 1981.

Davidson, David M. "Negro Slave Control and Resistance in Colonial Mexico, 1519-1650." In Richard Price. *Maroon Societies: Rebel Slave Communities in the Americas*. Baltimore: The John Hopkins University Press 1979: 82-103.

Davis, Angela Y. *If They Come in the Morning: Voices of Resistance*. New York: New American Library, 1971.

DeNoon, Donald. *Southern Africa since 1800*. New York: Praeger, 1972.

Desmangles, Leslie. *The Faces of the Gods: Vodou and Roman Catholicism in Haiti*. Chapel Hill: University of North Carolina Press, 1992.

DuBois, W. E. B. *The Souls of Black Folk*. London: Longman, 1995.

_____. *Pan-Africanism and the liberation of South Africa: International Tribute to William E. B. DuBois: Statements made at the Special Meetings of the Special Committee Against Apartheid held on 23 February 1978 in Tribute to Dr. William E. B. DuBois*. New York: United Nations Center Against Apartheid, 1982.

Edgerton, Robert B. *Like Lions they Fought: The Zulu War and the Last Black Empire in South Africa*. New York: The Free Press, 1988.

_____. *Mau Mau: An African Crucible*. New York : Free Press, 1989.

Engineer, Asghar Ali (ed). *Islam and Revolution*. Delhi: Janta Publications, 1984.

_____. "On Developing Liberation Theology in Islam." In Asghar Ali Engineer (ed.) *Islam and Revolution*. Delhi: Janta, 1984.

Equiano, Olaudah *Equiano's Travels. The Interesting Narrative of the Life of Olaudah Equiano or Gustavus Vassa, the African*. Abridged and edited by Paul Edwards. Oxford: Heinemann, 1996.

Esedebe, P. Olisanwuche. *Pan-Africanism: the Idea and the Movement, 1776-1991*. Washington, D. C.: Howard University Press, 1982.

Fanon, Frantz. *The Wretched of the Earth*. New York: Penguin, 1967.

Fax, Elton. *Garvey: The Story of a Pioneer Black Nationalist*. New York: Dodd, Meed & Company, 1972.

Fauchard, Jean. *The Haitian Maroons: Liberty or Death*. New York: Edward W. Blyden Press, 1981.

Fick, Carolyn E. *The making of Haiti: the Saint Domingue Revolution from Below*. Knoxville: University of Tennessee Press 1990.

Fraginals, Manuel Moreno (ed.). *Africa in Latin America: Essays on History, Culture, and Socialization*. New York: Holmes and Meirs, 1984.

_____. "Cultural Contributions and Deculturation," in Manuel Moreno Fraginals (ed.). *Africa in Latin America: Essays on History, Culture, and Socialization*. New York: Holmes and Meier, 1984.

Furedi, Frank. *The Mau Mau in Perspective*. Athens: Ohio University Press, 1989.

Gallen, David. *Malcolm X as they knew Him*. New York: Carroll & Graft, 1992.

Gann, L. H. and Peter Duignan. *Colonialism in Africa, 1870-1960*. London: Cambridge University Press, 1970.

Gibson, Richard. *African Liberation Movements: Contemporary Struggles Against White Minority Rule*. New York: Oxford University Press, 1972.

Geiss, Imanuel. *The Pan-African Movement*. London: Methuen, 1974.

Genovese, Eugene D. "Herbert Aptheker's Achievement and Our Responsibility," in Okihiro, Gary Y. (ed.) *In Resistance: Studies in African, Caribbean, and Afro-American History*. Amherst: The University of Massachusetts Press, 1986: 21-31.

George, Nelson (ed.). *Stop the Violence: Overcoming Self Destruction*. New York: Pantheon Books, 1990.

Gerhart, Gail M. *Black Power in South Africa: The Evolution of Ideology*. Berkeley: University of California Press.

Grant, Joanne. *Ella Baker: Freedom Bound*. New York: John Wiley, 1998.

Gwassa, G. C. K. "African Methods of Warfare During the Maji Maji War 1905-1907" in Bethwell A. Ogot (ed.) *War And Society in Africa: Ten Studies*. London: Frank Cass, 1972: 123-48.

_____ and John Iliffe *(eds) Records of the Maji Maji Rising* Part 1 Nairobi: East African Publishing House, 1967.

Hagan, George P. "Nkrumah's Cultural Policy," in Kwame Arhin (ed.). *The Life and Work of Kwame Nkrumah*. Accra, Ghana: Sedco Publishing Limited, 1991.

Hamilton, Anthony. Father Amdee. "Kill," Black Voices on the Streets of Watts, 1971. (Reproduced in Cross, *It's Not About A Salary*).

Hargreeves, J. D. "The European Partition of West Africa" in J. F. Ade Ajayi and Michael Crowder (eds.) *History of West Africa, Vol. 2.* New York: Columbia University Press, 1976.

Harris Jr., Robert L. "Coming of Age: The Transformation of Afro-American Historiography," in Abdul Alkalimat (ed.) *Paradigms in Black Studies: Intellectual History, Cultural Meaning and Political Ideology.* Chicago: Twenty-first Century Books and Publications, 1990: 53-72.

Haskins, James. *"Voodoo and Hoodoo": Their Tradition and Craft as Revealed by Actual Practitioners.* New York: Stein and Day, 1978.

Heinl, Robert, and Nancy Heinl. *Written in Blood: The Story of the Haitian People, 1492-1971.* Boston: Houghton Mifflin Co., 1978.

Hiskett, Mervyn. *The Development of Islam in West Africa.* London: Longman, 1984.

Hopkins, Elizabeth. "The Nyabingi Cult of Southwestern Uganda," in Robert Rotberg and Ali Mazrui (Eds.) *Protest and Power in Black Africa.* New York, Oxford University Press, 1970: 258-336.

IDAF Research, *Women Under Apartheid in Photographs and Text.* London: International Defence and Aid Fund for Southern Africa, in Co-operation with the United Nations Center Against Apartheid, 1981.

Igbafe, Philip. "Western Igbo Society and Its Resistance to British Rule: The Ekumeku Movement, 1898-1911," *Journal of African History* 12, no 3. 1973, 441-59.

Iliffe, John. "The Organization of the Maji Maji rebellion," *Journal of African History.* 8, no. 3 1967, 495-512.

Inikori, Joseph E. and Stanley L. Engerman (eds.) *The Atlantic Slave Trade: Effects on Economies, Societies, and Peoples in Africa, the Americas, and Europe.* Durham: Duke University Press, 1992.

Isaacman, Alan. *The Tradition of Resistance in Mozambique: The Zambesi Valley 1850-1921.* Berkley: University of California Press, 1976.

Jackson, John G. *Introduction to African Civilizations.* New York: Carroll, 1993.

Jacques-Garvey, Amy (ed.) *Philosophy and Opinions of Marcus Garvey Vol. 1 & 2.* New York: Atheneum, 1973.

James, C. L. R., *The Black Jacobins: Toussaint L'Ouverture and the San Domingo Revolution*. New York: Vintage Books, 1963.

_____. *World Revolution, 1917-1936: The Rise and Fall of the Communist International*. Atlantic Highlands, NJ: Humanities Press, 1993.

Jean, Clinton M. *Behind the Eurocentric Veils: the Search for African Realities*. Amherst: The University of Massachusetts Press, 1991.

Jones-Quartey, A. K. B. *A Life of Azikiwe*. Baltimore: Penguin Books, 1965.

Kanya-Forstner, A. S. *The Conquest of the Western Sudan: A Study in French Military Imperialism*. London: Cambridge University Press, 1969.

Keyes, Cheryl L. "At the Cross Roads: Rap Music and the African Nexus." *Ethnomusicology*, Vol. 40. No. 2, 1996: 223-48.

King, Jr., Martin Luther. *I have a Dream: Writings and Speeches That Changed the World*, edited by James M. Washington. San Francisco: Harper, 1992.

King, Richard H. *Civil Rights and the Idea of Freedom*. New York: Oxford University Press, 1992.

Kiple, Kenneth F. and Brian T. Higgins. "Mortality Caused by Dehydration During the Middle Passage" in Joseph E. Inikori and Stanley L. Engerman (eds.). *The Atlantic Slave Trade: Effects on Economies, Societies, and Peoples in Africa, the Americas, and Europe*. Durham: Duke University Press, 1992: 321-37.

Klein, Herbert S. *The Middle Passage: Comparative Studies in the Atlantic Slave Trade*. Princeton: Princeton University Press, 1978.

Knight, Franklin W. *Slave Society in Cuba during the Nineteenth Century*. Madison: University of Wisconsin Press, 1970.

Knight, Ian. *The Anatomy of the Zulu Army from Shaka to Cetshwayo, 1818-1879*. London: Greenhill Books, 1995.

Kanogo, Tabitha M. *Squatters and the Roots of Mau Mau, 1905-63*. Athens: Ohio University Press, 1987.

Kwitny, Jonathan. *Endless Enemies: The Making of an Unfriendly World*. New York: Penguin, 1986.

Langley, J. Ayodele. *Pan-Africanism and Nationalism in West Africa, 1900-1945: A study in Ideology and Social Classes*. Oxford: Clarendon Press, 1973.

Lanternari, Vittorio. *The Religions of the Oppressed: A Study of Modern Messianic Cults*. New York: New American Library, 1965.

Lasisi, R. O. "Africa and the League of Nations: The Marginality of the Continent in the International Search for Peace" in A. E. Ekoko and S. O. Agbi (eds.) *Perspectives in History: Essays in Honour of Obaro Ikime*. lbadan: Heinemann Educational Books, 1992.

Leakey, L. S. B. *Defeating the Mau Mau*. London: Methuen, 1954.

Levine, Lawrence W. *Black culture and Black Consciousness: Afro-American folk thought from Slavery to Freedom*. New York: Oxford University Press, 1977.

Lavine, Michael L.. *African Americans and Civil Rights*. Phoenix: The Oryx Press, 1996.

Lee, Margaret C. *SADCC: The Political Economy of Development in Southern Africa*. Nashville, TN: Winston-Derek, 1989.

Lewis, David Levering et. al. *The Civil Rights Movement in America: Essays*. Jackson: University of Mississippi Press, 1986.

Lewis, J. Lowell. *Ring of Liberation: Deceptive Discourse in Brazilian Capoeira*. Chicago: University of Chicago Press, 1992.

Lewis, William F. *Soul Rebels: The Rastafari*. Prospect Heights: Waveland Press, 1993.

Leyburn, James G. *The Haitian People*. New Haven: Yale University Press, 1966.

Leys, Norman. *Kenya,* London: Frank Cass, 1973.

Light, Alan (ed.) *The Vibe History of Hip Hop*. New York: Three River Press, 1999.

Lincoln, C. Eric. *Black Muslims in America*. Boston: Beacon Press, 1973.

Logan, Rayford W. and Michael R. Winston (eds.). *Dictionary of American Negro Biography*. New York: Norton, 1982.

Love, Edgar "Legal Restrictions on Afro-Indian Relations in Colonial Mexico." Journal of Negro History, Vol. 45 January 1970, 131-9.

Luthuli, Albert. *Let My People Go: An Autobiography*. New York: McGraw-Hill, 1962.

Mabee, Carleton. *Sojourner Truth: Slave Prophet, Legend*. New York: New York University Press, 1993.

Malhotra, Veena. *Kenya Under Kenyatta*. Delhi: Kalinga Publications, 1990.

Manuel, Peter Lamarche. *Caribbean Currents: Caribbean Music from Rumba to Reggae*. Philadelphia: Temple University Press, 1995.

Mapunda, O. B. and G. P. Mpangara. *The Maji Maji war in Ungoni*. Nairobi East Africa Pub. House 1969.

Marable, Manning. *DuBois W. E. B. Black Radical Democrat*. Boston: Twayne's Twentieth-Century American Biography: no. 3, 1986.

Margarido, Alfredo. "The Tokoist Church and Portuguese Colonialism in Angola" in Ronald H. Chilcote (ed.). *Protest and Resistance in Angola and Brazil: Comparative Studies*. Berkley: University of California Press, 1972: 29-52.

Marley, Bob and the Wailers. "Confrontation," Island Records, 1983.

_____. "Exodus." Produced by Bob Marley and the Wailers, Distributed by Island Recording Inc. New York.

_____. "War." Produced by Bob Marley and the Wailers, Distributed by Island Recording Inc. New York.

Marsh, Clifton E. *From Black Muslims to Muslims: The Transition from Separatism to Islam, 1930-1980*. Metuchen: The Scarecrow Press, 1984.

Martin, Marie-Louise. *Kimbangu: An African Prophet and His Church*. Oxford: Basil Blackwell, 1975.

Martin, Tony. *Marcus Garvey, Hero: A First Biography*. Dover: The Majority Press, 1983.

Mathurin, Owen Charles. *Henry Sylvester Williams and the Origins of Pan -African Movement, 1869-1911*. Westport: Greenwood Press, 1976.

Miers, Suzanne. *Britain and the Ending of the Slave Trade*. New York: Africana, 1974.

Miller, Douglas T. and Marion Nowak. *The Fifties: The Way We Really Were*. Garden City, New York: Doubleday, 1977.

Morrish, Ivor. *Obeah, Christ and Rastaman: Jamaica and its Religion*. Cambridge, England: J. Clarke, 1982.

Mugambi, J. N. K. *African Christian Theology*. Nairobi: Heinemann, 1989.

Murphy, Joseph M. *Working the Spirit: Ceremonies of the African Diaspora*. Boston: Beacon Press, 1994.

Mzala, *Gatsha Buthelezi: Chief with a Double Agenda* London. Zed Books, 1988.

Nettleford, Rex M. *Dace Jamaica: Cultural Definition and Artistic Discovery: the National Dance Theater Company of Jamaica, 1962-1983.* New York: Grove Press, 1985.

Nicholas, Tracey. *Rastafari: A way of Life.* New York: Anchor Books, 1979.

Nkrumah, Kwame. *The Autobiography of Kwame Nkrumah.* Edinburgh: Thomas Nelson, 1961.

_____. *Africa Must Unite.* London: Heinemann, 1963.

_____. *Neo-colonialism: The Last stage of Imperialism.* New York: International Publishers Co., 1969.

Oates, Stephen B. *The Fires of Jubilee: Nat Turner's Fierce Rebellion.* New York: Harper and Row, 1975.

Ogot, Bethwell A. (ed.) *War And Society in Africa: Ten Studies.* London: Frank Cass, 1972.

_____ and William Ochieng, "Mumboism--An Anti-colonial Movement" in Ogot, Bethwell A. (ed.) *War And Society in Africa: Ten Studies.* London: Frank Cass, 1972.

Ohadike, Don C. *The Ekumeku Movement: Western Igbo Resistance to the British Conquest of Nigeria, 1883-1914.* Athens: Ohio Univ. Press, 1991.

Okihiro, Gary Y. (ed.) *In Resistance: Studies in African, Caribbean, and Afro-American History.* Amherst: The University of Massachusetts Press, 1986.

Okwoli, P. O. *A Short History of Igala.* Ilorin, Nigeria,1973.

Oliver, Roland and John D. Fage. *A short History of Africa.* Baltimore: Penguin Books, 1962.

Omer-Cooper, J D. *The Zulu Aftermath; a Nineteenth-century Revolution in Bantu Africa.* Evanston: Northwestern University Press, 1966.

Omari, T. Peter. *Kwame Nkrumah: the Anatomy of an African Dictatorship.* London: C. Hurst & Co., 1970.

Okpewho, Isidore. *African Oral Literature: Backgrounds, Character, and Continuity.* Bloomington: Indiana University Press, 1992.

Osemene, Rhoda. *Zik, The African Legend.* Lagos, Nigeria: Time Books, 1996.

Padmore, George. *Pan-Africanism or Communism.* Garden City: Doubleday, 1971.

Palmer, Colin A. *Slaves of the White God: Blacks in Mexico, 1570-1650*. Cambridge: Harvard University Press, 1976.

Patterson, Charles. *The Civil Rights Movement*. New York: Facts on File, 1995.

Paris, Peter J. *Black Religious Leaders: Conflict in Unity*. Louisville: John Knox, 1991.

Pearson, Hugh. *The Shadow of the Panther: Huey Newton and the Price of Black Power in America*. Reading, Mass.: Addison-Wesley, 1994.

Pearson, Yves. "Guinea—Samori," in Michael Crowder (ed.). *West African Resistance: The Military Response to Colonial Occupation*. New York: Africana Publishing Corporation, 1972.

_____. "Samori and Resistance to the French," in Robert Rotberg and Ali Mazrui (Eds). *Protest and Power in Black Africa*. New York, Oxford University Press, 1970: 80-112.

Perham, Marger. Foreword to Josiah Mwangi Kariuku. *"Mau Mau" Detainee: Account by a Kenyan African of his Experiences in Detention Camps 1953-60*. Oxford: Oxford University Press, 1964.

Price, Richard. *Maroon Societies: Rebel Slave Communities in the Americas*. Baltimore: The John Hopkins University Press 1979.

Ranger, T. O. "Connections between Primary Resistance Movements and Modern Mass Nationalism in East and Central Africa," parts 1 and 2, *Journal of African History*. Vol. 9 nos. 3 and 4. 1968: 437-53 & 631-41.

Ranger, Terence O. *Revolt in Southern Rhodesia, 1896-97: A Study in African Resistance*. Evanston: Northwestern Univ. Press, 1967.

Reis, Joàs José. *Slave Rebellion in Brazil: The Muslim Uprising of 1835 in Bahia*. Baltimore: Johns Hopkins University Press, 1993.

Richard, Pankhurst. *"The Battle,"* In *One House: The Battle of Adwa 1896—100 Years (ed) Pamela S. Brown and Fassil Yirgu*. Chicago: Nyala, 1996.

Robinson, Roland. "Non-European Foundations of European Imperialism: Sketch for a Theory of Collaboration." In *Imperialism: The Robinson and Gallagher Controversy,* ed. William Roger Louis. New York: New Viewpoint, 1976, 128-51.

Rodney, Walter. *How Europe Underdeveloped Africa*. Washington DC: Howard University Press, 1981.

Rosberg, Jr. Carl G. and John Nottingham. *The Myth of "Mau Mau":
Nationalism in Kenya*. New York: Meridian Books, 1966.

Rose, Tricia. *Black Noise: Rap Music and Black Culture in Contemporary America*. Hanover: Wesleyan University Press, 1994.

Rotberg, Robert and Ali Mazrui (eds). *Protest and Power in Black
Africa*. New York, Oxford University Press, 1970.

Rubin, Vera. Foreword to Michel S. Laguerre. *Voodoo Heritage*. Beverly
Hills: Sage, 1980.

Rublowsky, John. *Black Music in America*. New York: Basic Books,
1971.

Sartre, Jean-Paul. "Preface" to Frantz Fanon. *The Wretched of the Earth*.
New York: Penguine, 1967.

Schwartz, Frederick A. O. *Nigeria: The Tribes, the Nation, or the Race.
The Politics of Independence*. Cambridge: M. I. T. Press, 1965.

Schwartz, Stuart B. "The Mocambo: Slave Resistance in Colonial
Bahia," in Richard Price (ed.). *Maroon Societies: Rebel Salve Communities in the Americas*. Baltimore: The Johns Hopkins University Press, 1979: 202-26.

_____. *Slaves, Peasants and Rebels: Reconsidering Brazilian Slavery*.
Urbana: University of Illinois Press, 1992.

Shaw, Arnold. *Black Popular Music in America: From the Spirituals,
Minstrels, and Ragtime to Soul, Disco, and Hip-Hop*. New York:
Schirmer Books, 1966.

Small, Christopher. *Music of the Common Tongue: Survival and Celebration in Afro-American Music*. London: John Calder. 1987.

Sobel, Mechal. *Trabelin On: The Slave Journey to an Afro-Baptist Faith*.
Westport: Greenwood Press, 1979.

Steward, T. G. *The Haitian Revolution, 1791 to 1804*. New York:
Russell & Russell, 1971.

Stockwell, John. *In Search of Enemies: A CIA Story*. New York: Norton,
1978.

Stuempfle, Stephen. *The Steelband Movement: the Forging of a National
Art in Trinidad and Tobago*. Philadelphia: University of Pennsylvania Press, 1995.

Sweetman, David. *Women Leaders in African History*. London: Heinemann, 1984.

Takaki, Ronald. *A Different Mirror: A History of Multicultural America*.
Boston: Little, Brown and Co., 1993.

Temu, Arnold J. "Tanzanian Societies and Colonial Invasion 1875-907," in *Tanzania Under Colonial Rule*. Ed. H. Y. Kaniki. London, 1969: 86-127.

Tibebu, Teshale ."Adwa and Menelik's Ethiopia. " *In One House: The Battle of Adwa, Adwa1896—100 Years (Ed) Pamela S. Brown and Fassil Yirgu*. Chicago: Nyala, 1996.

Thompson, Vincent Bakpetu. *Africa and Unity: the Evolution of Pan-Africanism*. New York: Humanities Press, 1970.

Thornton, John K. *The Kongolese Saint Anthony : Dona Beatriz Kimpa Vita and the Antonian movement, 1684-1706*. Cambridge: Cambridge University Press, 1998.

_____. "African Dimensions of the Stono Rebellion," *The American Historical Review*. Vol. 96; no. 4. October 1991, 1101-13.

Thorpe, Edward. *Black Dance*. Woodstock: Overlook Press, 1990.

Trimingham, J. Spencer. *Islam in the Sudan*. London: Frank Cass, 1965.

Tyson, George F. *Toussaint L'Ouverture*. Englewood Cliffs, N. J: Prentice-Hall, 1973.

Uzoigwe, G. N. *Britain and the Conquest of Africa: the Age of Salisbury*. Ann Arbor: University of Michigan Press, 1974.

Voeks, Robert A. *Sacred Leaves of Candomblé: African Magic, Medicine, and Religion in Brazil*. Austin: University of Texas Press, 1997.

Wachanga, H. K. *The Swords of Kirinyaga: the Fight for Land and Freedom*. Kampala: East African Literature Bureau, 1975.

Washington, James M. (ed.). *I Have a Dream: Writings and Speeches that Changed the World*. San Francisco: Harper, 1992.

Washington, Margaret (edited with an introduction). *Narrative of Sojourner Truth*.New York: Vintage Books, 1993.

Watt, William Montgomery. *Islamic Fundamentalism and Modernity*. London: Routledge, 1988.

Webster, J. B. "The Civil War in Usuku" in Bethwell A. Ogot. *War and Society in Africa*. London: F. Cass, 1972.

Weisbrot, Robert. *Freedom Bound: A History of America's Civil Rights Movement*. New York: Norton, 1990.

Williams, Eric. *Capitalism & Slavery*. Chapel Hill: University of North Carolina Press, 1994.

Williams, Juan. *Eyes on the Prize: America's Civil Rights Years, 1954-1965*. New York: Viking, 1987.

Wolf, Eric R. *Peasant Wars of the Twentieth Century.* New York: Harper & Row, 1969.

Young, Crawford. "Decolonization in Africa" in *Colonialism in Africa, 1870-1960. Vol 2. The History and Politics of Colonialism, 1914-1960.* Edited by L. H. Gann and Peter Duignan. London: Cambridge University Press, 1970: 450-502.

Index